Global Inequalities

Global Inequalities

Robert J. Holton

palgrave

First published 2014 by
PALGRAVE

Palgrave in the UK is an imprint of Macmillan Publishers Limited, registered in England, company number 785998, of 4 Crinan Street, London N1 9XW.

Palgrave Macmillan in the US is a division of St Martin's Press LLC, 175 Fifth Avenue, New York, NY 10010.

Palgrave is a global imprint of the above companies and is represented throughout the world.

ISBN 978-1-137-33956-0 ISBN 978-1-137-33958-4 (eBook)

DOI 10.1007/978-1-137-33958-4

This book is printed on paper suitable for recycling and made from fully managed and sustained forest sources. Logging, pulping and manufacturing processes are expected to conform to the environmental regulations of the country of origin.

A catalogue record for this book is available from the British Library.

A catalog record for this book is available from the Library of Congress.

Contents

Tables

Acknowledgements

The topic of global inequality evokes anger, passion, perplexity and dismay, despair as well as hope. These arise in many different ways, both in relation to the scale of the problems and challenges involved and because of the seeming lack of current success in resolving grave inequalities and injustices. This book navigates a course between hope and despair drawing on theory, evidence, and policy evaluation, while avoiding ideological partisanship.

I have drawn on wide reading and on conversations about globalization with a range of scholars. I am indebted to Roland Robertson, Supriya Singh, Chris Rumford, Sandra Holton, Steve Edwards, Kevin O'Rourke, Anthony Elliott, and John Braithwaite for their stimulating ideas over the last decade, well before the idea of this book emerged in 2012. Anna Marie Reeve first suggested that I write a book on global inequality, and I am very grateful for her perspicacity in putting the project to me.

The electronic journal library of Trinity College, Dublin, has been a wonderful resource in giving me access to journal literature across many disciplines. Mid-way through the writing I became Adjunct Professor of Sociology at the University of South Australia, and I thank the University and the Hawke Research Institute for their support for my work. I also turned increasingly to reading novels as I wrote this book, feeling that academic writing could be far more imaginative and aesthetically pleasing than it is. I don't think I have in any way transformed my writing style as a result. But I am very glad to have had contact with the work of Ivan Turgenev, Penelope Fitzgerald, and David Mitchell, all of whom have crafted powerful narratives out of complex and uncertain social circumstances. In my own case, this book also attempts to locate the threads of plausible narratives out of complex and uncertain features of global inequality, and to reach out, however fleetingly, into the experience of particular persons.

Sandra, George, Flora, and Anthony have provided love, encouragement, and many kindnesses during the writing of this book. I am, as ever, in their debt in so many ways.

Abbreviations

BRIC	Brazil, Russia, India, China
CPE	Cultural Political Economy
CRT	Critical Race Theory
DALYs	Disability-Affected Life Years
FAO	Food and Agriculture Organization
FX	Foreign Exchange (as a basis for foreign currency conversion)
GDP	Gross Domestic Product
HDI	Human Development Indicators
HIE	High Inequality Equilibria
ILO	International Labor Organization
IMF	International Monetary Fund
LIE	Low Inequality Equilibria
MDG	Millennium Development Goals
NGO	Non-Government Organization
OECD	Organization for Economic Cooperation and Development
PPP	Purchasing Power Parity
WHO	World Health Organization
WTO	World Trade Organization
UN	United Nations
UNICEF	United Nations Children's Fund (originally United Nations International Children's Emergency Fund)
UNCTAD	United Nations Commission on Trade and Development
UNDP	United Nations Development Program
UNODC	United Nations Office on Drugs and Crime

1 Introduction

The world is a very unequal place. The gap between rich and poor is getting wider rather than narrowing. Wealthy individuals and households from business, politics, and celebrity culture live in a comfortable elite world of pleasure, prestige, and power. Meanwhile millions of children starve, tens of thousands of women experience domestic violence, and poorly paid workers struggle to survive. Behind these stark interpersonal contrasts lie powerful institutions, customs, and ideologies, each strongly implicated in structures of inequality. This state of affairs generates anguish and misery, social criticism and conflict, and for many, a strong sense of moral outrage.

A vital point to make at the outset is that inequality is global as well as national in scope. We often think of inequality as a feature of individual countries. Yet there are profound contrasts in income, wealth, health, and social participation between countries as well as within them. Many also believe that global inequalities are very much the product of globalization. The suggestion is that unless globalization is radically reformed or countered by some alternative set of social institutions, levels of global inequality will get worse.

Alongside these issues, there is a growing sense that the scale of global inequality is undermining the legitimacy of the global economy and the way it is organized through global markets, corporations, and forms of governance. This was reflected at the January 2014 World Economic Forum at Davos. Here a number of elite participants expressed concern that global inequality had reached a level that could intensify social conflict and increase pressure on governments to regulate global business (Kennedy and Martinuzzi 2014). The status quo, it seems, is unsustainable.

Global inequality is then a matter of extremes. One way of summing this up, suggested by Philosopher Thomas Pogge (2002, 2007), is through the notion of *radical inequality*. This has the following five elements:

1. The worse-off are very badly off in absolute terms, evident in poor health and vulnerability to insecurity of food supply.
2. They are also very badly off in relative terms, because the gap between rich and poor is widening.
3. It is difficult for the very badly off to improve their position.
4. Inequality is multidimensional affecting all aspects of life, not income alone.
5. Inequality is avoidable because the better off could easily afford transfers to the poor.

The idea of radical inequality encapsulates the challenge that this book takes up. Put simply, I ask how and why radical inequality has arisen? What types of global inequality are most important and how far are they increasing or decreasing? Is there one dominant pattern and, if so, is there one basic reason for inequality? Or are there many types of inequality and multiple causes to be taken into account?

Not everything about the world is bleak. Long-term aggregate income growth and better access to health and education have been achieved. Social and human welfare are amenable to social reform, and some inequalities can and have been challenged and addressed. What then can be done about global inequality? How successful is development aid? And which policies and programmes work and which do not? The answers to such questions turn out to be not quite as simple as rival ideologues of 'free markets' and 'state regulation' would have us believe.

This book offers a critical guide through evidence of global inequality, but it offers more than that. What is added is an extensive search for the intellectual resources – be they theories, concepts, research strategies, or critical research findings – that are most useful both to understanding inequality and taking practical measures to combat it. While there is a vast literature on inequality, this book offers a distinctive response to the many challenges involved, for three main reasons:

(a) It takes a multidisciplinary approach to inequality centred on sociological analyses of the reasons behind it.
(b) It looks at inequality historically and how the past influences the present.
(c) It takes a global rather than purely national perspective on what causes inequality and what can be done about it.

(a) The Need for a Multidisciplinary Approach

Most academic accounts of inequality begin with inequalities of income and look to economists to provide insights into trends in inequality and explanations of these trends. This book takes a different approach. Income inequality as studied by economists is very important. Yet it is not by itself sufficiently broad to take in the multiple dimensions of inequality beyond income. This requires that attention be given to the wider social, political and historical context in which markets function.

Due regard must be given to the pioneering work of economists on inequality. We may start with the contribution of the American economist Simon Kuznets (1955). He developed an inverted U-shaped theory of the trajectory of inequality over time. Kuznets argues that inequality of income was relatively low in pre-industrial societies, where most were poor, rose in the early phases of industrialization, but then declined again in the 20th century with increased education and state redistribution of resources. This has become a major middle-range theoretical reference point in subsequent debates.

Like most economists he focusses on income as the key to understanding inequality. This is because income is a key resource for access to many kinds of human welfare, including health and education, as well as food, clothing, and shelter. It can also be measured, at least for societies that care to and can afford to assemble statistics.

This model is optimistic and does fit the trajectory of some Western countries where income inequality follows something like an inverted U-curve. It has also been extended by economists onto a global scale in the study of economic development. Here economic openness to trade, deregulated markets, and efficient financial institutions are seen as a key to greater opportunity and rising income right across the world. The main problem with it, as argued by a less optimistic school of economic reasoning, is the widespread evidence of increasing global income inequality over the long term, both between countries and within many countries.

One way of capturing this is to compare the ratio of the income of the top 10% with the bottom 10% of the world's income distribution. Milanovic (2011, 152) calculates that the top 10% receive 56% of the world's income, while the bottom 10% receive 0.7%, meaning that the ratio between the two is around 80 to 1. If allowances are made for different price levels between rich and poor countries, the relative shares of the top group expands and the bottom group contracts further, worsening the ratio in the process.

Global inequality has then worsened for most of the 19th and 20th centuries during the phase of industrialization and Western global dominance. Statisticians measuring inequality use an indicator called the Gini coefficient to provide a headline number on a scale where 100 equals complete inequality and 0 complete equality. (More discussion of this measure is available in Chapter 3.) For the moment, we use this index to underline the historical worsening of global inequality, from a figure around 50 around 1820, rising to 61 in 1910 and 66 in 1992 (Bourguignon and Morrison 2002). In the last 20 years, the rise seems to have been halted, but at a very high level of around 70 (Milanovic 2011, 150). This is higher than any individual country, where the index varies between highs of around 60 in Brazil and South Africa to over 40 in the United States and Russia and the low to mid 30s in the EU, lowest of all in Scandinavia.

The worsening of inequality over this period occurred during the phase of global market expansion associated with industrialization, global mobility of capital, labour and commodities, and the freeing of markets from intrusive political regulation. This process has been very dynamic economically, but has persistently failed to reduce global inequality. Markets may or may not be efficient, but they do not contain mechanisms which necessarily distribute economic rewards in a manner that is fair, just, or able to guarantee a decent life. They also create periodic instability and crisis, like the recent Global Financial Crisis.

This is not to deny that market liberalization can and does increase opportunities and income in a number of countries and sectors of the economy. However, such optimistic stories coexist with darker and more depressing evidence of extreme poverty and a growing gap between the richest and the poorest. Consequently market solutions clearly have limits as means to reduce global inequality, and it is an important task of this book to determine why this should be.

Economists are not of course apologists for any necessarily optimistic account of patterns of global inequality. They vary in assessments of just how much inequality there is and whether things are getting better or worse. The evidence here is quite complex, and we shall explore the relevant literature when examining global income inequality in more depth in Chapter 4. Income trends are very important, but social inequality and human welfare more generally are not simply matters of income derived from employment or business. Other forms of income transfer matter, such as welfare payments and public subsidies (such as food or energy price controls) which cheapen the cost of living. And beyond this are a range of other aspects of social life which bear upon human welfare, including educational and health provision, rights to social participation, and freedom from violence and abuse. These must all be taken into account in assessing what inequality means, including aspects of life that cannot be easily or clearly measured.

The case for moving beyond economistic accounts of inequality

It is helpful then to clarify the reasons why an income-focussed account of global inequality, as studied by economists, is inadequate. The following issues are relevant here:

- Economics says very little about the broader social and philosophical standards by which welfare and inequality are judged.
- Economics does not take sufficient note of the social as distinct from economic origins of inequality.

Broader social and philosophical yardsticks for considering inequality

The need for a broader approach to human welfare quickly becomes apparent if we ask the question 'what exactly do we mean by inequality?' or, put more starkly, 'inequality of what?'. To speak in terms of inequality presumes some sense of difference in the welfare of individuals and households, both within and between nations. But what kinds of differences matter most, and are all differences relevant to issues of inequality?

One common answer is that differences of income and wealth matter most. This approach is widely held because material resources are seen as critical to all aspects of human well-being, including access to health, education, and effective social inclusion within community life, as well as consumer goods regarded as necessary to leading a decent life. This economic focus is shared both by economists and many other social scientists, but there remain a variety of views about which kinds of economic difference are most salient.

For many it is poverty and the extremes of economic inequality that matter most, rather than broader patterns of differences in income and wealth across the board. Some economists believe that much inequality is simply a product of different human skills and assets, and is inevitable in any system which relies on the incentives of higher incomes for those who possess skill and capital. The focus on poverty directs attention to the large proportion of the world's population with an income of US$1 or US$2 per day, rather than systemic disparities in the distribution of income and wealth per se. Inequality in outcomes is less troubling to this school of thought than inequality of opportunity (Wade 2007, 104–105).

Such approaches were associated in the latter part of the 20th century with the development policies of international organizations like the World Bank and International Monetary Fund (Woods 2006). Founded originally to underwrite balanced global growth, the role of these organizations has expanded over time to include crisis-intervention and policy advice together with loans of various kinds. They have also been great globalizers, supporting market deregulation and free movements of capital, which is assumed to have a buoyant effect on the lowest incomes. Critics felt that the policy discourses involved centred on growth and economic development rather than income redistribution or broader social and political rights. The World Bank, over the last few decades, has undoubtedly expanded its social outreach in areas such as education and social infrastructure, with social development and inequality reduction becoming far more prominent objectives.

Certainly the challenges of reducing global inequality require a broader developmental perspective beyond earlier emphases on economic growth alone. The alternative approach focusses directly on all those types of inequality which undermine the capacity of individuals, households and communities to enhance their life chances. This includes obstacles like lack of access to literacy, education, and social participation or lack of access to clean water, effective sanitation, and good health.

The Indian economist and philosopher Amartya Sen (1985, 1996, 1999) and the American social philosopher Martha Nussbaum (2000, 2011) are associated with what has been termed the 'human development' or 'capabilities' approach to global welfare. For Sen, rights to enter markets to choose consumer goods supplied by processes of economic growth are too narrow an approach to freedom. What matters more is the freedom to 'choose a life one has reason to value' (1999, 74–75). For Nussbaum (2011), human welfare focusses on the struggle for 'human dignity', and this centres on 'what each person is able to do and be' (ibid. 18). This enlargement of the idea of human development goes well beyond economic growth to include all aspects of well-being. It also goes well beyond the sphere of statistical measurement, to evidence about human lives drawn from personal histories.

Sen's concept of choice warrants further attention. This is not only because it goes beyond market choice or electoral choice, but because it even extends to the choice of a way of life that entails inequality. This particular version of the human development approach seems to

privilege choice over equality (Walby, op. cit. 9), or at least ec
opportunity over equality of outcome. This has led to criticism
emphasis on choice may entail the maintenance of inequality. An alternative way of thinking about broader human development goals is then in terms of direct reduction of inequality, focussing on outcomes rather than choice. This is the approach to global inequality taken up by the United Nations Development Programme (UNDP) and enshrined in the UN's Millennium Development Goals.

The case against a primary focus on economic welfare is, as we shall see in this book, a strong one. It relies on the point that welfare is not measured by income alone. Better incomes, for example, do not necessarily correlate with better health. Thus, the health of low-income groups and nations can vary considerably, depending on variations of diet or community education as much as income, while the health of higher-income groups and nations can also vary depending on lifestyle choices in matters such as exercise, alcohol consumption, or smoking. This is not an argument against reducing income inequality, rather it is an argument for taking factors additional to income into account, such as chronic illness, premature death, or vulnerability to violence and environmental crisis, when investigating inequality. Put another way, there are multiple types of inequalities, not one single overarching form of inequality.

In the light of this, throwing material resources at problems is either not enough or not always relevant. Inequalities based on cultural and political prejudices involving race, gender, and ethnicity, for example, require legal, educational, and cultural changes to better regulate abusive behaviour within institutions and interpersonal relationships. These in turn may reduce aspects of economic inequality in the functioning of labour markets, but their main impact is likely to be on those broad issues of human dignity and the right to do and be what one wishes that lies at the heart of the human development approach.

A second general point about social differences is that they are not in and of themselves equivalent to inequality. The sociologist Sylvia Walby puts this well when she asks, 'when is something a positively valued difference and when is it inequality?' (2009, 21). This question draws explicit attention to the crucial importance of values in the way that inequalities are perceived and understood. There are several aspects to this. One is that concern about inequality depends in large measure on the positive valuation of equality. Social differences in income, access to education or to political power, only become live social and political issues if such differences are regarded as unjust, unfair, and unnecessary.

This in turn presumes some kind of moral or evaluative yardstick against which such differences are assessed and judged. In an epoch of intensifying globalization, such yardsticks have come to include the population of the world as a whole. Inequality manifest anywhere in the globe is taken to be unjust when judged against standards such as human rights to a decent life free from want and oppression, or human development capable of realizing the human potential of everyone.

The connections between inequality and valuation are however more complex than this, because different and sometimes conflicting ways of life and forms of social organization are valued. A second set of problems arise from this. Is someone who chooses a way of life that values cultural or spiritual values above material goods suffering inequality in the same way as those who have little or no effective choice? In the lives of women, do social differences arising from the contrasts in material resources available from paid work as against unpaid domestic labour simply represent a case of gender inequality? Or are they to be seen rather as two valued but different social activities?

In the absence of value consensus about the merits of different ways of life, there seems to be no universal standard by which inequality can be separated out from valued social difference. Even ostensibly universal yardsticks like 'human rights' are typically relativized to the social or cultural situation of particular groups to which they might be applied, such that there are 'women's human rights' or human rights according to different cultural yardsticks influenced by religion or political tradition. In all of this inequality and difference are co-present features of social life, a state of affairs Walby describes as one of 'complex inequality' (ibid. 21). One implication of this kind of complexity is that rights to difference should be taken into account in discourses about improving human welfare or implementing human rights, rather than pursuing highly abstract universalistic formulae that purport to be culture-free.

The valuing of difference is evident in many bodies of thought. These include traditions of cosmopolitanism (Appiah 2006) and the 'group rights' focus of philosophers like Young (1989). But it is also found within the economic liberalism that informs mainstream economics, whereby it is for individuals and households to decide what constitutes their own welfare. Though written by a sociologist and historian, this book is written very much as a critical dialogue with economic liberalism. It remains to be seen how far the liberal recognition of difference, which in one sense seems very progressive, is ultimately capable of recognizing and addressing the multiple inequalities that currently mark the human condition.

This foray into questions of what is meant by inequality and human welfare shows that there is much more at stake than measuring incomes available to individuals, important as they are. Broader social and philosophical yardsticks matter too. But there are further reasons for taking a broader multidisciplinary approach to global inequality.

Inequality is generated within society, not simply within the economy

This is the second reason for moving beyond an economistic account of global inequality focussed on incomes generated through markets. Mainstream economics tends to bracket out most social issues, to focus on how resources are allocated in markets, how economic growth emerges, and what patterns of income distribution arise under different conditions. This allows a greater focus and precision by concentrating on what can be measured via prices and incomes. Most other issues are regarded as external or 'exogenous' to economics proper. The world is far more complex, however, than simple economic models allow for. Consequently a wider approach is required. This is able to draw on traditions of political economy and economic sociology, which include power and political sources of inequality, alongside sociocultural reasons for inequality.

The following three examples indicate how and why the analytical breadth available within a broader multidisciplinary approach to society matters to the study of global inequalities.

The first example surrounds the economic sociology of the Hungarian historian Karl Polanyi (1957). He noted that free or radically deregulated markets are historically anomalous. At most times in both the past and the present, social and political institutions have been necessary to create social integration in the face of economic instability. Free-standing markets cannot create their own order, let alone wider social stability, since they tend to tear apart political and cultural regulation based on broader social principles and values of community and welfare. This is essentially why welfare states were created as a response to the failures of 19th-century laissez-faire capitalism. This insight remains powerful especially in the light of the recent global financial crisis and widespread rejection of banking practices produced by the misguided deregulation of finance in the 1980s and 1990s (Holton 2012). Globally deregulated markets, however, pose new problems of social integration, since they operate across the borders of nation states. National welfare states are no longer enough. Polanyi's approach draws attention to the unresolved issue of how global governance can contribute to new forms of social organization able to restore some kind of political and cultural order and legitimacy to global social relationships.

Second is world system theory developed first by Immanuel Wallerstein (1974, 1979, 1991), partly under the influence of Polanyi, and elaborated further by a thriving international group of scholars (see Chapter 2). This theory explains global inequality between countries not in terms of the intrinsic characteristics of each country but in terms of the power relationships that govern the exchange of commodities and division of labour between countries and regions. The powerful 'core' countries, in this model, dominate the weaker 'peripheral' countries, such that inequalities of income and life chances are perpetuated. What remains unresolved is how far peripheral countries and regions can break out of this location and what kinds of institutions and policies might help bring this about. This question is an intriguing one in terms of the recent economic rise of China, India, and Brazil, which was not predicted by world-system theory, yet has also not been achieved by recourse to economic deregulation alone. Power-centred theories remain important, but their more precise value and limits will be explored further in later chapters.

A third alternative set of resources involves the integration of gender and feminist perspectives into accounts of global social inequality. Building on earlier work on distinctive gender-based inequalities in the global arena (Enloe 1989), the volume *Globalization and Inequalities* by Sylvia Walby (2009) represents a major sociological contribution to multidimensional analyses of contemporary global inequality. One key feature is the emphasis given to violence as a fundamental aspect of inequality, alongside more conventional approaches that see inequality as economic, political, and cultural. This innovation stems in large measure from feminist accounts of patriarchal violence against women, but integrates this focus with the analysis of violence in international relations and in the operation of globalization. Violence is endemic in the contemporary world in both public and domestic arenas. Its emergence as an analytical theme in the study of global inequality is one of a number of ways that sociological approaches extend the intellectual framework beyond an economistic framework.

These three examples begin to indicate the explanatory potential of a wider sociological and historical focus on global inequality. They are not the only perspectives of this kind. Nor do I wish to prejudge their capacity to deal with the inadequacies of economistic thinking. These issues will be debated below. What is important for the moment is to emphasize that there are alternative resources to the influential and prominent theoretical work of economists.

(b) Looking at Global Inequality Historically

The *second* distinctive feature of this book is its focus on historical patterns of social division and their consequences for the present. While spatial inequalities are integral to global social divisions, there are comparatively few accounts which link past inequalities to those of the present. Much public commentary on global inequality reaches straight for the latest evidence or stories about inequality, attributing current problems and crises simply to contemporary institutions and activities. This has the merit of being relevant and topical. Yet it forecloses on some very important questions about long-term rather than short-term patterns and explanations of inequality.

In this book, a strong argument is made that historical inequalities are important to any understanding and explanation of current inequalities. Without a historical perspective, it is difficult to determine how far contemporary inequalities are the product of contemporary capitalism and globalization, how far the effect of patterns of inequality established in the past, and how far these processes interact. This focus is pursued in part because there is some evidence that different nations seem to have distinct long-term patterns of inequality that stretch across decades and even centuries. Put another way, patterns of within-country inequality do not appear to be converging on a single general pattern that is true across all countries.

But there is another reason why a historical approach is significant for the study of inequality, which sheds light on why social inequality is such a major political and moral preoccupation. As the sociologist Ulrich Beck has pointed out, 'in a historical perspective, social inequalities become a political scandal relatively late' (2010, 167). The point here is that objective social differences only become inequalities when they are understood as violating social norms and when they are seen as socially generated and thus amenable to social reform. For much of history, inequality was seen as natural and a product of God's will. It was part of the order of things.

The shattering of this order, Beck argues, began with the 18th-century Enlightenment which prized individual reason, liberty, and equality above religious faith, and above the authority of monarchs and aristocrats. From this point onwards, equality, the obverse of inequality, has become a major social, political, and cultural value. This provides the yardstick by which inequality is perceived as unjust and unnecessary, which in turn legitimizes a new politics of inequality reduction through social action.

Ideals of equality take many forms and have a longer history than Beck supposes. As the late medieval commentator Piers Plowman asked in a celebrated question posed on the eve of the Peasants Revolt of 1381, 'When Adam delved and Eve span, who was then the gentleman?' The implication here is that social hierarchy and inequality are not natural features of an unchanging order. There may then be subaltern religious routes into the emergence of discourses of social inequality well before the Enlightenment. Traditions of communitarianism from below are also relevant to criticisms of inequality, both historically and in the present day. Yet suitably amended for a less schematic approach to history, Beck's general approach to social evaluation and the historic emergence of concerns about inequality is a valid one. Put simply, such concerns do not arise when the rich get richer and the poor get poorer, but only when social norms of equality arise and spread (ibid. 166).

(c) Taking a Global Rather than National Approach

The *third* distinctive feature of this book is that it rejects the exclusively nation state approach to inequality taken by most sociologists of social inequality and social stratification over the last three or four decades. Inequality within nations is a very important aspect of social inequality and is one that has a strong resonance in the rise of democracy and the welfare state, especially in Western Europe. However, as we shall see in detail below, a growing proportion of global inequality over the last 200 years has been due to between-country inequality rather than within-country inequality (Bourguignon and Morrison 2002, Milanovic 2011). This striking research finding gives credibility to theorists of globalization who argue that the image of a world of separate nation states or 'societies', within which social life takes place, has become misleading in a world of intense interdependencies between regions, nations, organizations, and households.

This image, often branded 'methodological nationalism', remains the focus of much sociological research on social stratification and social mobility (Beck 2007). A nation-focussed approach is certainly defensible in that nation states remain a robust part of the international order (Mann 1993, 1997) and provides much of the context for struggles over nation-based inequalities. This defence is however inadequate if we want to know how much inequality exists between nations, and ho border mobilities of capital, commodities, and labour affect p... of inequality and opportunity. Methodological nationalism is therefore inadequate as a basis for understanding global inequality, though quite what replaces it remains a matter for continuing debate.

Beck (2007, 2010) prefers to think in terms of methodological cosmopolitanism, implying that cross-border connections are more central to global inequality than nationally bounded inequalities. Yet cosmopolitanism is a normative term as much as an analytical one, whereby transnational connections and allegiances are privileged over bounded national frames of reference. It may therefore be less contentious to adopt a methodology which takes both national and cross-border processes and relationships as central to the analysis of global inequality. Instead of methodological nationalism or methodological cosmopolitanism, we might think of methodological glocalism (Holton 2009, 106–110), whereby global and local aspects of inequality are treated simultaneously and conjointly. This serves as a productive framework for thinking of global inequality not simply as an amalgam of between-country and within-country inequality, but also as a product of processes that transcend the economic and political life of nations.

Global inequality: A provisional definition

On the basis of the discussion so far, I now provide a working definition of what is meant here by global inequality.

Inequality refers to differences in the circumstances, opportunities, life chances, and characteristics of populations of individuals. Social inequality refers both to causes of inequality thought to lie in human society and to characteristics of individuals and groups that are regarded as socially meaningful. The populations of individuals said to exhibit inequality are typically grouped, whether in social classes, by country or region of residence, or by gender, race, or ethnicity. Meanwhile, identification of inequality requires criteria whereby populations are differentiated, whether these involve measurement and quantification, or rely on more qualitative indicators of social status and access to life-enhancing resources. These are considered historically, not simply by reference to contemporary trends.

Global inequalities take the population in question to be the world's inhabitants. Inequalities in this sense can be thought of simply in terms of differences, especially income differences between separate individuals, wherever they live. However, this neglects the social relationships and networks within which people live, including families and households, communities, villages, cities, and migrant networks of various kinds.

I shall explore what difference it makes to examine inequality between individuals and inequality between households later in this book. I shall also explore the limitations of using income alone to understand global inequality. For the moment, attention is drawn to a further issue of definition. This concerns a distinction that has become of increasing importance in recent debates, in which inequality within countries is distinguished from inequality between countries. Whereas most attention has previously been given to the former, the latter has in fact grown to represent the major sources of inequality in the world today (Bourguignon and Morrison 2002, Milanovic 2011). This reinforces the importance of considering global as against purely national sources of global inequality. The underlying question here is why between-nation inequalities have become so significant?

Taken overall, global inequality may be thought of as the sum of within-country inequality and between-country inequality. It may also be seen as open to both global and national influences affecting the distribution of income and broader life chances among world citizens.

Plan of the Book

Chapter 2 is concerned with theories of social inequality developed within social science. This chapter will identify three general approaches characteristic of economics, political economy, and sociology. These broad approaches are not monolithic and contain varieties of analysis and internal intellectual conflict. Nor should they be regarded as entirely separate from each other, since they have emerged in large measure through mutual debate and critical engagement. They are nonetheless a helpful way of simplifying complex debates over the scope, causes, and policy options arising in the study of global inequality.

Economics will be discussed via a critical evaluation of the positive claims made for markets and their impact on economic growth, development, poverty reduction, and enhanced human welfare. The development of global markets and huge flows of capital and commodities have seen an extension in economic development and expansion of economic growth over the last 200 years. Yet markets left to themselves do not distribute the benefits of economic growth equally or fairly. Long phases of global capitalist development have not produced a steady and regular convergence of incomes among market participants. Why then are many aspects of inequality still growing? Market liberals often attribute this simply to non-market factors such as cultural conservatism or lack of resources. Yet the possibility has to be faced that market capitalism and associated policies, such as economic deregulation, can generate inequality and instability in some respects, even while it may be a source of development and improved productivity in others. If there are weaknesses as well as strengths in market-based accounts of economic growth then what additional intellectual resources are available to meet these deficiencies.

Discussion then turns to political economy and economic sociology as two broader sets of resources. Political economy focusses on power-centred accounts of the functioning of markets and the origins of inequality, and on the necessarily political processes whereby inequality is reproduced or resisted. Key work in this tradition includes world system theory and theories of imperialism and globalization, including work by Wallerstein (1974, 1979, 1991) and his associates and Bob Sutcliffe (2007). This approach analyses markets as structures of power and deals directly with between-country inequalities. The policy implications involve major structural reform to global governance of markets, requiring changes to institutions such as the World Bank and World Trade Organization. A major problem here is whether all sources of inequality may be reduced to inequalities of economic power. The discussion here opens up the idea of power inequalities to wider extension beyond capital ownership to examine state power and the discursive politics of gender and race.

Attention shifts finally to a third sociological option able to integrate markets, states, households, and cultural practices into the study of global inequality. Until very recently sociology had far more to say about within-country inequalities, including class, gender, race, and ethnicity, than about global inequalities between countries and regions. It was left very largely to radical political economists and interdisciplinary scholars in development studies, geography, and international relations to generate accounts of global structures of inequality. In the last two decades sociologists have played an important and growing part in debates around globalization. This has brought together analyses of political and cultural as well as economic and technological aspects of global processes. Important sociological contributors to analyses of global inequality include Walby (2009), Beck (2007, 2010), Castells (1996), and Therborn (2006).

The major strengths of the sociological approach are to integrate the study of power inequalities with other features of social relationships and institutions. Sociology shares with political economy an emphasis on linkages between markets and states, including the relevance of policies of regulation and deregulation, taxation, and social redistribution to outcomes of inequality. It has, however, been more likely to focus on patterns of inequality associated with gender and race, as well as having a more explicit focus on global migration and its implications for inequality. Sociology also has a long-standing concern with problems of social integration as well as problems of inequality and conflict, and is thus more able to theorize how we might grasp ways of generating a greater element of cross-national and inter-cultural harmony in the face of radical global inequality. This links debates more explicitly with moral philosophers' concerns with the injustices of global inequality, together with the activist climate of negative opinion towards the global economy.

Having outlined the strengths and limitations of three important theoretical traditions, Chapter 3 offers a brief historical sociology of global inequality. This sets out from the proposition that globalization has a long history pre-dating modern capitalism. This has involved processes of empire, slavery, and migration, as well as the eventual emergence of the capitalist world system, free trade, and recent phases of migration. Several key issues follow from this. One is that global social inequality in the past may have causes unrelated to modern capitalism. In this sense capitalism or deregulated markets did not invent global inequality, nor are 'free markets' necessarily always the major source of present global inequalities. To be sure, historical processes are complex. Institutions like slavery may in some settings, like 18th-century plantation agriculture, be integral to global markets, even if in older periods they were primarily political and imperial in character. The implication here is to treat long-run comparisons in global inequality with caution.

A second issue to be explored is how far divisions and inequality from the past may still influence contemporary experience. In this respect the experience of slavery and colonization are clearly still reference points in cultural relations between post-colonial and post-slave countries and populations on the one side, and countries, usually wealthier countries, with an Imperial or slave-owning past on the other. This issue has current resonances in conflicts over migration, where wealthier countries try to limit immigration from poorer countries, including those which were previously colonized. In the United States, meanwhile, a kind of internal colonialism has been detected in relations between the 'white' racial core and the 'African-American' population, relations which 150 years after the abolition of slavery remain characterized by inequality.

Chapter 3, therefore, offers a historical perspective on global inequality today, which is useful both for comparative purposes across time and for the analysis of historical legacies in the present.

Chapters 4, 5, and 6 are concerned with contemporary aspects of global inequality in its widest senses. They are largely evidence based and contain material on both economic and broader aspects of inequality. They discuss forms of inequality that can be quantified statistically, as well as qualitative evidence based on the life-experience of individuals and groups.

Chapter 4 discusses global inequalities of income and wealth, applying both within countries and between them. This literature is extensive and dominates discussions by economists. Drawing on the historical approach in Chapter 3, this chapter first examines how far income inequality has grown or lessened since the acceleration in industrialization and global economic development over the last 200 years. The approach will be non-technical. A major question in this section is how far income gaps between rich and poor countries may be narrowing or widening further. This will include reference to the rise of China, which appears to be bridging part of the gap between poorer and somewhat wealthier countries, as well as to the failure of poverty reduction in many of the poorest countries.

The chapter goes on to discuss major innovations in recent research including the distinction between within-country and between-country inequality and the growing use of household-based survey evidence. A key reference point here is the work of the economist Branko Milanovic (see below). This will be examined in depth as a contribution to current debates about whether global inequality is increasing, decreasing, or stable. Will between-country inequality continue to be the largest contributor to global inequality or is within-country inequality now widening in significance, as proposed by Goran Therborn (2011)?

In Chapter 5 the analysis of inequality extends the focus from income and wealth to issues of life expectancy and morbidity, health, education, disablement, discrimination and exclusion, and political participation. These wider measures of inequality are necessary to broaden the economistic focus on income into social relations within households, communities, and the political sphere. Here, non-income based aspects of inequality remain highly significant. Conceptually, this broadening connects with the idea of human development rather than individual welfare, taking us beyond the excessively thin and abbreviated accounts of individual well-being provided in most schools of economic theory.

This broader approach also extends the focus beyond economic analysis, bringing in wider social science literatures, using qualitative as well as quantitative evidence. A major aim here is to clarify what difference inclusion of social processes makes to an understanding of global inequality. While income and non-income aspects of inequality are, of course integrally connected, they are discussed here in separate chapters to aid analysis and to correct the primary emphasis on income in the economic literature.

Gender inequality affects not only income but the health of women and children and wider rights to social participation. It has been a consistent feature of global inequality over the broad sweep of history, although there has also been some progress in narrowing the gender gap. The discussion will consider how far this has occurred and what major obstacles remain. Another major theme is race, ethnicity, and migration. This extends the analysis beyond atomized households towards global mobilities and the overlay of imperial and colonial hierarchies on current post-colonial populations.

Chapter 6 draws together analytical themes developed in earlier chapters and is centred around the question, 'How far does globalization cause global inequality?' This question is fundamental to many current debates and to activist politics like the well-known protests at the 1999 meeting of the World Trade Organization in Seattle or the more recent challenges posed by the Occupy movements to symbols of corporate power in New York and London. The presumption that contemporary globalization is mainly responsible for global inequality is however problematic and too simplistic. Global inequality does not necessarily get worse when economic globalization intensifies. A far broader and more subtle analysis is required to get at the complexity of the many different reasons for different types of inequality. Economic globalization is connected with some features of global inequality. Yet it represents only part of the story. And its influence has in some ways been positive rather than fundamentally negative.

The discussion here will assess how far global corporate activity, backed up by global institutions and policies, is responsible for global inequalities. What aspects of global inequality can be attributed to free trade, foreign direct investment, and global migration? And what effects have policies of economic deregulation had on lifting poor countries out of poverty. Conversely, what positive contributions have emerged from economic globalization?

As it turns out, economic openness through free trade is not invariably connected with a worsening inequality, especially in the medium to long term. Global markets can and do however worsen the position of the poorer countries under certain circumstances and this discussion explains how. Foreign direct investment also has positive as well as negative effects. On the other hand the enforcement of programmes of deregulation and privatization in ways that ignore the social and political features of poor countries often also make things worse. The case of sub-Saharan Africa, one of the poorest regions of the world, is investigated at a number of points in the analysis to illustrate the relevance and limits of global influences on intractable levels of inequality.

Having analysed the complex connections – positive as well as negative – between globalization and inequality, the analysis in the second part of the chapter examines a wider set of themes. These include environmental processes that contribute to inequality, which are themselves linked with demographic changes. Further attention is then given to the cultural politics of racism and patriarchy which is central to explaining forms of inequality that affect human potential and self-esteem. Finally issues to do with local political institutions are also taken into account. Once again the underlying analytical emphasis is on the multidimensional nature of global inequality and the value of a broad sociological approach in explaining the complex reasons for it.

The concluding chapter, Chapter 7, asks what can be done about global inequality? This question is linked back to the explanations of inequality discussed in the previous chapters. The chapter is concerned with general features of development aid and broad policy strategies and policies rather than more detailed blueprints. Which general policy responses might work and which have proven less fruitful?

One of the main analytical findings of the book is that globalization is not in and of itself the general overarching cause of global inequality. The causes are multiple and relate to both global and national processes and policies. This suggests that policies of anti-globalization or de-globalization will not reduce global inequality, and certainly not between-country inequality. Meanwhile there are some aspects of globalization that may in many circumstances stimulate development and incomes in poorer countries. The evidence suggests that trade openness and foreign direct investment may often have a positive impact. What doesn't work is the rigid Washington Consensus model of enforced deregulation and privatization, without adequate social supports and reforming political institutions. Market autonomy is simply not enough to reduce inequality. Left to themselves, 'free markets' may exacerbate development problems and increase inequalities. So there remains the problem of how to make global capitalism more consistent with inequality reduction and delivering fairer and more just ways of distributing incomes and public resources.

Global inequality still seems to many to be entrenched. Yet there are some signs of movement, notably the rise of the so-called BRIC countries of China, India, Brazil, and Russia. While internally unequal, their successful economic development, especially that of China, has made some inroads into global between-country inequality when measured by income and considered on a per capita basis. Yet this has not been achieved on the basis of radical deregulation but on a state-managed basis of selective and partial deregulation. This process also indicates that the contemporary capitalist world-system is not so rigidly unequal that change is impossible, such that all poorer nations are trapped forever in inequality and poverty. The BRIC countries are nonetheless relatively powerful nation states compared with many of the smaller poorer nations in Africa and Asia. Consistent with world-system theory the BRIC countries themselves may already be creating newer inequalities of power and influence in their relations with weaker nations and regions.

The chapter then goes on to discuss how far national initiatives can also work and how far recourse to a reformed system of global governance is necessary. Two particular policy measures relevant to inequality reduction are discussed which depend on a more intensified intervention by international organization and states into economic affairs. These are the proposal for a global financial transactions tax and the idea of a greater deregulation of global migration.

Contrary to the argument of Nussbaum and others, nation states are not enough to ensure the global co-operation implement measures in pursuit of enhanced human development. These issues are discussed through a detailed review of the policy-relevant work of the Harvard economist Danni Rodrik. These focus on his theory of a trilemma between economic globalization, national sovereignty, and democracy – the trilemma being having all three of these simultaneously seems impossible.

One potential way forward is through a social-democratic rather than neo-liberal form of global governance. The merits of this are considered as a possible contribution to a post-Washington Consensus world. Social-democratic initiatives are relevant to many dimensions of inequality including violence and cultural exclusion as well as income.

The argument in this chapter consistently warns agains
general policy recipes for global inequality. It also uses a case
successful global health policies in favour of a pragmatic element i
icy responses. This focusses on what works and why? The case stu
indicates that elite-sponsored top-down approaches to global inequality in this sector do not work. Rather multiple actors operating from below as well as above are central to health improvements that work to release poor populations from the baneful effects of chronic disease and demoralization. In this arena political willingness to act makes a huge difference, as does community participation. The chapter concludes with six specific recommendations for global inequality reduction.

·ies of Social
ality

This chapter examines theories of social inequality developed within social science. Such theories typically develop general explanations of the origins and consequences of inequality. This chapter identifies three such approaches: the work of economists on markets and globalization, the perspective of political economy centred on power, and sociology centred on interactions between economic, political, and cultural life. (For further insight into these traditions see Holton 1992.)

These three approaches are neither entirely uniform nor sharply separate from each other. There is therefore some overlap and common ground to the questions asked, concepts used and evidence analysed, but also some striking differences and contrasts in theoretical breadth, and analytical focus. Such differences also generate somewhat differing accounts of the scope, causes, and consequences of global inequality. This chapter does not provide a comprehensive account of the economics of markets, the political economy of power or the sociology of globalization. What I set out to do is to analyse the ways these three distinctive approaches understand global inequality. The aim is to identify and evaluate their analytical strengths and weaknesses, and, more specifically, to establish what a sociological account adds to economics and political economy.

Economics

Key themes and issues

Economists have made much of the running in analysing global inequality. They have been instrumental in advancing theories of the causes of inequality, and why inequality varies between nations (Kuznets 1955). They have also provided accounts of the historical patterning of inequality (Bourguignon and Morrison 2002), and analysed data on income inequality for both individuals and households (Milanovic 2011). Economists have also given considerable attention to analysing how far and in what senses globalization is responsible for contemporary patterns of global inequality. Economists have also been instrumental in policy advice and evaluation in relation to global development and the amelioration of global poverty, involving institutions like the World Bank. Economists have not, however, spoken with one voice, but remain divided over the relationship between deregulated markets, and their effect on patterns of equality and inequality. Much of the work on recent increases in inequality has been done by economists.

The orthodox neoclassical position among economists, dating from the last 19th and early 20th centuries, claims that deregulated or at least lightly regulated markets are a critical source of economic efficiency and thus higher productivity. This is because they can draw on the dynamic potential of self-interest applied rationally by producers and consumers to fuel economic expansion. Compared with alternative economic systems that involve higher levels of political regulation, including socialist or communist systems, markets are seen as more efficient and therefore able to better enhance economic opportunity and raise incomes. In the 20th century this approach was extended further in analyses of economic growth and global economic development. The dominant characteristic underlying most work by economists is one of economic liberalism.

The criticism that markets do not guarantee an equitable distribution of resources adequate to meet needs of entire populations has been around for at least two centuries. Yet optimism about market-based prosperity revived after the world wars and economic depression of the first half of the 20th century. This was most evident in the United States among economists and many sociologists. Modernization theory arose in this context around the varied work of Rostow (1960), Parsons (1971), and Blau and Duncan (1967). The broad argument of modernization theory was that Western societies undergoing successful industrialization were making a transition from traditional to modern society. Modernity meant deregulated markets, coupled with political democracy and a culture of individualistic achievement. The personality structure of modernizing societies was integral to economic success and upward social mobility through the medium of education to enhance marketable skills. Society, still thought of in terms of individual nation states, would become more egalitarian as productive markets and achievement-oriented and better educated individuals transcended traditional limitations. Such achievements were thought to be transferable to all parts of the world through diffusion of Western institutions.

This optimism about markets and modern institutions drew in part on the historical record of long-term economic growth and social transformation achieved in Western Europe and North America. Market-based economies, so it was argued, performed better than alternative systems like the command or Communist economies of Eastern Europe. This viewpoint seemed to be confirmed by the crisis and collapse of Communist economies in the late 20th century. Market optimism was further consolidated by the economic benefits associated with the renewed phase of economic globalization since the Second World War. Global markets, so the argument went, provided an even more productive and dynamic economy capable of lifting living standards around the globe not simply for the wealthiest societies. Such assumptions were built into the so-called Washington consensus – a principle of global governance enshrined in the operations of the International Monetary Fund, World Bank, and World Trade Organization. This linked market deregulation, privatization of public enterprises, and cross-border mobility of capital and commodities with economic growth and global prosperity.

The orthodox view among economists is well summarized by Martin Wolf, a leading financial journalist, who claimed that economically successful countries share 'a move towards the market economy', based on 'private property rights, free enterprise, and competition', rather than 'state ownership, planning and protection'. In short 'they chose... the path of economic liberalization and international integration. This is the heart of the matter. All else is commentary' (Wolf 2004, 143–140).

The emphasis of economic liberalism on market efficiency as the key to modernity and improved human welfare ran into increasing problems in the last third of the 20th century for failing to lift the life chances of large segments of the world's population. The problem of distribution, namely how to spread the benefits of economic innovation to all, inherited from the 19th century, was evident on a world scale despite a huge economic upswing after 1950. Once again greater economic efficiency did not automatically guarantee an equitable distribution of income, wealth, and broader living standards. Hubris among economists and modernization theorists re-emerged in the financial upswing of the 1990's, only to be deflated by the global financial crisis of 2008–2009, which was both a crisis of regulatory failure *and* market failure (Holton 2012). Economic value was destroyed on a colossal scale, as governments stepped in to provide the stabilization that markets could not.

A critical evaluation of economic liberalism

A more balanced evaluation of the strengths and limitations of economic liberalism than the one summarized by Martin Wolf requires a greater recognition of complexity. On the one hand, markets driven by rational self-interest and entrepreneurial zeal are dynamic and greater economic productivity does lift aggregate incomes over time. Yet there are public as well as private contributions to productivity in areas such as legally secure property rights, war-derived technological innovation, human capital upgrading, and infrastructural support. So it is simplistic and utopian to argue that free markets are the heart of the matter. And beyond this, it is also clear that the benefits of market dynamism do not flow inexorably through to all sections of the population and all parts of the world.

Underlying this criticism of economic liberalism are three key propositions. The first is that social inequality as measured by the gap between the wealthiest and the poorest has widened rather than narrowed over time. In 1820, as Milanovic (2011, 100), points out, the richest countries in the world, Great Britain and the Netherlands were only three times richer than India and China. Today the richest are a hundred times more wealthy than the poorest, while Britain, far from the richest country is six times wealthier than China, in spite of China's economic development over the last decade. Another way of making this point is to compare the shares of the wealthiest 10% and the poorest 10%. At a global level Milanovic calculates that the richest 10% of the world's population receive 56% of global income, while the poorest receive only 0.7%, making a ratio of around 80 to 1 (ibid. 152).

The counter-argument by economic liberals is that the poorest are those least well integrated into the global economy, as in much of sub-Saharan Africa. Their plight cannot therefore be attributed to markets or economic globalization. They suffer from too little globalization not too much. This defence is not, however, all that convincing for a number of reasons. True there may be local causes of slow growth and extreme poverty linked with adverse climates, poor resource endowment, and government corruption (Sachs and Warner 1997). Yet this is not the entire picture. To argue simply for local causes of distributional failure excludes the possibility that there are external causes too. These have to do with the actions of external interests including corporations, Western governments and institutions of global governance. Growth rates and by implication a lessening of inequality could have occurred even with poor resource endowment, according to Sachs and Warner (ibid. 27–28), if public policies had been different. Nor should it be assumed that local political circumstances always reproduce inequality. In later work by Sachs et al. 2004, evidence about positive features of many African political institutions renders the common stereotype of poor African governance across the board highly misleading.

Rich country governments typically protect their home markets by restrictions on immigration from poorer countries, thereby cutting one route to a better life. A number of countries including the United States and nations within the EU also protect their agricultural markets by subsidizing home producers, restricting the capacity of poorer food-producers to trade their way out of poverty. Finally the operations of IMF and World Bank programmes in areas such as sub-Saharan Africa, have, despite their best intentions, produced more negative rather than positive consequences (Stiglitz 2002).

An underlying problem behind radical market-centred remedies in such situations is often that market supporting resources such as transport infrastructures or institutions such as local suppliers of credit are scarce. To rapidly reduce state initiatives and to assume that markets will readily pick up a self-sustaining developmental momentum in such circumstances has often made things worse. The anti-government bias here contrasts with the largely successful combination of market and state-based economic development of China over the last three decades.

The failure of market-centred approaches to agriculture is made clear in Stein's (2011) study of World Bank agricultural policies in sub-Saharan Africa. Over the last three decades, poverty and the inequality gap with the rest of the world have generally worsened in this region. Stein links this very largely with anti-government bias and poorly designed market-centred programmes. When the World Bank required cuts to public expenditure, investment in roads or irrigation declined from already low levels, as did research and development in agriculture. Similarly when fertiliser supply was deregulated and subsidized provision to farmers ceased in countries like Tanzania, market prices rose so high than many farmers stopped using fertiliser and productivity fell. Meanwhile private credit provision did not quickly emerge as an incentive to efficient producers to innovate and expand. There is then a large gap here between an efficient world of rational self-interested farmers following flexible price signals to raise production and the reality of farmers lacking access to credit, and good roads to get produce to market. In such settings, information costs involved in learning about new techniques are high, as are climatic risks to successful harvesting.

The conclusion that should be drawn here is not that markets cannot contribute to economic development or create opportunity for people to lift themselves out of poverty. Nor is it that globalization is the source of all development problems. It is rather that economic liberalism has significant limits as the underpinning for a strategy for successful development and reduction of the grossest forms of global inequality.

The second proposition involved in the critique of economic liberalism is that there has only been limited convergence between the inequality profiles of the world's nations over time. This issue matters for both economic liberalism and modernization theory because it was assumed that as economic transformation from traditional to modern practices took place this would tend to produce similar patterns of income distribution for the countries involved. One theoretical underpinning for this projection is the argument that globalization produces convergence in the prices of factors of production like capital and labour and that this should also mean that per capita incomes across the world tend to converge. This is of course a matter both for within-country inequality, where the national income distribution profiles of individual countries should come closer together, and between-country inequality, where cross-border wage rates should converge with the normal rider – other things being equal.

In economic thought the assumption of convergence of global income profiles is largely based on the neo-classical theory of international trade developed by Heckscher and Ohlin (for more detailed discussion of this see O'Rourke 2002, 40ff). This theory contains large numbers of assumptions. In basic form it is assumed that trade patterns reflect differences in endowments between nations. Increased global market integration should therefore increase the demand for abundant factors of production (e.g. types of capital and labour), raising returns to them, and reduce demand for scarcer more expensive factors reducing their price. To simplify, using a two-country model based on the United States and Mexico, 'If the US is abundant in skilled labour and Mexico in unskilled labour, trade will increase US skilled wages and Mexican unskilled wages, while lowering US unskilled wages, and Mexican skilled wages' (O'Rourke 2002, 41). Thus trade should increase wage inequality in the United States and reduce it in Mexico.

However in the real world things are more complicated. First, there is the issue of cross-border migration from South to North. Unskilled migration from Mexico to the United States may have the same effects as trade, raising wage inequality between skilled and unskilled in the United States. However skilled labour migration from Mexico will have the reverse effect, reducing wage inequality in the United States, and increasing it in Mexico. The more general implication of this point is that cross-border trade is not the only economic mechanism that can influence patterns of global inequality. Labour flows are another.

A second complicating issue is that patterns of economic development vary across time as well as space, and may not then be susceptible to a single general theoretical analysis. The best evidence for a positive impact of cross-border migration on the lessening of inequality through convergence in the profiles of different countries comes not from the contemporary world of immigration controls, but from the expanding late 19th century global economy. Here within-country inequality decreased over the period 1850–1914 during a period of relatively uncontrolled migration, especially prior to 1900. Such labour flows had an egalitarian effect because most migration was from poorer to richer countries (O'Rourke 2002, 55). At the same time, as the Heckscher-Ohlin model predicts, the predominately unskilled labour flows from Old World Europe to the New World, saw inequality lessen in the Old World and increase in the New.

Interestingly, this point about the possible egalitarian effects of unskilled global migration is germane to current policy debates about global poverty reduction. If global labour flows were as deregulated as flows of capital and commodities are, then considerable inroads might be made into global inequality. The reason this does not happen is more to do with the self-interest of richer countries (including the interests of their poorer unskilled populations fearing job competition), than with markets or capitalism per se.

There is a another complicating issue in the analysis of trade, globalization, and inequality. This is the obvious point that developing countries vary considerably in factor endowments and in the distribution of these endowments between citizens. It matters who has marketable skills, who owns resources such as land and industrial capital, and how political power is distributed The impact of deregulated globalized trade on such countries, depends therefore on far more than supply and demand for commodities and its impact on incomes. In the case of land ownership in the Old World, for example, a rise in the ratio of wages to rents, contingent on outmigration of labour would have an adverse effect on the income of large landowners and a more egalitarian effect on the income distribution. If land ownership was smaller scale, by contrast, a worsening of conditions for poorer producers would have the opposite effect.

Attention now turns to a third proposition in the critique of economic liberalism. This, following on from the second proposition, is that economic liberalism fails to deal satisfactorily with the social context to economic activity. This neglect is in a sense deliberate and partly understandable. Economics is after all founded on a simplified account of human behaviour and social life, in which wider complexities are bracketed out in favour of postulates of rational self-interest and income or welfare maximizing behaviour. This approach treats as external (or exogenous), questions as to where wants or interests or cultures of entrepreneurial innovation come from, what kinds of relationships people enter in the course of conducting economic life, and what consequences follow for social stability and cohesion.

This conceptual parsimony is thought to be justified according to the following logic, namely, 'If the world operated according to the postulates of rational self-interest, then under any given set of conditions, markets would be efficient and maximise incomes'. Inasmuch as this doesn't happen, then recourse is had to augmented models. So if many sub-Saharan African countries today remain trapped in poverty, this must be because other factors are interfering with the market, rather than due in some way to the market itself. The suspicion in the recourse to ad hoc augmentation often arises that perhaps markets can never fail theoretically, in which case we seem to be dealing with market utopianism rather than evidence-based social science.

At the same time, the more recourse is had to ad hoc augmentation to the basic model, the more the underlying problems with conceptual parsimony are dramatized. This is not to say that has market economics has stood still. It hasn't. It has been theoretically extended in recent decades in a number of ways. These include the use of game theory to analyse strategic behaviour that takes account of others moving us beyond the solipsistic world of atomized market actors. It has also made inroads into the functioning of non-market institutions and imperfect information through the economics of transaction costs. Economics has also inspired historically informed analysis of the relationship between property rights, economic growth, and inequality (North 2005). Economists now think of markets in a more sophisticated way than before, speaking of markets and hierarchies or markets, hierarchies and networks (Thompson 2003). Some of this work is labelled 'new institutionalism' to signify new ways of thinking about the interplay of markets and institutions.

Many of the remaining problems with the application of economistic models to the real world, according to Stiglitz (2002), former chief economist of the World Bank, are because new insights have not been applied. He cites problems of information affecting areas like unemployment and credit (xi–xii). Markets were assumed necessarily to be efficient in any context – whether in Europe, Africa, or Asia, leaving aside a broader understanding of obstacles to market functioning, or opportunities for governments to guide economic development in a market-supporting way. For Rodrik (2011, 12) insufficient attention has been given to the preconditions for market-based trade. 'Ultimately', he says, 'someone has to take responsibility for peace, security and the framework of laws and regulations that makes trade possible'. Such preconditions are 'social arrangements' (14), a notion which we may develop further by thinking in terms both of political institutions of state and law, and underlying normative and cultural principles, like respect for the rule of law or willingness to comply with legitimate political authority. While it is clearly possible for capitalist enterprise to function in relatively lawless, corrupt, and authoritarian contexts in Russia, parts of Asia, and Africa, over the long term markets generally depend more on stability and the minimization of uncertainty.

It is one thing to augment economic theory with further elements to cope with the complexities of the real world and quite another to theorize interactions between economy and society in a more systematic way. A broader and more persuasive way of approaching this problem is to construct a better understanding of systematic connections between economy, polity, and culture.

Missing elements in economic thought

There are a number of missing themes that need attention here. Power is an obvious starting point because the dynamics of global inequality depend on who owns or has control over economic resources, and how far that power is exercised in a unilateral manner rather than subject to checks, balances and resistance by other social forces. Power is however not simply an economic matter, but extends beyond to military, political, cultural and ideological processes (Mann 1986). This means that there are multiple sources of power-based inequality. These may be based on institutions of empire which seek territorial as much as economic control over populations. In the ancient Roman Empire, extreme wealth was held in the hands not only of the Emperor but of administrators and officials who plundered the provinces of resources (Milanovic 2011, 48–49). Inequalities of power may also arise from forms of social exclusion and domination based on gender and race as much as economic or military power. In the case of gender, systematic inequalities in income and in social participation have depended across history on a range of political and cultural forms of exclusion. These have involved a major divide in social status, regarded by feminist scholars such as Cynthia Epstein (2007), as the 'most fundamental social divide' (1), founded on male-dominated 'systems of ruling and governing...on national and local [and I would add global] levels' (4) [my parentheses].

Another theme generally neglected by economic thought is social order or integration. This is relevant to questions of global inequality, inasmuch as patterns of inequality come to be regarded as unacceptable sources of social tension, political conflict, and instability. It is very superficial to argue, as some ideologists of free markets do, that protest against social inequality is driven only by the politics of envy. This is to deny the integrity of the differing values people may hold, and is, ironically, a very illiberal position for supposed defenders of liberalism to take up. In any case egalitarianism, has both a long history in one shape of form, and plays a major role in contemporary modernity, including political liberals in the European sense, as much as parties of the Left and campaigners against global inequality. It will not go away. Accordingly, analysts of inequality are obliged to take such views into account as an aspect of the social setting in which processes of inequality arise and are played out.

This broader line of argument embraces the different world-views (or 'imaginaries', Jessop 2010), with which analysts frame an understanding of global inequality. For most economists, typical world-views centre on assumptions and narratives about the necessity of deregulated markets to sustain global competition, create greater efficiency, and wealth creation. These have been described here as economic liberalism. But they are also widely referred to as neo-liberalism. This is because they have implications for government and policy as well as markets. So what then are the alternatives to neo-liberalism? What options are available to provide a better understanding of global inequality and the social setting in which it has arisen and is reproduced over time. What alternative narratives have been articulated? And how do these contribute to alternative understandings of what forms of government, policy, and social action might mitigate or transform existing levels of global inequality?

Alternatives to Economics

Two major alternatives are discussed here. One is political economy, the other sociology.

Political economy

Political economy in the sense used here, may be defined as a power-centred approach to markets and economic life. Political economy in the 18th and 19th centuries was a tradition of thought that included writers as diverse as Adam Smith, Ricardo, and Karl Marx (for further background, see Winch 1996, Walton and Gamble 1972). What they shared was a wider sense of the political and social context to economic development than was later to emerge in neo-classical economics developed in the late 19th century. Ricardo and Marx were interested in inequality as it was manifest in the distribution of income between social classes rather than its distribution among individuals. And it was Marx, in particular who made the unequal power of social classes a centre point of his analysis of the capitalist mode of production. This power-centred approach has thrived over the last 150 years in work on imperialism and the capitalist world-system, as reviewed below.

Major themes linking political economy and global inequality

Political economy is considered here in relation to problems of global inequality in general, and the continuing reproduction of inequality in particular. While Marx's influence is still significant in the analysis of globalization, political economy approaches have had to engage with a major problem with his work. This is the assumption that global capitalism is sufficiently dynamic as to transform all parts of the world. Capitalism would emerge everywhere in an advanced form. However expansive it has been, this has simply not happened. Instead the development of the global economy is characterized by profound differences across regions and countries in levels of development, and by profound forms of social inequality between as well as within countries.

Power-centred accounts of the global economy, labelled here as political economy, typically focus on one or more of the following processes (Table 2.1):-

Table 2.1 Political economy and power

- The power relations operating in an international division of labour where high-value activities (such as research and development) are primarily located in wealthier countries while low-value activities, such as component assembly are mostly to located in poorer countries.
- The power to influence the terms of trade between countries such that interests based in richer countries are generally able to secure primary products at a cheap price, maximizing their incomes and profits, while interests in poorer countries must accept lower prices adversely affecting their incomes and development potential.

- The power to control technological innovations through intellectual property rights held by multinational companies which disadvantage poorer countries who wish to gain access.
- The power of wealthier interests to negotiate advantageous deals with poorer countries short of capital, in matters such as tax concessions on incoming investments, thus lowering the fiscal revenue available to such countries.
- The repatriation of profits made through foreign investment in poorer countries to wealthier metropolitan nations.
- The power of richer countries to protect their home markets in sectors such as agriculture disadvantaging poor country food exports, while simultaneously enforcing free trade for rich country products on poorer nations.
- The power exerted by institutions of global economic governance such as the International Monetary Fund and World Trade Organization, such that the rules of international finance and trade tend to favour the interests of the powerful and wealthy.

These various processes are of course interrelated in many respects. They combine economic and political power, augmented on occasions with military power. Three particular aspects of political economy are significant for power-centres accounts of global inequality.

The first involves theories of imperialism and empire, the second is dependency theory, while the third is world-system theory. While there is considerable overlap between all three, they also exhibit interesting contrasts.

Theories of imperialism from the late 19th century onwards, have taken a different road to neo-classical economics and economic liberalism. Markets are seen not as beacons of efficiency illuminating the pathway to economic growth and poverty reduction. They function rather within structures of economic and political power that depend on and reproduce profound social inequalities. As Sutcliffe (1999) points out, there have been two waves of imperialism theory. In the first between 1890 and 1920 the concern was more with the dynamics of European expansion across the globe and conflict between leading nation states. It was only in the second wave over the last 60 years that the focus shifted to inequality between nations.

While many political theories of empire tend to be concerned with territorial control manifest through formal processes of colonization, more economic accounts of empire are as concerned with informal empire. The focus here is on the ways in which multinational enterprises backed by powerful states control cross-border trade and investment (Hardt and Negri 2001). This is done in a way that is more to the advantage of Western-based interests and countries rather than the peoples of poorer countries generally deployed as cheap labour in mining, plantation agriculture, and manufacturing.

Global inequality is thus a consequence of inequalities of power and control rather than market failure and weaknesses in deregulatory strategy. For theorists of Imperialism seeking to reformulate and revise Marx, it is inequalities of power in relations of production that matter most, and which help to explain why so-called Third World countries find themselves in a position of social inequality.

Power differentials clearly matter, though in the contemporary post-colonial world older mechanisms of Imperial control via colonization are clearly less relevant than before. Historically, the fact that Japan was never formally colonized suggests one reason why its economic development in the second half of the 20th century was more successful than other more thoroughly colonized parts of Africa and Asia. Yet it is also possible that the impact of power differentials can be exaggerated especially for the post-colonial period where China and to a lesser extent India have been part of the dynamic expansion of the so-called BRIC economies, moving some way towards bridging part of the inequality gap with wealthier countries. Negative colonial legacies are not therefore sufficient to obstruct all further development.

Theories of empire may also have over-emphasized the external power factor as a source of developmental obstruction and of the gross social inequalities facing poorer countries. Such theories neglect internal or endogenous causes of inequality such as poor resource endowment or political instability and corruption, and often regard any reference to such causes as a form of apology for Imperialism.

An alternative way of thinking about power inequalities in the global economy was developed by a second school of interpretation, namely dependency theory. This emerged from the 1950's onwards (see especially Prebisch (1950), Baran (1957), and Frank (1971)). It was designed to explain why it was that poorer countries were failing to secure steady economic and social advance to viable industrial nation status, as predicted by modernization theory. This theory emerged very largely from Latin America, where a long history of political independence had not been sufficient to produce regional economic development that would allow the continent to bridge the gap with North America and Western Europe. Analysts identified historical inequalities in the terms of trade between the region and wealthier European and North American interests as a key factor in dependency. As with theories of Imperialism, there is no single unified version of dependency theory, with the main proponents located in Latin America and the United States.

Theories of Imperialism and Dependency theory are both critical of economic liberalism and modernization theory, but they differ in their main conceptual focus. While the former approach focusses in the main on dominant state expansion across the globe, the latter is more concerned with inequalities in the international division of labour that create a dichotomy between development for some and underdevelopment for others (Ferraro 2008, 58–64). The state of underdevelopment is then caused by the developmental dynamic and power of the wealthier countries.

The central proposition here is that economic resources are transferred from poorer 'peripheral' locations (including nations and regions) lacking economic power to richer more powerful locations at the core of economic development. Instead of a general advance of all countries within the international economy as predicted by modernization theory, or a crisis of Imperialism leading to Revolution as envisaged by Marxists, the future was seen in terms of a divergence between developed and under-developed parts of the world. The under-development of some was explained by the political-economic dominance of others.

A key element of dependency, as analysed by early theorists, was pressure to accept imports of manufactured goods from wealthier regions which had benefited from cheap resources such as raw materials or labour in underdeveloped countries. To overcome this unequal exchange it was assumed by writers like Prebisch that nationally focussed import-substitution policies should be adopted. This would create an autonomous developmental momentum, and help to reduce poverty and inequality. Marxist dependency theorists like Baran were more sceptical believing obstacles to the development of poorer peripheral countries needed to be away through political revolution before real progress could be made. As it turned out, the import-substitution alternative to market-centred economic liberalism, followed in much of Latin America from the 1930s to the 1980s, has not led to self-sustaining industrialization or significant reduction in poverty (Milanovic 2011, 182–186).

Wallerstein and world-system theory

The political economy of global inequality was reformulated and reinvigorated by Immanuel Wallerstein with the development of world system theory (see especially Wallerstein (1974, 1979)). This retained the core–periphery focus of dependency theory to understand global inequality, but posited a more complicated hierarchy based on regions as much as nation states. This hierarchy included a semi-periphery which was able to achieve some developmental success without becoming integrated in the wealthy and powerful core group. This emphasis on complexity went some way towards meeting the objection of some critics of dependency theory that limited forms of development were possible even within an unequal international division of labour.

Wallerstein's approach is certainly deeply historical and comparative. He distinguishes between older (attempts at) world-empire tied together politically and militarily, and a capitalist world economy tied together through an international division of labour. He sees this as emerging from the 16th century onwards. As it has developed over five centuries, he believes this system has been driven by forces of capital accumulation. The net result is a system which powerfully allocates resources, incomes and wealth in highly unequal ways. Rather than economic convergence and a reduction in global inequality, the system generates a complex system of interdependent regions and nations at different levels of development.

Wallerstein recognized that the core does not monopolize development and hence rejected the idea of a uniformly underdeveloped Third World. Yet it is not clear that his approach predicted the recent rise of China and the BRIC nations, who have been able to bridge some of the gap between themselves and the core Western countries. In this way the core–periphery model may contain an underlying theoretically imposed rigidity in spite of Wallerstein's more subtle treatment of diversity compared with early dependency theorists.

Another line of criticism involves the question of endogenous (or internal) as against exogenous (or external) causes of global inequality. Economics has tended to take a largely endogenous view of the reasons for global inequality, linking causes back to the internal characteristics of nation states. Nations with a more dynamic economic record have internal structures more conducive to growth and rising incomes, whereas poorer countries have significant internal obstacles. For Wallerstein and the earlier dependency theorists, by contrast, it is exogenous developments at a world-system level that is the key to explaining economic performance and inequality.

Sanderson (2005, 2011), among others, claims that this biases explanation towards the exogenous as if all national or local phenomena can best be understood holistically in terms of the overall characteristics of the system. He takes the example of sub-Saharan Africa (already discussed earlier), as a case of a region only weakly integrated into the global economy with only a short history of colonization, yet one whose poor economic performance and abject poverty remains largely intact. How, in such circumstances can the power differentials of the global system be primarily responsible for this state of affairs. The claim is that Africa is too marginal to the system to be dominated by it. Civil wars and political authoritarianism seem mostly local in origin and link with social and cultural struggles for power, even if western interests supply arms. Against this, more recent world system theorists like Chase Dunn (Chase-Dunn and Lawrence 2010, 473), dispute that their approach necessarily privileges the exogenous, arguing that the exogenous/endogenous distinction is often unhelpful. What matters more is global/local interactions. World system theory is also far from monolithic or static, moving into newer areas not fully elaborated in Wallerstein's original work, such as global migration (Sassen 1988a, Sassen 1988b), or the long-run multi-millennial evolution of world systems prior to the rise of Europe (Frank and Gills 1993).

A further interesting issue arises in relation to the policy implications of world-system theory. Wallerstein, like most theorists of imperialism and dependency is deeply critical of capitalism for its incapacity to resolve human problems including poverty and inequality. While the capitalist world-economy is seen as a very dynamic historical phenomenon able to surmount the economic limitations of political empire, it faces serious contemporary crises (Wallerstein 2011). These include economic instability and uncertainty as well as fiscal crisis, where the social costs of managing the system clash with the requirements of capital accumulation. Markets by themselves cannot solve this crisis, so what can? If political revolution now seems very remote, what other processes might assist in producing social change that could address global inequality more effectively?

This question raises many issues. One consistent emphasis in Wallerstein's work has been that changes in forms of knowledge and ways of thinking are important in guiding social action. He was therefore an early advocate of thinking globally rather than in terms of a nation state focus (1974). Inequality arises through evolving structures of power operating at a global level within the international division of labour. These structures include knowledge and culture. Thus the capitalist world-system has a dominant culture based on liberalism, as witnessed in the Washington consensus. Race and gender inequalities also derive from the structural inequalities of the international division of labour (Balibar and Wallerstein 1991). Anti-systemic movements arising from the inequalities of capitalism exist, as represented in bodies like the World Social Forum and the anti-globalization movement, but it is very hard for them to breakdown dominant ways of thinking.

The underlying social theory here remains close to Marxist materialism in that social life is constituted through economic relationships and institutions, which structure politics and culture in their image.

Chase-Dunn and Lawrence (2010), in discussing the role of human action, within world-system theory, portray in a positive light the a-cultural structuralism at its heart. Action is thereby focussed on the logic of the system transmitted and reproduced via the emergent properties of institutions rather than the meaningful actions of individuals and groups, including capitalists and workers. This approach sets out from a critique of the methodological individualism of economics, whereby structures are grounded in rational self-interest rather than power and domination. In rejecting this particular account of social action, however, no alternative ways of thinking about action are considered. So structuralism rules supreme. Social life is thereby over-simplified but in a different way to the simplifications of economics.

The over-riding difficulty with this simplification, which is general within political economy, is that it remains unclear why the unequal structures of domination within the global economy do not produce the kinds of social change that Marx supposed would arise from conflict between capital and labour. The challenge raised by this problem is sometimes explained by the supposed existence of a dominant ideology of liberalism, in spite of considerable evidence of the scope of anti-globalization movements and nationalism. But beyond this the remoteness of Socialism or of a world-state designed to replace capitalism, cries out for a deeper analysis of why social actors think and act as they do, how far they regard inequality as a salient political and cultural issue, how far globalization is linked with benefits as much as problems, and how far cosmopolitan openness to the plight of the global poor matters. These questions take us well beyond the analytical confines of conventional economics, and beyond political economy too.

Evaluation of political economy

Where then does all this leave the tradition of political economy as a guide to global inequality.

Its major strength is to discuss unequal economic power within the global economy and its consequences for economic development and the distribution of income. Markets are not simply based on transactions between rational self-interested individuals but incorporate powerful institutions like global corporations and powerful processes like the international division of labour. The various theories of empire and dependency construct this institutional framework in somewhat differing ways, but share a macro-level focus on power inequalities as the source of global inequalities.

Political economy is therefore rightly critical of the policy prescription that sees market deregulation by itself as a necessary element in developmental progress and the lessening of global inequality. If we take the recent economic advance of China as a test of the relative merits of market and power-centred approaches, some interesting observations apply. Firstly market approaches claim that Chinese advance is because it has begun to embrace the market economy, which indeed it has. Political economists on the other hand can point to its use of neo-mercantilist state sponsored forms of nation-building by a large country with considerable geo-political power. China has attracted large amounts of foreign capital, but never embraced the Washington consensus of economic deregulation. The state remains a very powerful economic manager able to devise its own national trade and fiscal policies, while evading much of the intellectual property rights regime developed by Western capitalism. All this suggests that the political economy approach can tell us more about Chinese development than market-centred economic liberalism. Yet there is also a paradox here, namely that most dependency and world systems theorists failed to predict the rise of China, believing that global economic obstacles built into core–periphery relations would stand in its way.

If political economy in the period culminating in the work of Wallerstein has strengths, it also has weaknesses. Three general problems may be identified. First there are problems with the tendency to see economic power as the primary form of power, leaving out alternative forms of social and cultural power around race and gender, which affect inequality. These require a view of society able to embrace the idea of multiple social divisions and sources of social inequality that stretch beyond markets, economic institutions, and states.

Secondly, much political economy in this epoch tended to be excessively structuralist, such that inequality is rooted in the global division of labour and institutions of corporate power. This makes it unclear exactly how social and cultural meanings are constructed in daily life and how these influence patterns of social action and inequality. How far does power operate through cultural assumptions and narratives. When do these take the form of cultural hegemony, as analysed in the earlier tradition of Gramsci, and in what circumstances social actors can influence patterns of domination and inequality? To produce an excessively structuralist interpretation of cultural hegemony, over-simplifies social complexity and forecloses on the possibility of multiple causes of inequality. It also undercuts exploration of the potential of social actors and movements to transform the situation, tends to undermine policy recommendations, leaving a gap between analysis of the causes of inequality and the achievement of a more just and egalitarian world. So how equal could a country or the global array of countries be, and how would they get there?

One relevant issue here is the potential of state-centred Socialist societies for lowering inequality below levels typically found where capitalism is dominant. Comparative data on income inequality developed by Milanovic (2011) shed some light on this issue. They indicate that levels of income inequality within the post-war Soviet bloc were lowered to a Gini coefficient in the upper 20's and lower 30's, which is around 6–7% lower than levels in capitalist countries of Western Europe (53–54). This shows that Soviet-style Socialism was more egalitarian in an economic sense, but not on wider measures of inequality embracing access to political participation. This once again raises the need for a wider account of multiple aspects of social inequality, requiring a broader account of social processes.

There are two ways of proceeding from here. One is to move straight to alternative intellectual resources, including those found within sociological traditions. Before I take this step, it is important to note that political economy like economics has not stood still. Neither current of thought is monolithic, and attempts to respond to problems with earlier analyses are available.

In the case of political economy, the last decades have seen a number of interdisciplinary (or perhaps post-disciplinary) ventures in understanding the social and political context to economic activity. One of the foremost of these is cultural political economy (Sayer 2001, Jessop 2010, Jessop and Sum 2014). This has been described in terms of a 'cultural turn' in political economy.

Cultural political economy (CPE), as a relatively new current of thought, has not solidified into a new orthodoxy around a few key propositions. It may nonetheless be seen as an eclectic attempt to bring cultural issues into political economy while retaining the pre-existing emphasis on power and inequality. The main emphasis in CPE is on the social construction of meaning, and how this both feeds into the ways social actors understand, construct, and reproduce kef forms of social life. Structures still matter, but so to cultural processes that create meaning. Culture here is not regarded as a separate domain to be bolted on to the economy or polity, but as an integral part of social life, part of our very being.

The strength of cultural political economy lies in drawing attention to the ways in which dominant world views of economic globalization influence corporate actors and policy-makers, helping to create a deregulated world in which narratives of social improvement depend on deregulation, competition, and how to lift populations out of poverty. Power is mediated through ideas or discourses bringing Gramsci's account of cultural hegemony into contact with Foucault's notion of discursive power (Jessop 2010). In this perspective inequality arises as much as an effect of world-views and discourses that understand the world in a particular neo-liberal world, rather than through structural imperatives of capital accumulation.

The cultural turn in political economy cannot be reviewed in great depth here, but it can be said that political economy has shown the capacity to revise and rethink certain of its key intellectual assumptions. This has been achieved with respect to the structuralism of earlier work, but not fully applied to issues of gender and racial inequality as autonomous dimensions of power. CPE also remains rather generalized and abstract, making it hard to integrate with more empirical literature on patterns of inequality across time and space. And beyond this the intellectual benefit of a closer engagement with work on power and multiple inequalities within mainstream sociology, has not yet been properly explored.

International political economy post-Wallerstein has also extended and refined its repertoire of power-centred approaches to global inequality in a number of important ways. These include more highly elaborated accounts of historical patterns of inequality (Korzeniewicz and Moran 2009), work on contemporary phases of global capitalism around notions like financialization (Epstein 2005), and on structures of trade and inequality (Kaplinsky 2005), work on tax havens and money laundering (Palan, Murphy, and Chavagneux 2010), (Sharman 2011), and analyses of global economic governance (Wade 2003, Bernstein 2011). Many of these more recent studies will be built in the more detailed analyses of global inequality in the following chapters. The legacy of political economy is therefore highly significant. But it still lacks a broader approach to power, and to the complex relationships between markets, states, and cultures that may be found within sociological analysis.

Sociology

Sociology, in a general sense, examines social processes in their widest manifestations, linking economic, political, and cultural processes together rather than treating them as separate and distinct domains.

So culture and politics matter to markets. Meanwhile power has multiple elements rather than being reducible to economic power alone. Sociology explores interactions between markets states and culture; between power and social divisions; between economic organizations, hierarchies and networks; and between power, social action, knowledge, and policy.

In the contemporary world, much of this work takes in sociological debates around class, gender, ethnicity, sexual preference and age, linked with arguments about globalization and the dynamics and discontents of modernity. Sociology like anthropology and philosophy also has a methodological sensitivity to qualitative as much as quantitative aspects of inequality. This takes in the lived experience of global poverty and injustice than simple recourse to comparisons of incomes and wealth across the.

I have already noted an overlap between economics and sociological discussions of modernization and social mobility at various points in the second half of the 20th century. This legacy has however been criticized both for the excessive evolutionary optimism in its account of modernization, and for the skewing of analysis to wealthier Western nations, presumed to be models for the rest of the world. A stronger overlap has therefore grown up between political economy and sociology, manifested in work like Offe (1985) on capitalism and democracy, Castells (1996) on network society, Sassen (1998a, 2001) on global cities and migration, and by Martell (2010) on globalization.

In this section of the chapter I make no attempt to provide a systematic discussion of all possible connections between sociology and the analysis of global inequality. The focus is more selective, concentrating on two specific connections that are of major importance.

Sociology and multidimensional approaches to power

The first sociological route into global inequality focusses on power, but broadens enquiry beyond economic power. Michael Mann's work on power, quoted briefly earlier in this chapter, is a very useful starting point here. Mann sees social power operating in four modes rather than one single mode (1986, 2–3). These comprise ideological, economic, military, and political processes. These are analytically distinct but usually interrelated in social life. All become effective through organization, but organizational forms vary including states, particularly relevant to political power, but also armies, markets, and churches. *Ideological power* arises from the search for meaning that underlies social action, this can involve rational self-interest linked to acquisitive individualism, but it can also involve a range of collective and communal movements and networks where religions or secular ideologies like socialism are involved in struggles for power. *Military power* arises from the search for collective defence and from aggressive strategies pursued by social groups grounded in the exercise or threat of physical force. *Economic power* is more diffuse, and derives from struggles over the satisfaction of needs involving class relationships and networks of economic activity. Meanwhile *political power* is associated with centralized states operating from within a bounded territory, and centres on the use of states by various groups to realize their goals.

Political economy, following Marx, has tended to assume that one type of power – the economic – broadly structures the others, such that armies, states, and ideologies reflect economic processes and divisions, which are primary. This connection need not be thought of in a rigid or mechanistic way, as debates around the idea of economic primacy have made clear. This approach has many merits, and can illuminate aspects of political, military, and ideological processes. A powerful example in the field of inequality is the argument that inequalities between ethnic and racial groups in wage levels or social status and access to political participation reflect strategies of divide and rule, whether by employers or colonial regimes.

This may be the case in some settings, but this does not prove a necessary connection between economic power and forms of inequality based on the cultural status of individuals and households. Ruling class and state strategies, as Mann (1987) points out, vary considerably including liberal and reformist as well as authoritarian options. Patriarchy and racism do not necessarily emerge only from economic interests, but rather from the ideological or cultural power and interests, acting as autonomous influences on patterns of inequality.

Mann and Riley (2007) have developed this argument further in study of macro-regional trends in global inequality. They link the four types of power identified by Mann with four sources of inequality. Thus ideological power, for example, generates ideological inequality. Two ways are suggested for this to happen. First ideologies like Christianity and Islam influence state social policies and the types of inequality that populations will accept. Second, ideologies influence social hierarchies, by legitimizing patterns of group closure in areas such as caste or racial categories. In each case there are consequences for inequality. The same logic is applied by Mann and Riley to economic, political, and military power. This approach is then applied to what are called macro-regions such as Nordic Europe (the Nordics), the Anglo world, Latin America, and so forth. The claim is that particular profiles of intra-regional inequality are best explained in terms of the interaction of multiple forms of power. It is noteworthy that this approach militates against a singular general theory of social inequality, where the explanatory framework is identical for all cases.

This argument about multiple dimensions of power in relation to social inequality has been further elaborated in the very stimulating work of Sylvia Walby (2009) on social complexity and inequality in an epoch of globalization. Walby like Mann focusses on diverse forms of power and inequality, and the need to recast social theory to grasp the complex forms in which inequality is generated and reproduced. There is no single structure of power, but a complex set of social relationships in which power is used for purposes of domination. 'Class is not the only significant inequality... [others include]... gender, ethnicity, racialization, nation, religion, able-bodiedness, sexual orientation, age, generation, linguistic community and more' (18). Unlike economics and political economy, sociology sees most of these dimensions of inequality as involving a sense of cultural difference. They cannot be reduced to class, any more than ethnic difference can be reduced to culture. This multidimensionality is characteristic of most recent sociological accounts of inequality (see also Therborn 2006).

For Walby, power is articulated in what she terms 'regimes of inequality', a concept that refers to basic aspects of social life – or, in more philosophical parlance, ontology, referring to the nature of social being. Like Mann, there are four dimensions to this, namely economy, polity, violence, and civil society. Economy is not simply about market-based incomes but also non-monetary relationships which help to sustain material life, while polity is far more than government extending to governance and social movements. Violence is included here because it is seen as an omnipresent feature of social life and social domination, whether in official state-based or unofficial communal forms. This broadens Mann's notion of military power to include micro-level violence at the communal and domestic levels. For Walby, violence is not simply a reflection of different social forces, but helps to constitute social relations in an autonomous way. Civil society, meanwhile is used as a proxy for culture, which she feels is to narrow a term to include 'the media, arts, sport and knowledge creation' (18). Civil society is also privileged as the sphere of social creativity. Inequality pervades all these dimensions of social life, while at the same time also provoking response, conflict and the search for alternatives.

One intellectual challenge that arises from this more complex approach is to find a way of acknowledging the multidimensionality of power and inequality that goes further than a shopping-list of different forms of inequality. Walby addresses this problem by means of the concept of inter-sectionality (Walby 2009, 60–65, see also Walby 2011). This has been used in recent years both as a way of recognizing the complex array of different forms of social inequality, and as a way of trying to integrate them together. This kind of integration is required because each dimension of inequality does not operate in isolation from the others, but rather they mutually influence and change each other. Inter-sectionality may also be conceived in terms of structures, symbolic representations, modes of identity construction, and political (in the sense of policy-focussed) processes (Verloo 2006, Winker and Degele 2011).

Inter-sectionality is then a way of responding to the complexity that arises when different forms of social inequality interact. Walby goes on to rehearse a range of possible ways of working with this concept. These include a turn from general approaches, the search for a single underlying cause underlying complexity, or the connection of each specific form of inequality with a particular cause. All of these have problems. Her own solution tries to retain a general framework while recognizing a distinction between relational and institutional processes. Following the work of Lopez and Scott (2000), this distinction opens up the possibility of particular regime of inequality being spread across institutions, rather than linked with a single institutional location. Thus 'the economy includes both free wage labour but also domestic labour…the polity…not only states, but the EU, and organized religions that govern specific areas of life (such as aspects of intimacy)…(65)'. Meanwhile regimes of violence occur both at an interpersonal level as well as that of organized military violence.

These general theoretical considerations indicate just how wide-ranging the sociological approach to social inequality has become, and how far it has moved beyond the discourses of mainstream economics and political economy focussed primarily on income and wealth.

Sociology and globalization

Beyond this first general issue of recognizing multidimensionality and complexity in the operation, there is also a second sociological route into global inequality through sociological contributions to the study of globalization. As in the study of inequality, this focus has extended accounts of globalization beyond an economistic or political economic framework, important though these are, to a broader social framework. This embraces the study of socio-cultural identity, religion, networks, risk and the environment, again considered in interaction with markets, states and economic power (Robertson 1992, Castells 1996, Therborn 2006, Beck 2000, 2010, Sassen 1998, 2007, Holton 2005, 2011). This point can be illuminated further through comparisons and contrasts in the work of Mann, Beck, and Walby.

Mann's work, as we have seen, disputes the adequacy of an exclusive focus on the nation state as the primary container of social power. His argument is rather that that the 'societies' within which power is exercised are not limited to nation states, but are better seen as 'constituted of multiple overlapping and intersecting socio-spatial networks of power' (1986, 1). This leaves space for the cross-border movements typical of globalization, but not at the expense of abandoning the contemporary centrality of nation states, as the primary locus of political power. In consequence 'state, culture and economy... almost never coincide' (ibid. 2). The implication of this position is that power operates through a range of processes and organizations according to multiple logics. It cannot be deduced from a unitary account of society, whether this is centred on the nation state or the world market.

This general argument does not deal explicitly with global inequality. Where it is helpful is as a way of thinking of the possibility of a range of forms of power that may influence inequality, whether within a given nation, or within process that occur between or outside of national institutions. The multidimensionality of this approach is especially helpful because the current epoch is both a period of more intensified globalization, but also an epoch in which the nation state remains a key player in social life. It is therefore preferred to the recent influential approach of Ulrich Beck (2007) which calls for a move 'beyond class and nation', to a 'cosmopolitan sociology of inequality' (ibid. 689).

Beck's substantive work on globalization includes discussion of environmental risk and cosmopolitan governance. He also argues that the dominant sociological approaches to inequality over recent decades have been trapped in 'methodological nationalism'. This he sees as outmoded in view of a profound trans-nationalization of social relationships. A wholesale reframing of the study of inequality is required to focus on trans-national relations. This largely persuasive argument is pursued in a passionate and iconoclastic manner, but downplays the continuing robustness of nation states, and nationally based public policy interventions in key areas affecting inequality, such as equal opportunity and citizenship, welfare provision, industrial relations, health, and education. An endogenous focus may be inadequate by itself because it downplays the limits of nation state autonomy from external processes and pressures arising within the global economy. Yet it should not be rejected altogether. What is needed then is not a wholesale reframing of approaches to inequality, but a broadening of focus to capture global–national interactions.

Walby (2009, 117–131, 199–208, 228–247), provides an analytical framework that avoids methodological nationalism, by including global and national intersections. The global focus includes flows of capital, trade, and people together with the operations of global institutions like the World Bank, hegemonic centres of power like the United States, and to a lesser extent the EU, with China close to occupying such a position. She also includes 'global waves', a term which approximates to politico-cultural movements of opinion and action, linking civil society with political practice. Both neo-liberalism and movements for global justice are included here. The influence of globalization is not that of a unitary force as projected in world-system theory, but requires the disaggregation and intersection of many such elements. Each, singly and in combination, has implications for inequality.

But it also includes what are called 'country processes'. These include the types and balance of economic sectors in a country (covering primary production, manufacturing, and services), degree of involvement in the knowledge economy and technology, the extent of decline of a domestic non-market economy and expansion of wage labour, together with more political processes. These include the extent to which social-democratic politics has an economic and social base able to support political measures to address inequality, and the extent to which individual states may be in fiscal crisis setting limits to public expenditure. Finally Walby looks at national and regional (e.g. EU) political configurations to see how far alliances and movements influence the balance of liberal and social-democratic projects and policies. This in turn affects the extent of economic regulation and the allocation of resources between social groups, once again influencing levels of social inequality.

Intersecting with this barrage of processes are processes of violence, and movements associated with the social creativity of civil society. Patriarchal violence at a communal and domestic level influences patterns of gender inequality, while the violence of military power at the inter-state level may act to enslave of liberate social groups and populations with considerable implications for social inequality. Civil society, often defined as the space between states and markets, is for Walby, a space where 'new ideas, practices, visions of alternative social formations' develop (228). These can be authoritarian or democratic, of the right as well as the left. Their significance for the analysis of global inequalities is that they help to create the ideas and mobilize social groups to support projects such as neo-liberalism, social democracy, feminism, and environmentalism. All of these have to be taken into account when we analyse both the prevailing state of global inequality, the under-researched issue of how inequalities are perceived (Reis 2006), and how social action is conducted in ways that change, reform, perpetuate, and reproduce inequality. This sociological framework is fuller and analytically richer than the approaches of economics, and political economy.

Conclusion

This chapter has been primarily theoretical. It has identified three analytically distinct general ways of theorizing global inequality, located in economics, political economy, and sociology. Some reference has been made to empirical evidence that different theories have generated or relied upon, but a more detailed empirical survey of the complex dimensions of global inequality remains to be explored later in this study.

The main conclusions that are drawn here are three-fold.

First neither economics nor political economy are adequate to the explanation of global inequality, in spite of undoubted strengths. Second, sociology, in conjunction with other cognate disciplines, has provided some broader perspectives on inequality, which are able to meet a number of problems with the other general theories. The sociological contribution is not theoretically unified, but it has generated an analytical framework that is distinctive, together with methodological features especially helpful to the study of globalization.

Third, there remains a distinct possibility that no single general theory is as yet able to account for the multiple and complex set of processes that lie behind global inequality. This latter point will be investigated further in the chapters that follow, looking first at the history of global social divisions and in later chapters at the empirical contours of global inequality in diverse settings across the world.

3 A Short Historical Sociology of Global Inequality

Much commentary on global inequality plunges straight into current contrasts between enormous wealth for some and massive poverty for many others across the world. Inequality is sometimes represented visually in juxtapositions of photographs of shanty towns and the homes of the wealthy (see the cover of Held and Kaya 2007). It is also encapsulated in bold statistical contrasts between the small percentage of the world's population who receive most of the income and the huge percentage that receives very little (see Table 3.1). This contemporary focus makes sense, because it is here and now that matters most to those suffering from the effects of inequality, as well as to commentators, analysts, governments, and social movements seeking change and reform.

Yet understandable concerns for the present may well be an obstacle to fully comprehending patterns of global inequality, and the reasons why inequality happens. How, in other words, did we get to the current state of affairs? Has income inequality always been this enormous across history? And if it has does that mean that the causes of today's global inequality are as much historical as contemporary?

These important questions cannot be taken very far without some understanding of the evidence available to us, and of the ways that social scientists try to measure and compare inequality across time and space. Relevant evidence really only exists for the last 200 years, and that is very patchy and uneven for most of the 19th and early 20th century. Income inequality is only one dimension of global inequality, but it is one than can be measured and compared across time and space. Analysts use a number of statistical measures to compare inequality, the most widely used one being the Gini coefficient. This can be used to compare inequality profiles of different countries, regions within countries, and for the world as a whole. They can therefore assist the understanding of both within-country and between-country inequality.

A more detailed account of this measure is provided in the box below; for the moment, I simply note that the Gini coefficient can be expressed as a simple number between 0 and 100, with zero being absolute equality and 100 absolute inequality. The higher the number the greater the

Table 3.1 Income inequality between haves and have-nots

Income Recipients		Share of Total Income
Top	5%	37%
Top	10%	56%
Bottom	10%	0.7%
Bottom	5%	0.2%

Source: Derived from the discussion in B. Milanovic (2011, 152)

inequality. If the Gini is used to track global inequality across recent history, there is a sustained and marked increase from a figure of around 50 in 1820, rising to 61 in 1910 and 66 in 1992 (Bourguignon and Morrison 2002). In the last 20 years the rise seems to have been halted, but at a very high level around 70 (Milanovic 2011, 150). This is higher than any individual country, where the index varies between highs of around 60 in Brazil and South Africa, to over 40 in the United States and Russia, and the low to mid 30s in the EU, lowest of all in Scandinavia.

Firstly, this material demonstrates the obvious point that global inequality is not new, which confirms that historical causes matter. Secondly, it shows that global inequality worsened across the critical period of industrialization and global capitalist expansion, even while aggregate incomes per head of population showed a tendency to increase. In other words the income gap worsened in a period of plenty. Thirdly, the fact that inequality is greater for the world as a whole than in any individual country indicates that between-country inequality was growing faster than within-country inequality. This indicates that the quest to explain global inequality should concentrate on historical processes linking the fate of countries in the global arena, as much as internal national factors. Lastly, the differences between countries own inequality-profiles suggest that national factors still matter. This national dimension, however, also requires historical as much as contemporary analysis. This is because the contrasts between the Gini numbers reported above for the recent period turn out to be similar across recent history, as the work of Korzeniewicz and Moran (2009) reviewed below makes clear.

The Gini coefficient

Gini was an Italian statistician and economist interested in measuring inequality. The Gini coefficient compares the attributes of each individual with the attributes of all other individuals within a given population. It is the most widely used statistical construct in studies of inequality, though there are additional types of measures, such as the Theil index, with different technical properties, The Gini coefficient is only useful in gauging inequality in individual attributes, such as income, that can be measured. Its utility also depends on the accuracy of data assembled.

Ginis are constructed in a series of stages. First, the sum of all inequalities in income between individuals within a population is calculated. This is usually for a nation state, which also allows regional and local as well as national patterns to be calculated. Where data are not available for each individual, then some proxy is used, such as mean income from sets of individuals within different income brackets. These typically include mean incomes for all those within 10% bands in the income distribution, from the top 10% down to the bottom 10%. Second this sum total is divided by the number of people in the population plus the average income of this group.

The results fall between 0 (complete equality) and 1 (complete inequality). Most national Ginis vary between around 0.20 and 0.60. These figures are sometimes expressed in percentages, that is, a range from 20% to 70%, or multiplied by 100 to give convenient whole numbers, that is, 20 (relatively low inequality to 70 (far greater inequality).

One of the main problems with the Gini coefficient is that the same final number is compatible with very different income distributions. The index also focusses on cross-sectional data at specific points of time and thus fails to get at processes of change in the structure of populations, such as income distribution across the life-span. Interpreting the analytical significance of the Gini coefficient is therefore not at all straightforward. For further elaboration of these points, and deeper technical discussion, see Milanovic (2011) and Atkinson (1970).

Inequalities of individual income do not, in and of themselves, give us the full picture of inequalities of household income, since most households are composed of more than one income recipient. Nor do they deal with other material assets such as home ownership. Gini coefficients based on individual income can therefore be augmented with additional data, whether on household income or by including financial estimates of the benefits of home ownership (for which rent levels are an obvious proxy). Other complex issues involve variations in tax structures and the impact of transfer payments arising from social security.

So what difference does a historical perspective on global inequality make? There are basically two kinds of considerations at stake here. The first are substantive and have to do with long-term patterns of social division and inequality connected with a range of cross-border as well as local processes. The second are theoretical and methodological, and concern the assumptions made and techniques used when collecting evidence and interpreting it. I shall consider each in turn.

Part One: Social Division and Global Inequality: Some Historical Themes

Social distinction and inequality have very long histories. The idea of golden age of equality in hunter-gatherer societies in the distant past is widely held, but appears to be a myth. This is partly because differentials in access to material resources necessary to sustain life foster inequalities between groups (Burch and Ellanna 1994). It is also because cultural processes of status formation also create differentials. It did not take money and markets for inequality to first develop. Nor have patterns of economic taken a standard form or scope throughout the long-history of economic life over the last four millennia. And throughout this period, economic inequality has generally been embedded in political institutions and cultural practices.

Inequality can be traced across the rise of agrarian societies based on private land-owning, the empires of ancient Greece and Rome, medieval Europe, and the empires of China and Mughal India, prior to the development of modern Western capitalism. They are however very hard to measure because relevant data are sparse. Much of what we can say is qualitative rather than quantitative. Inequality arose from a complex mixture of economic, political, and cultural sources. These included imperial colonization, resource extraction and sometimes enslavement of populations. But all societies had elites whose power and income-generating activities derived from a range of activities including political domination and forced taxation, inherited wealth connected with social status, trade, and the exploitation of the labour of subservient social groups.

Inequality in the Roman Empire

In the early Roman Empire roughly 2000 years ago, the elite represented around 1% of the population, that is 200,000–400,000 people, while most of the remaining 50–55 million lived at little beyond subsistence. Spatially the ration of income between the richest (e.g., Italy and Egypt) and poorest parts of the Empire (e.g., North Africa and lands around the Danube) was around 2 to 1. The Gini for the Empire has been calculated at around 40, roughly the same as the United States and enlarged EU today (Milanovic 2011, 49–52).

It is beyond the scope of this study to examine pre-modern inequality in any depth.

What is significant here, is firstly that inequality has a long history, and secondly that the causes of inequality in the past let alone the present, cannot be explained simply in terms of the internal characteristics of countries or regions in question. External factors matter too, and these may be connected with Empire, colonization, trade, and migration. One way of thinking about these external processes is through the idea of globalization. This, in one form or another, influences the long-history of inequality.

Processes of globalization are not something new of relevance only to contemporary inequality. Rather they emerged over centuries if not millennia, rather than being a recent entirely novel feature of social life (Hopkins 2002, Holton 2005, 2011). Globalization may be defined as cross-border connections and interdependencies in economic, political, and cultural life, together with consciousness of the world as a single space. Aspects of globalization, such as long-distance trade, cross-border slavery, imperial conquest, trans-continental and trans-regional migration, and expansive religious movement across cultural divides, have been around for several millennia (Frank and Gills 1993). Such processes differ in geographical scope and intensity from the rapidly moving globalization of today, tied together by virtually instantaneous communications technology. Early globalizations (perhaps better thought of as proto-globalizations) were therefore patchy, uneven, and liable to over-extension and collapse. Yet they left influences and residues behind that strongly influence the present (Hopkins 2002).

Empire and the historical sociology of global inequality

One leading example is the institution of empire, seen by Wallerstein as the major cross-border social institution prior to the capitalist world-economy (1974, 1979). Empires across history have typically been founded on powerful territorial cores, as in ancient Greece or Rome, 17th century Spain, or 19th century Britain. These sought to control or dominate wider areas, extracting wealth and resources like foodstuffs or treasure, and dominating, sometimes enslaving, populations. All this was enforced by coercive power and justified by a strong sense of superior cultural mission. The cultural politics of Empire, from a European perspective included a range of religious, scientific, and racial elements. Empires were always far more than economic entities.

Global inequality throughout history has many causes, including the natural resource endowments of particular regions and localities, as well as locally generated hierarchies of power and status within tribes and emerging cities. Beyond this Empires were perhaps the first major source of global inequality arising from cross-border activity as such. This involved both economic inequality and politico-cultural domination, sometimes in extreme form as in the attempted genocide of indigenous populations. Empires also created demographic change through the settlement of colonizers, the co-option of segments of compliant local populations in administration, and the importation of labour whether into new colonies or the core imperial heartland. In the ancient Roman Empire, both food and slaves were imported into Rome from other parts of the Empire in Europe and North Africa.

Winant (2001) sees the historic sociology of Empire in terms of three major elements. Firstly, Empire is significant in changing relationships between capital and labour, which included enslavement and other forms of indentured labour. Secondly, Empire represents forms of state-building and territorial control including military coercion. Thirdly, Empire generates new forms of culture and cultural identity. For Winant these come together in modern Europe from the Renaissance onwards in creating forms of modernity that were both dynamic and fundamentally implicated in cross-border inequality. The relevance of historical processes such as these to contemporary patterns of social inequality is considerable.

One major line of argument derived from political economy links contemporary inequalities with the initial resource endowments of different parts of the globe, and the way these influenced the construction of social and political institutions during colonial settlement (Engerman and Sokoloff 2000, Hoff 2003, van de Walle 2009, Korzeniewicz and Moran 2009). Where natural endowments favoured plantation agriculture or intensive mineral extraction, coercive control of labour was greater and control of the institutions of the state passed into the hands of landowners. Those who owned land and resources controlled the state and judiciary. This created highly unequal social structures which have persisted to this day, in settings such as South Africa, much of Latin America, and the southern states of the United States. Put simply the countries with higher inequality in the past are often those with higher inequality today. This was not simply a product of the economic interest of landowners but also involved cultures of racism. Frederickson (2001), writing on South Africa and the southern states of the United States, argues that a history of racial subordination perpetuated negative stereotypes of limited black competence. This reinforced long-term patterns of limited access to education, and concentration in unskilled work. Blacks were 'lacking in rights' and therefore 'ultraexploitable' (9).

Drawing on political economy and world-systems theory, Korzeniewicz and Moran (2009), in their fascinating book *Unveiling Inequality*, identify two distinct historical patterns of inequality going back over several centuries. Because these patterns are constant they are seen as forms of equilibrium. One pattern involves a relatively high level of inequality equilibrium (HIE) by world standards, the other a relatively low level of inequality equilibrium (LIE). These relate in turn to different forms of economic activity and patterns of social institutions, as indicated in Table 3.2.

Spatially these contrasting patterns do not conform to assumptions that the Western world has been the exclusive home of more egalitarian democratic historical processes, while the world beyond is typically more despotic and authoritarian. The contrast is rather between regions and countries with differing resource endowments and economic, social and political institutions. Most of those in the HIGH inequality category were not only significant historical centres of extractive industry, such as Latin America, South Africa, and the southern states of the United

Table 3.2 Two historic patterns of income inequality

	Economic Activity	Social Institutions	Locations
HIGH [HIE]	Mining/plantations	Colonization and slavery	Latin America South Africa Southern USA
LOW [LIE]	Abundant land	Greater social and political autonomy	Western Europe East Asia

Source: Derived from the discussion in Korzeniewicz and Moran (2009)

States, but locations where Western interests fostered colonization and slavery from 1500 onwards. In the case of the diverse set of countries in the LOW inequality category, spanning Western Europe, areas of white settlement like New England and Australia, and certain East and South East Asian places like Japan, it is not easy to find a simple common feature. In addition to more abundant endowment of land in relation to labour, mentioned by a number of writers, most of this grouping typically retained greater social and political autonomy from external control. In the case of Western countries, this meant that the prosperity fostered in part by very high inequality outside the core countries fostered lower levels of inequality at home.

Income inequality in sub-Saharan Africa

Van de Walle (2009) has applied a different version of the historical argument about colonial institutions to sub-Saharan Africa, where inequality has been high yet does not fit the HIE pattern identified by Korzeniewicz and Moran. Here plantation agriculture was more weakly developed and mining concentrated in a relatively few areas. In the tropical areas, in particular, colonial states and settlement of colonizers were less developed, while local labour was scarce. Colonial states were less entrenched and their main institutional impact was in the spheres of taxation and law and order rather than economic development. This has adversely effected the capacity of post-colonial states to improve human welfare because state-led experience of development has been lacking.

What Korzeniewicz and Moran add to existing accounts is a focus on the institutional arrangements that sustained and reproduced patterns of higher inequality over several centuries into the present. The focus is on changing power structures and the way these were exploited to the advantage of the powerful and the disadvantage of subordinate groups, whether plantation slaves, indentured labour or mine-workers. This approach sets out to explain both within-country inequality and between-country inequality. While it might be supposed that the former is a product of local factors and the latter the product of global ones, they argue that the two dimensions of global inequality cannot be separated so neatly. One key reason is that between-country inequality is largely 'an outcome of the comparative advantages that some nations gain over others in their inter-action' (Korzeniewicz and Moran 2009, 74).

Colonialism and slavery also involved the creation of intensive forms of social exclusion, violence, and psychological coercion that have had longer term consequences for patterns of inequality right into the present. These were sustained by regimes of racial classification, hierarchy, and subordination, based on white supremacy. As Frederickson (1981, 70), points out, this produced a sense of cultural solidarity among whites, 'that could become a way of life, not simply a cover for economic exploitation'. Such forms of solidarity, and the traditions associated with them, have fed into recent forms of racial mobilization which seek to defend the rights, privileges and welfare of whites. But the legacy of slavery also had profoundly negative consequences for the social organization and morale of those subjected to it.

Long-term effects of slavery

O'Connell (2012) has studied contemporary patterns of racial inequality in the southern United States using county-level census data. She finds a significant correlation between the scale of white-black inequality today, and the areas that had the highest concentration slavery in the mid-19th century. On a different tack, Nunn (2008) considers the adverse effects of the slave trade on those parts of West Africa upon which the Atlantic slave trade depended. Using statistical analysis he finds that the greater the number of slaves removed from any particular African location the poorer the record of economic development in that location in more recent times. This connection has to do with weakening of social ties between different villages and towns and a weakening effect on the development of broader political structures.

Empires through history have operated a complex set of forms of domination and rule, direct and indirect, through coercion but also co-option of colonized peoples that defy any single formula (Cooper 2001, 200–211). What is most relevant, for this study of global inequality, is the point that long histories of racial exclusion are hard to overcome, even when slavery and colonialism is dead and political independence achieved. This may be partly because economic dependency remains intact in post-colonial settings creating a limited resource platform on which to create and control greater income and wealth, and partly because post-colonial state structures and forms of social organization have been impaired by the legacy of the past. This does not, however, fatally undermine contemporary prospects for change or initiatives to reduce social inequality.

At political independence in the 1950's and 1960's new African governments inherited a situation of high inequality, the legacy of factor endowments and colonial administration. Authoritarianism and corruption persisted with limited democratic participation perpetuating much of this legacy. The colonial institutional legacy existed prior to recent phases of economic globalization which are often presented as the sole key to understanding sub-Saharan inequalities. Meanwhile continuing forms of post-colonial exclusion also owe a good deal to localized forms of racial and ethnic domination across many parts of Africa and Asia, the causes of which cannot simply be ascribed to Empire.

All this is not to downplay the range of historical legacies that colonizing empires have created, often unwittingly. In the longer-term, for example, imperial connections may have stimulated at least some of the conditions that facilitate far more positive inter-cultural engagement and cosmopolitanism (Appiah 2006). This may be expressed within inter-marriage and inter-faith dialogue, but also in communal politics, education, and leisure pursuits such as sport. Such developments tend to undercut cultural tensions and inter-cultural violence as sources of inequality. Empires, in this way, may have an ambivalent impact on global inequality, rather than functioning simply as generators and perpetuators of economic and racial divides.

The legacy of empire, is certainly a problematic idea, inasmuch as cultural perceptions of what the legacy actually means shift and change rather than remaining constant in some kind of primordial manner. Nonetheless various senses of an Imperial past – positive or negative – remain a contemporary influence. This applies both in old Imperial 'cores' like the United Kingdom, France, and the Netherlands or in decolonized regions in Africa, Asia, or the Caribbean. In the old imperial cores like the United Kingdom, the immigration of post-colonial populations from former Caribbean, Asian, and African colonies runs up against a cultural baggage of racial perception and exclusion. As Paul Gilroy (1987) put it in a striking book title 'There Ain't No Black in the Union Jack'.

Legacies of racial superiority persist in Imperial cores among segments of indigenous populations. They typically surface where immigration is seen as creating competition for jobs or where cultural tensions within localities are interpreted in racial terms. Recent examples in Britain include conflicts within the older industrial towns of Lancashire. Imperial legacies are also evident in countries of colonial settlement such as South Africa or Australia, where relations between white settlers and indigenous peoples continue to reflect historical experiences of exclusion and abuse.

Independent post-colonial nations created during the second half of the 20th century face a number of predicaments. One is the challenge of how to build new state capacity capable of fostering economic and social development when the institutional legacy of colonialism is often inadequate, and the power of external economic and political forces is great. Another is an internal predicament centred on challenges of social cohesion in the face of mixed populations inherited from the arbitrary colonial carve-up of territory, and more historic legacies of cultural and religious tradition. Within-country inequality in such settings undoubtedly has some external causes, but continuing inequality in post-colonial exclusion also owe a good deal to localized forms of racial, ethnic, and patriarchal domination across many parts of Africa and Asia. The causes of this cannot simply be ascribed to the historic legacy of Empire, or inequalities associated with global capitalism. The rhetoric of colonial independence, freedom, and justice has not been matched in much of post-colonial Africa, by reductions in economic segregation, spatial exclusivity, and elite privilege. Similarly gender inequality manifested in widespread rape and domestic violence, in India or the Middle East also cannot be attributed to macro-economic global forces (any more than similar processes in the United States or United Kingdom can).

The idea of a major global social division between North and South, terms first popularized by the Brandt Report, is strongly connected with inequalities of wealth and power that are associated with empire, and with continuing inequalities experienced in the post-imperial epoch (International Commission on Development Issues 1980). The language in which this divide has been conceived is partly geographic based on the divide between hemispheres, but also metaphorical, since some wealthier nations such as Australia or emerging countries like Brazil, are located in the South. In symbolic terms, the rich and powerful 'North' continues to dominate the poor and less powerful 'South'. However the mechanisms may have changed from 19th and early 20th century forms of territorial control to deregulated market-based exchanges skewed in favour of multinational corporations, markets supervised by North-dominated international organizations like the IMF and World Bank. As with any macro-level distinction of this kind, however, the North-South divide, by itself, is unable to do justice to the complexities of *both* global and local patterns and causes of inequality.

Migration and mobility

Long-distance migration through history has sometimes been connected with Empire as in forced forms of human mobility associated with slavery. Yet migration also has voluntary as well as coerced aspects, and this makes migration an issue in its own right in understanding the historical sociology of social division and global inequality. Its major contemporary significance for the analysis of global inequality is that it offers, or seems to offer, a way out of poverty and political insecurity for millions of people in Africa and Asia. In contrast to the deregulation of flows of trade and capital in the global economy, however, movements of population are tightly regulated in the wealthier countries. Immigration controls seek to limit new migrants to officially approved categories. Yet the continuing lure of a better life in Western Europe, North America, or Australia, results in massive flows of illegal immigrants who may die or suffer extreme abuse in their attempts to move. They represent further tragedies resulting from the perpetuation of global inequality.

Humankind, according to the anthropologist James Clifford (1992), has always been a travelling species. People migrate to find land and food, to secure ways of making a better living, to free themselves from political control and domination, and to enhance their way of life. Empires have sometimes been instigators of migration, as have processes of economic development, each requiring additional sources of labour, whether for plantation labour, military employment or factory work. Patterns of inequality were typically built into these processes, as the following example makes clear.

Migration and racial domination in late imperial cities

African migrants moved into colonial cities en masse in the late 19th and earlier 20th centuries to work in mines, processing of raw materials, and unskilled service work. Demissie (2007, 158–160) shows how in cities such as Johannesburg, Harare, Kinshasa, and Nairobi, colonial administrators saw Black Africans as a social and cultural threat, likely to spread, crime, disease, and disorder. Racialized discourses of public health were used to enforce racial segregation creating racial ghettoes with poor housing and little social infrastructure. Ironically it was these slums and shanties that helped to act as incubators of trade unionism and national liberation movements.

Flows of migrants have continued to expand in the post-colonial world, reaching over 200 million by 2010 according to official statistics assembled by the World Bank (2011a). This reflects both push factors such as poor economic prospects or political oppression in countries of origin as well as the pull factors of greater perceived opportunities and personal freedom in countries to which migrants head (Castles and Miller 1993). Such flows are responses to forms of economic and political inequality in the country of origin as well as being implicated in structures of inequality in receiving countries. Not all migrants are of course poor or unskilled. Nonetheless for those who are conditions in receiving countries are often difficult for a variety of reasons of which racial and cultural discrimination may be one (for a deeper analysis of this issue see Sassen 1998a).

The most relevant issues for the historical sociology of global inequalities, are threefold. First, migration is a recurring feature of globalization, but one that has always been associated with inequality as much as opportunity. Second, the recent history of Empire, slavery, and colonial independence influences the ways in migrants look for a better life, and the ways in which they are treated in new settings.

Third, the scale of attempted global migration speaks not simply to desires of the poor for a better life, but also the moral and political challenge facing richer countries whose immigration control policies deny the world's poor a major potential avenue of inequality-reduction.

Migration has generally taken place within family networks with shared cultural practices, rather than through isolated individual actions. Such networks (Holton 2008) often defined by a mix of ethnicity and religion have a particular history and social characteristics, which may contrast in real or imagined ways with other groups living in places to which they migrate. This creates a possible basis not simply for social tension, but also for social division and inequality. This occurred historically with processes of Jewish migration and settlement which sometimes occurred relatively peacefully, but in other contexts involved bitter social divisions and anti-Semitism (Dubnow 2000, Menocal 2002). As in all cases of social division based on cultural characteristics, the attribution of difference and division is based on evaluative criteria rather than objective criteria. This often takes the form of derogatory cultural stereotypes invented by dominant groups as ways of demeaning and dominating migrants. This has led in extreme cases to the Nazi genocide of the Jews, and to more recent ethnic cleansing in both central Africa and Balkan Europe.

Attempts to enforce racial or cultural domination may also be community-led rather than deriving from exclusively top-down initiatives. Fear of migrants who are perceived as culturally distinct may be associated with real or imagined competition for employment, but may equally have strong elements of emotionally charged cultural symbolism. And yet cultural mixture arising from migration, does not necessarily foster conflict and cultural inequality between different social groups. Under certain conditions, it may produce its opposite.

World religions

Religion performs a wide range of social functions. It can be harnessed to the interests of the powerful. An obvious example is the use of Christianity or Islam as ways of providing a religious justification for Imperial expansion and control over territory and populations. The role of Christianity to buttress the Spanish and Portuguese colonization of South America is well known. Religion can also be a consolation in the face of human suffering, and may therefore appeal to the poor and oppressed. In this mode it may underwrite resistance to structures of oppression and feed into liberation movements or struggles against racism. In the historical sociology of global inequality, the role that religion plays is a complex one, sometimes contributing to inequality, sometimes resisting it.

Religion, colonization, and indigenous peoples

Mignolo (2000) draws attention to religious debates in 16th century Spain that have a huge significance for world history and global inequality. These are the so-called Valladolid debates that dealt with religious doctrine and the Spanish conquest of South America. Debate focussed on the question – is it legitimate for Christians to declare war on and dominate indigenous populations? This was seen to depend on how far the AmerIndians were seen as fully human! To say 'no' as most were to do, saw the Church underpinning colonization and racial inequality. To say yes, as a few were to do, meant that Amerindians should have rights as peoples. This offered a kind of religious cosmopolitanism as an alternative to racism. But the majority position prevailed with fateful consequences for the peoples of South America.

Another way of describing global social division is through the contrast between the West and the world beyond, sometimes referred to as the East or Orient. This has its origins not so much in economic developments as in medieval and early modern religious conflict and division between Christendom and Islam. This occurred in the 'Christian' Crusades, resistance to the Moorish occupation of Spain, and to the expansion of the Ottoman Empire into south-east Europe. Subsequently the contrast between the West and its 'Others' extended after 1700, through religious as well as economic and political processes, with the global expansion of both Western Empires and capitalism into Asia and Africa.

This earlier religious sense of 'civilizational contrast' has nonetheless come to the fore again in the last two decades with the rise of radical Islam, the impact of 9/11, and the so-called 'war on terror'. One symbolic way of conceiving the contemporary position is through Benjamin Barber's (1995) vivid contrast between what he calls Jihad and McWorld. Jihad, the Arabic word for holy struggle encapsulates the broader Islamic challenge to what is perceived as Western materialism and spiritual emptiness, as much as the call to take up arms. McWorld, by contrast, stands for Western consumer capitalism, an amalgam of McDonald's fast foods, Apple Mac computers, and MTV entertainment. This social division between Jihad and McWorld has both geo-political dimensions, as witnessed in the 9/11 attack, as well as cultural ones.

Much of the geo-political dynamic behind radical Islamization is connected with a profound sense of political inequality in the global order, as Islamic nations fail to establish an effective international presence in world affairs. Their borders and sovereignty, as in Pakistan or Afghanistan are porous allowing Western military and political penetration and intervention. In this way, the struggle of Jihad against McWorld is not in the main, an other-worldy struggle against Western civilization. While not aimed expressly at material inequality it speaks to a sense of revolt against geo-political domination and the humiliations involved. Many Islamists look to the revival of the Caliphate, which at various points in the past acted as an expansive political and military institution. This is conceived precisely as a means of countering the political inequalities which drive much radicalization.

In the world as a whole, the lure of McWorld beyond Europe and North America continues to fuel attempts at upward social mobility. For the poorest this is partly to be achieved through attempted migration. But for those with education and skills, there are also expectations of living sustainable middle-class lifestyles, whether in Islamic countries like Malaysia or Indonesia or in China and India.

Gender inequality across history

In this chapter I have attempted to show why history matters to an understanding of global inequality. Attention has focussed on the emergence of economic, political, and cultural processes and institutions in past centuries, which continue to shape and influence the contemporary world. Yet there is another sense in which historical processes influence the present, and that is where very long-term and deep-seated structures of inequality persist from past to present. The leading case is that of gender inequality.

Fernand Braudel uses the term 'la longue durée' to refer to very-long term processes in history as distinct from shorter cycles of change across decades, as well as the flux of everyday life. Continuity in this view matters as much as change. This emphasis on continuity has been taken up by Judith Bennett (2006) looking at the very long-term dominance of men over women across centuries. This dominance represents a patriarchal longue durée. Women's experience may have changed during processes of modernization or industrialization, but it has not been transformed. Explaining how this has occurred is therefore a task for historians of continuity as much as analysts of the present-day.

The evidence used to support this historical point of view includes (Table 3.3):

Table 3.3 Dimensions of gender inequality across history

- Different material rewards and status accruing to the labour of men and women
- Restriction or denial of women's rights over their bodies in areas such as fertility
- Persistent vulnerability of women to domestic violence and rape
- Absence or restriction of rights of women to property ownership
- Prohibition or restriction of women's social and political participation in community life and government

The argument here is not one of total and invariant bleakness in women's social situation across history, nor that historical changes in the position of women are completely absent. The point is rather that patriarchy in more or less intense but varying forms has a very long history. It is in this sense that long-term processes of historical continuity matter a great deal to an understanding of global inequality whether in the past or present. Alongside the 'racial longue durée' identified by Winant (2001, 21), lies a patriarchal longue durée (Bennett 2006).

Historical legacies and path dependency

Historic patterns of inequality associated with phenomena like empires, slavery, migration and ethnicity, or patriarchy, occurred at a time when market-economies and cross-border capitalism were of limited significance. This warns us against the simplistic assumption that some singular process like the drive to global capital accumulation is always the prime mover behind global inequality. Familiar contemporary processes like the international division of labour founded on capitalist property rights and market deregulation may indeed be of vital significance today. Yet other processes that have been important in the past, may still be of significance too.

To give an obvious example, if gender inequality and patriarchy, have been important in both past and present, this suggests that any contemporary explanation based exclusively on capitalism as the key causal factor is likely to be unsatisfactory. This argument is not intended to deny any kind of linkage between markets, capitalism and inequality, only to caution against simplistic recourse to one over-arching explanatory framework. Rather there are reasons to be sceptical towards the application of any single grand theory to the analysis of global inequality, and hence a reliance on one single policy approach to achieve a more egalitarian social order.

Another version of this general argument about historical continuities speaks of path-dependency. This refers to the possibility that developmental pathways that have arisen in particular national and regional settings may have a longer term influence into the present. The concept of path dependency challenges one of the key assumptions of modernization theory, namely that particular nations will converge on a single pattern of modern institutions such as markets, democratic politics, and the rule of law. Those who modernize first – such as Western Europe and North America – help to diffuse modernity to late-comers. This is the broad logic behind the Washington Consensus operated by Western-dominated institutions like the World Bank and International Monetary Fund in the latter decades of the 20th century. This approach has however broken down, as many recent examples of successful economic development like that of China, have combined markets with political and cultural institutions drawing on Chinese legacies. Routes to modernity differ in part because historical legacies, such as those embedded in Chinese Communism matter in the present. They do not converge in any simple way.

Korzeniewicz and Moran (2009), whose work has already been discussed earlier, provide a more general example of this kind of analysis, identifying how it is that a contrasting set of 'high-inequality' and 'low-inequality' countries have emerged. This contrast, is not restricted to the present but goes back across decades and sometimes centuries (43–88). Their underlying argument, as we have seen, is that variations in patterns of economic activity or political rights at particular moments of social change have longer term consequences for patterns of inequality, which persist creating longer-term pathways of development. The mechanisms of continuity typically involve new institutions which create property rights, forms of social hierarchy, or democratic rights which lock-in particular patterns of inequality – high or low. A few countries, notably the United States, do not fit neatly into one of the two patterns, but the two contrasting profiles are remarkably constant.

This historical dimension is a warning against any single grand-theoretical perspective. This warning is all the more significant because these authors have been strongly influenced by world-system theory, but nonetheless develop a very nuanced approach alive to complexity and variations in inequality, as well as equilibria in inequality patterns sustained by local institutions. This is one example of a tension within social theory noted by Walby (2009, 79) between the search for explanations 'of the greatest power and range', and a 'concern with accuracy and particularity'.

Walby's time-frame is far less extensive than that of Korzeniewicz and Moran, since her underlying focus is on multiple forms of modernity associated with complex regimes of inequality in an epoch of globalization. Much of this concerns the last 25–30 years and the existence of a divergence between neo-liberal and social democratic versions of modernity at a time when global processes have often been associated with homogenization. One general question that arises here is whether this divergence will turn out to be only short term in character, with forces of global convergence becoming more important in the longer-term? Walby argues that the plausibility of divergence and its link with path-dependency is sustained both through the idea of different types of capitalism (Hall and Soskice 2001, Jackson and Deeg 2008) and different types of welfare-state regime (Esping-Andersen 1990).

It is important, of course, to clarify in more concrete terms how path-dependency influences contrasting historic patterns of social relations and inequality in neo-liberal and social democratic settings. Walby provides an example in relation to the issue of violence (208–212). Here characteristics like the depth of democracy, the extent of economic inequality, or the historical salience of militarism connect with path-dependent trajectories of particular countries. Democracy tends to be deeper in social-democratic countries as is a tendency to 'fuller criminalization of violence against women', and more opposition to militarism. In neo-liberal countries like the United States, by contrast, economic inequality is higher, as are crime rates and higher rates of violence (Halpern 2001, van Wilsem 2004). Walby also notes that there is a connection between higher levels of gender inequality and high levels of domestic violence against women (see also Yodanis (2004)).

Another important sociological contribution to the analysis of historical influences on current patterns of inequality has been developed by Mann and Riley (2007). Their focus, as we have seen in Chapter 2, is on macro-regions, rather than inequality within or between individual nation states. Such regions are defined as 'clusters of countries occupying geo-political niches... possessing similar political institutions, cultures, and similar economies' (82). Their argument is firstly that there are distinctive regional patterns of inequality, such that there is a high degree of convergence between the within-country inequality profile of the countries that constitute the regions. In other words, greater contrasts are found between regions than within them. But why should this be?

The second part of their argument is that historical processes such as success or defeat in war, colonial invasion of the spread of distinctive cultural practices have created legacies from past to present. East Asia for example has a more egalitarian profile as a region than Latin America. The East Asian pattern is attributed to relatively homogeneous populations, more inclusive education systems and higher literacy than in Latin America. Governance was also better co-ordinated in East Asia, with different power actors incorporated within it, while large landowners had been discredited by collaboration with European powers. In Latin America, by contrast, their power remained intact. Historically East Asia countries, according to Mann and Riley, came relatively late to global capital markets and problems of indebtedness to foreign interests compared with Latin America.

In Part One of this chapter, I have presented a brief historical sociology of social division and global inequality. Two broad conclusions follow from this. Firstly, it is clear that global inequality has existed across history as well as in the present day. This means there are historical as well as contemporary causes of inequality. The challenge facing this way of thinking is to identify which historical processes still exert an influence on the present, and which new or modified trends also matter. There is then an underlying issue here of continuity and change. The concept of path dependency helps to tease out issues of continuity beyond very generalized but often rather vague senses of long-term legacy. A second conclusion is there has never been a single overriding pattern of inequality that structures everything else. Theories that presuppose a prime mover responsible for inequality are therefore untenable.

Part Two: Methodological Difficulties in Using a Historical Approach

There are, nonetheless, some important methodological difficulties in thinking more historically taking due regard for complexity? The first concerns the existence of historical and cultural perceptions of and moral concern about inequality. The second concerns a mismatch between the static cross-sectional evidence most widely used in studies of inequality, and the need for more dynamic forms of evidence that allow us to better understand social processes over time. In this second part of the chapter I outline why these problems matter.

Historical and cultural variations in moral concern about inequality

Perceptions of inequality and the political or moral questions that arise from them vary across time. While it may be supposed that the poor have never enjoyed being poor and that this is something like a historical universal, it remains the case that the way poverty is understood, and the salience that it has for the rest of life varies considerably. Firstly perceptions of inequality are relative to the comparisons that are made – that is, unequal in relation to what? The comparator may involve other classes in society, or other peoples living elsewhere in the global arena, but it may also relate to a sense of ones rights, to the order that should prevail in God's universe, or to the capacity to live a life that is valued according to certain cultural standards. If some kind of social difference, such as differences based on gender or race, are regarded as part of the natural or god-given order of things then they are typically not defined as inequality, unless and until such concepts of the natural order are challenged politically and culturally.

Secondly, material inequality may be far less salient in some quarters than in others. An obvious case is that where spiritual concerns, such as the poverty demanded by monasticism, is seen as a higher matter than material wealth. Wherever material concerns take second place, material inequality is less culturally salient. But this is not all that is at stake.

Moral indifference among the wealthy and privileged may also reduce the salience of inequality both within nations or across the globe. If vast differences in income, wealth and life-chances are not seen as a problem by those that are doing well, then dominant social interests will not have much interest in identifying or measuring differences in well-being. The question of salience is an interesting one because official measurement of inequality is a comparatively recent historical phenomenon – traceable to the late 19th century (Milanovic 2011, 4–5). Before this time, nation states, and the social groups who dominated them, took some interest in the systematic wealth but far less in its distribution across the population. One of the emerging reasons for data collection was where social and political status affecting eligibility to vote, depended, in part, on income and wealth criteria. Such evidence that has survived from earlier times is therefore fragmentary and episodic. A leading example is that of ancient Rome, where measurement of inequality was based on data collected to meet one of the eligibility criteria for membership of the highest social classes, such as senators, and the equestrian order of knights (ibid. 46–50).

More systematic surveys of income distribution date from the last 200 years in a context influenced by growing fiscal demands created by war, increased public education, and of an expansion in political democracy to the working class. The public salience of income inequality increased however, not simply for reasons of greater economic justice reflected in the idea of progressive income tax, but also in relation to discourses about economic efficiency. The questions in debate here were how to set taxation levels that would not inhibit the functioning of markets through processes of saving and entrepreneurship. Underlying this are questions about the levels of inequality that are felt to be justified to achieve a dynamic economy. We are back to the question raised in Chapter 1, namely 'why does any given level of inequality matter?'.

Such debates have clearly influenced the collection of evidence on inequality over time, whether any data at all was collected, and if it was, in what form and for what purpose. Over the last 120 years data on inequality has proliferated, especially for wealthier countries, which have collected within-country evidence. But it has also waxed and waned depending on the political complexion of governments in power, with economically liberal administrations in the United States and United Kingdom in the last quarter of the 20th century collecting less than left-of-centre governments concerned with social justice.

Meanwhile the form in which evidence has been collected has also been influenced by the assumptions of economists. This has biased most research, until very recently to quantifiable evidence, that is to measurable data on incomes and wealth rather than broader social aspects of welfare. Here the unit of analysis is typically the individual rather than the household. Qualitative data, to do with the experience of those who experience inequality, including life-histories or accounts of how the poor and victimized cope with and struggle against their social subordination has generally been hidden from history, most of the time. A striking example of this are gender inequalities manifest in domestic violence and rape.

Qualitative research on violence and gender inequality in India

Gender violence arising from Keralan women's access to micro-credit for business and household purposes is explored by Valsala Kumari (2008), using the testimony of women. They reported how women's access to credit often provoked a violent response from male family or community members, given its destabilizing effect on men's patriarchal power and status. This example of interpersonal micro-level processes of patriarchy, is one of many qualitative dimensions of inequality that slip through the net of quantitative research.

The surfacing of such dimensions of inequality generally occurs from the bottom-up through social movements and protest rather than from top-down elite concerns. Labour movements, feminism, environmental campaigns and movements for colonial freedom have all contributed to this broadening of focus. Issues involved have included sweat-shop labour, violence against women, and toxic environmental practices in poor countries – all of which are major themes in global inequality (Bahun-Radunovic and Rajan 2008, Carmin and Agyeman 2011).

Concern with inequality within nation states generally pre-dates concern for global inequality. Again silence about such matters may reflect moral indifference, a characteristic which may be compounded by a sense that the global social order reflects god's will or the inevitability of market forces. Whatever the reasons, it is only with the extension of political democracy, decolonization, and the development of global organizations and social protest movements, that shifts in moral and political concern have brought global inequality onto the agenda, in the half-century since the end of the Second World War. This has led to bodies like the World Bank, the International Labour Organization, the United Nations Commission on Trade and Development (UNCTAD), and the Organization for Economic Cooperation and Development to collect data on a broader spatial and thematic basis. Such efforts have reached their widest published expression in the statistics that support the UNDP Human Development Index.

Until very recently data from wealthier countries has also been difficult to match with income data from poorer countries. It is only with decolonization and political independence processes since the Second World War that interest in, and capacity to collect data in Latin America, Asia, and Africa has emerged. This has permitted measures of income inequality across the world to be constructed as the number of nations for which comparable data exist has expanded rapidly. But once again, the form and scope of data collection has been influenced by both local political and global considerations.

One potential way around some of this is the systematic identification of the widest possible data-base across history, and the judicious use of estimation to fill in some of the gaps. Mention should be made here of the work of economic historian Angus Maddison. Over a 30 year period, Maddison and his colleagues assembled data on national accounts and population across time and space going back 200 years where possible, and spatially well beyond Europe and North America (Maddison 2006, 2007). Much of the historical evidence reviewed in the following chapter is based on the data-base that Maddison assembled.

What the methodological issues point to here is the familiar sociological proposition that the sum total of all available evidence on global inequality is marked by political, cultural, and intellectual interests and assumptions. The raw data, as in all social enquiries, do not speak for themselves, but require active interpretation.

Problems with cross-sectional data on inequality

A second methodological dimension to the historical study of global inequality concerns the primarily cross-sectional form that most quantitative evidence about global inequality takes. Cross-sectional data take a static look at patterns of global inequality at a given point in time, usually organized in terms of the distribution of income and other aspects of human welfare and well-being across nations and the world. Where data exist, this is usually combined with other cross-sectional evidence at different points of time. This enables account to be taken of trends and not simply of inequality at one moment of time. The methodology of multiple cross-sectional 'slices' is of course historical in the sense that it takes place over time, though the time-frame itself is typically shorter because available data tapers off the further back in time we go.

Most of the data cited in the public domain and taken up in political debate takes a cross-sectional form. There is often a tacit assumption behind the inferences drawn from this approach, namely that the people who occupy the different levels of the distribution of income over time roughly stay the same. This assumption may well be warranted in some cases, but not necessarily in all. The underlying difficulty here is whether those occupying particular positions in the income distribution at one moment in time are in the same situation at subsequent moments. To the extent that they are not, then typical inferences drawn from cross-sectional data become very misleading.

Esping-Andersen (2007, 217–220) raises this difficulty with particular reference to cross-sectional data on inequality within 'advanced industrial' nations. One dimension of inequality that cross-sectional data omit is the stage in the life course that the different individuals involved currently occupy. To have less income at one stage in your life, as a student or retiree, for example, does not necessarily mean lower income across a life time of paid work. A great deal depends therefore on how transient or persistent occupancy of particular positions in the cross-sectional distribution of income turns out to be (Whelan, Layte, and Maitre 2004). This work found that persistent or chronic income poverty among a large set of specific households over a period of five years between 1993 and 1998 varied between 7 and 12% across the countries of Western Europe. Those who never experienced persistent poverty across this time frame varied between 64 and 82% of the households tracked. Factors seen as most salient to persistent poverty included precariousness of income, large size of family, and experience of marital breakdown.

In an epoch of expanding economic development and increased opportunity, transient deprivation is likely to be far higher than in a phase of economic recession and structural crisis in opportunity. Where individuals face short-term poverty, consumption expenditure is smoothed over the bad times and the good. Where individuals face more persistent economic challenges, such as those facing young unemployed people in austerity Europe the position is far tougher. Esping-Andersen does not extend this point to the world beyond Europe and North America, but the same general methodological problem remains with all cross-sectional data, whether for United Kingdom or China, Brazil, or Germany.

Longitudinal data on income and lifestyle deprivation are available, enabling distinctions to be made between chronic and transient poverty at the lower end of the income distribution. This methodological shift has enabled new insights the nature of poverty, although technical issues to do with different types of measurement can produce different results.

Transient or persistent poverty? A complex problem

Duclos, Arrar, and Giles (2010) looking at household poverty in China over a 17-year period between the late 1980s and the early 21st century found that the majority of poverty was transient rather than chronic. Earlier studies of India (Gaiha and Deolaiker 1993) and Pakistan (McCulloch and Baulch 1999) yielded similar results. It may however be that the scale of chronic poverty has been underestimated in this kind of approach. McKay and Lawson (2003), for example, claim that the qualitative depth of poverty on a household way of life is not fully gauged in this work. This discussion also deals with poverty rather than inequality per se. Issues of transient low income across the life-cycle must then be balanced by other data indicating the cumulative effect across-time of those who start off in advantageous locations in economy and society (Willson, Shuey, and Elder 2007). Such persistent advantages also matter to the analysis of inequality.

At this stage, my concern here is not to resolve disputes about the relative numbers of those in persistent and transient poverty. The issue is rather a methodological one, that takes account of the factor of time in discussing the incidence of poverty, low income, and economic advantage. Concerns about whether the same or somewhat different sets of people are at the bottom of the income distribution across time are very important, but they do not affect the cross-sectional data on inequality which is used to establish the general profiles of inequality within different countries and the world as a whole. It is these profiles to which attention turns in Chapters 4 and 5.

Conclusion

The major purpose of this chapter has been to demonstrate how important it is to take a historical approach to the study of global inequality. In this chapter I have considered both substantive and methodological issues. Substantively history matters because of the importance of legacies from the past that affect inequality in the present. These may be connected with empire, slavery, migration, and religious expansion, whose legacies often extend into the present-day. Such processes affect the political and cultural history of social division as much as economic aspects of globalization. A historical sense puts into perspective the complex relationships between globalization and inequality. Above all, it suggests the importance of caution in attributing contemporary global inequality to contemporary processes of globalization. Continuity matters as well as change.

There are also key methodological problems arising from a historical approach. These include changing cultural perceptions of inequality and its salience for social life, and the importance of path-dependency to an understanding of continuities as well as change. Historical processes are not simply about structures and institutions but also about social actors and the lives of those involved in the construction of and resistance to inequality. This has implications both for the theme of continuity and change and for the life-course of individuals, questions which are not well captured by exclusive reliance on cross-sectional data, and quantitative evidence.

In the following two chapters attention turns to contemporary patterns of economic and social inequality.

4 Global Inequalities of Income and Wealth

The most widely used approach to global inequality is based on evidence about income. It is statistics of income inequality that are most likely to be cited in public debates on economic development and social justice. Measures of the huge disparity between the richest and the poorest countries or between the top 1% of the world's population and the rest typically cite statistics on income in support of the policy prescriptions that are favoured. Underlying this focus is the work of economists and sociologists on levels and trends in income inequality and how they are to be explained. In this first of two chapters on evidence of global inequality, I look in more depth at income and wealth, moving on in the following chapter to consider wider social measures of inequality.

How far is it possible to make bold judgements about the scale and patterns of global income inequality in the contemporary setting? Is it rising or falling? Does it follow a consistent pattern and trend? And how reliable is the evidence base on which such judgements rest?

In the first part of this chapter, the focus will be on general features of global inequality which command a high level of consensus among analysts. In the second part attention shifts to those issues about which there is more disagreement and uncertainty.

Some Very General Features of Global Income Inequality

It is possible to make some bold judgements about global income inequality about which there is general agreement. The evidence on which these judgements rest is primarily quantitative in form, depending on statistical evidence collected or assembled in a variety of ways. Accurate data is sometimes difficult or impossible to locate, especially for poorer countries lacking the resources to collect adequate data (Jerven 2013). Also the assumptions used in statistical analysis also vary. I shall return to some of these methodological issues later. For the moment, attention is given to four propositions which sum up the general features about which there is most agreement.

First, the contemporary world exhibits very high levels of inequality of income and wealth both between countries and within countries. Income is concentrated in the hands of the top 5% of the world's population who hold 37% of the global income, while the poorest 5% hold only 0.3%. The ratio in income between the top and bottom 5% groups is just short of 200 to 1 (Milanovic 2011, 152). Another way of showing just how high global income inequality has become is to calculate a Gini coefficient for the world as a whole. The Gini coefficient, described in Chapter 3, ranges from 0 (for no inequality) to 100 (highest possible inequality). This measure now stands at around 70 for the world as a whole, making global levels of income inequality higher than the inequality within any single country. Within-country Gini measures vary between 30 and 35 points in most of western Europe, rising to 40+ in the United States, China, and Russia, around 50–55 in Latin America and Africa to around 60 in Brazil and South Africa (ibid. 30–31, 152).

These high levels of inequality in income are taken as significant not simply because they limit the consumption of commodities available to individuals, but also because of the negative social consequences of low income levels on other aspects of well-being including health, education, and social participation. Wade (2007, 115) sees income inequality as closely linked with higher poverty, unemployment, crime, worse health, weaker property rights, and skewed access to public services.

Income inequality and the position of children and women

Ortiz and Cummins (2011, 20–21) in a discussion paper for the United Nations Children's Fund (UNICEF) note that nearly half the world's children and young people aged less than 25 are located in households within the bottom 20% of the global income distribution, having access to only 9% of global income. The global gender gap in income levels also remains significant. World Bank figures for 2009 indicate that women's wages in manufacturing across the globe remain around 10% lower than men's, while women in agriculture generally work smaller plots growing less remunerative crops (World Bank 2012).

Recent research by Babones (2008) across 100 countries over several decades finds strong statistical connections between income inequality, lower life expectancy, and higher infant mortality. This work is based on correlations between income inequality and other adverse social outcomes, not direct causal links. This distinction between correlation and causation matters if we wish to make sense of the complex intersection of different types of inequality and different causal influences. This issue will be pursued further in the next chapter within the context of a broader analysis of social dimensions of well-being beyond income. For the moment I simply make the point that patterns of income inequality have wide-ranging social dimensions and consequences.

Even greater inequalities are found when wealth, that is, the stock of assets owned by individuals, as distinct from income, is estimated. A 2008 discussion paper produced under the auspices of the United Nations University found that in the year 2000, the richest 2% of adults in the world owned more than half global household wealth, while the top 10% owned around 85%. This contrasts with the bottom 50% of adults who own only barely 1% of the world's wealth (Davies et al. 2008, 7–10). Such huge differences reflect the difficulty of those in poverty being able to accumulate wealth through saving.

Inequalities of wealth more extreme than inequalities of income

Whereas the global Gini coefficient for income lies around 70, the Gini coefficient for wealth in 2000 was around 80 when measured for households (Davies et al. 2011, 243) and 89 for individuals (Davies et al. 2008, 7–10). In the more recent Credit Suisse Global Wealth Report of 1912, these sharp inequalities are confirmed with the top 8% of adults owning in excess of 82% of wealth, while the bottom 70% owning just in excess of 3% (Credit Suisse 2012).

Wealth inequalities also vary within countries, even among those in the wealthier bracket. Thus the top 10% individual wealth-holders in the year 2000 owned around 70% of the national wealth in the United States and Switzerland, compared to around 53–56% in the United Kingdom, Canada, and India, and around 45% in Australia and Germany (Davies, ibid. 4, 9). What is interesting here is that national variations in wealth inequality are not correlated with levels of national wealth. Thus wealth inequality is somewhat similar in China, Ireland, and Spain where the top 10% of wealth-holders receive 41–42% of national wealth, even though actual levels of wealth differ markedly. Similarly the UK position where the top 10% receive 55% of wealth is not dissimilar to the figure for India, even though actual wealth levels vary significantly.

Global inequalities in wealth are evident at both the individual, household, and national level and in terms of contrasts between corporate wealth and the wealth of nations. Here the top 1% of corporations have larger revenues than quite sizeable and reasonably prosperous countries. This measure of income and wealth is often also taken as an indicator of global corporate power, though this kind of evidence is more illustrative than analytical. Thus the considerable power of corporations applies even in relation to countries that are larger than they are. This is reflected in low corporate tax rates in the United States and in favourable US government treatment during the global financial crisis when the largest banks and automobile companies were bailed out with public money.

Wealth of corporations and wealth of countries

According to *Business Insider* magazine in 2011, General Electric was larger than New Zealand, Walmart bigger than Norway, and Chevron bigger than the Czech Republic (Trivett 2011).

Second, economic inequality is spatially concentrated. It is well known in a general sense that the lowest-income areas of the globe are concentrated in Africa and Asia, while the wealthiest are in North America and Western Europe. Recent research, however, has generated a more precise map of the distribution of global income by country and region (for the following account see Korzeniewicz and Moran 2009, 91–96). Based on a sample of 85 countries, this shows that virtually the entire population of income recipients in richer countries like the United States and Sweden are concentrated within the top 20% of the world's income receivers, while in poor countries like Zimbabwe around 90% of income receivers lie within the bottom 20% of global recipients.

One implication of this evidence is that even the poorest sections of the richest nations are well-off by world standards. This applies even when the higher cost of living in wealthier countries is taken into account. Such radical differentials in income are also the primary reason why so many of the world's poor seek to migrate to the richer societies, even though there is no certainty of work or guarantee of a secure settlement free from discrimination. This is also a striking reminder that patterns of income inequality may look very different when moving from national within-country comparisons to global between-country differentials.

Further dimensions of global spatial inequality apply to cities. While shifts of the very poor from the countryside to the city may lessen within-country inequality, such processes have also seen a trend to the urbanization of global poverty. Between 1993 and 2002, the numbers of rural poor living on less than US$1 per day declined by an estimated 150 million, whereas the numbers of urban poor defined in the same way rose by 50 million (Ravallion, Chen, and Sangruala 2007). This process was also regionally skewed, with the highest numbers of urban poor in Latin America, and the least in East Asia. Meanwhile in Eastern Europe and Central Asia at this time, there was a greater ruralization of poverty.

In the case of global cities, meaning those most integrated into worldwide mobilities of capital and labour, Sassen (2001, 2011) identifies further dimensions of inequality. New urban structures in such settings involve both high paid corporate managers and professionals and a poor largely migrant and often feminized workforce of cleaners, domestic servants, janitors, and hospitality workers. Others point to growing exclusion of the poor from any niche within urban labour markets (Kilroy 2009). Such trends reproduce inequalities not so much between countries, but within global cities such as London, New York, Tokyo, and most recently Shanghai (Chen 2009). Sassen sees this as a new kind of social polarization. What is less clear is whether the low-income recipients in global cities are worse or better off than low-income recipients in other cities within the same country (Elliott 1999).

In this kind of global city analysis, flows of capital and flows of labour are integrated through global networks that are both virtual and physical. Social and electronic networks are interconnected features of a new kind of social structure that is both dynamic and highly unequal. This kind of thinking helps to break through the rather static nation state frameworks of much thinking on global inequality.

Most of the measures of income and wealth inequality considered so far are composed of static cross-sectional snapshots. A great deal, however, depends on trends over time. Are inequalities getting greater or lesser when we look across history? And can countries or regions change their relative positions in the distribution of inequality in contemporary world? These are vital questions, but many are fundamentally contested. Where there is most agreement is on the historical patterning of inequality.

Third, taking up the historical theme, social inequality as I argued in the previous chapter has always existed. In this particular chapter attention is focussed more specifically on very recent historic patterns of economic inequality. These can be pinned down with increasing accuracy across the 19th and 20th centuries, as a wider range of countries began to collect statistical data. Relevant evidence includes census data, national output and income statistics, taxation data, and more recently household income surveys. Historical statistics painstakingly put together by the economic historian Angus Maddison (2006, 2007) expand in scope from around 50 countries in 1820 to 160 – including China – in the first decade of the 21st century. What this material indicates, however, is that the scale and composition of global inequality in income and wealth has changed over time.

In terms of scale, the gap between the richest and the poorest has grown within the world as a whole over the last two centuries (Bourguignon and Morrison 2002, Milanovic 2011, 158–160). This does not mean that the poorest have got worse off in absolute terms between the early 19th century and today. This would be surprising in view of the productivity gains associated with industrialization and technological innovation and inconsistent with the rapid growth in the world's population over the last two centuries. What it does mean is that the relative gap between the richest and the poorest has widened, indicating that the benefits of enhanced productivity are very unequally distributed. This still leaves many facing crises of subsistence, food insecurity, and starvation, made even worse by growing environmental risks associated with climate change.

The UN-based Food and Agriculture Organization (FAO) defines malnourishment in terms of 'persons whose food intake regularly provides less than their minimum energy requirements'. On this basis, 868 million people were suffering malnourishment between 2010 and 2012, representing some 12% of the world's population. In parts of sub-Saharan Africa around 30–35% of the population of many countries was considered malnourished. There is, however, some evidence of improvement in global malnourishment rates which 20 years ago stood at 19% of the world's population (FAO 2013).

In terms of composition, the relative importance of within-country and between-country inequality has also changed over time. In the early 19th century it is estimated that within-country inequality composed the greater part of global income inequality. In the last 200 years, however, as capitalist industrialization expanded and the developmental trajectories of different parts of the world diverged, between-country inequality has grown in relative importance.

Growing divergence in global incomes between richest and poorest countries

Milanovic notes that the gross domestic product (GDP) per head of the Netherlands – the world's richest country in 1820 – was three times that of China the world's poorest. By 1913, the United States had become the world's richest country, and the ratio between the United States and China, which remained the poorest, had expanded to ten to one. Today the ratio of richest to poorest now stands at one hundred to one, though China is no longer the poorest (2011, 100, 109,143).

To say that between-country inequality now forms the largest component part of global inequality does not mean that the relative position of different countries and regions in the between-country mix remains the same. Thus if some countries successfully lift their rates of economic development, they may raise themselves out of the poorest group and maybe narrow the historic ratios of difference in GDP. This is precisely what has happened in China, India, much of south-east Asia, and Brazil, in the period since the 1980s (Dollar 2007). This more successful developmental trajectory has not been universal, however, across countries regarded as underdeveloped. However, the complex and dynamic processes involved in sorting out patterns and trends in between-country inequality, make secure generalizations difficult to determine.

Some Outstanding Areas of Dispute about Global Inequality

Beyond this point disagreements as to the nature of global inequality take over. The first and most immediate area of dispute concerns the current trend in global inequality. The question in dispute is whether income inequality is lessening, getting worse, or has reached something of a stable plateau. All three possibilities have their supporters. Answers to this key question depend to a significant degree on problems of how best to measure inequality in incomes. Different procedures and assumptions yield somewhat different results. Should the unit of analysis be individuals, households, or nations? How do we compare incomes across different countries with differing costs of living measured in different currencies? How accurate is data collected in poorer countries including most of sub-Saharan Africa, where few accurate data exist, and many cited figures are based largely on guesswork (Jerven 2013). And finally is there one simple trend at work, or a mixture of trends in the different component parts of global income inequality?

The disarray in opinion about current trends is not merely of academic interest, but affects policy-making and political action. For those who see a trend towards greater equality, there is no need to radically change current policies. For those who are more pessimistic, current policies have largely failed and new ones are needed. This applies to nation states and international organizations keen to promote economic growth and non-government organizations seeking to achieve a greater degree of global justice. As it happens there are probably more pessimists than optimists across this range of institutions, looking at the last 30–40 years. Yet it remains to be established whether a sharp divide between optimists and pessimists offers the most convincing insights into recent trends.

The *optimistic case* for a reduction of global income inequality since around 1980 has been developed by Bhalla (2002) and Sala-i-Martin (2002, 2006). They used national account figures on income per head together with more limited surveys of the distribution of income across households. This procedure has been criticized because some national accounts appear to exaggerate rates of economic growth and hence national income growth. This point has been made of key countries like China and India (see the discussion in Dollar 2007, 84). Other technical problems with this approach are identified by Milanovic (2007, 38) and Anand and Segal (2008). Sala-i-Martin (2006) nonetheless extrapolated a continuing phase of lessening inequality up until around 2015 if the high growth rates of China and India continued. Milanovic (2012) in later work dealing with the period up to 2008, relates improvement to a convergence of countries' mean income levels, but argues that continuing decline in global income inequality also depends on within-country inequalities being kept in check.

Others writing about the 1980s and 1990s have been more *pessimistic*. Gottschalk and Smeeding (1997, 636) identified increased income inequality across a number of industrialized economies. Similarly Cornia, Addison, and Kiiski (2003) in a wider study of 73 countries making up 80% of the world's population found 2/3 of developing countries, especially those in sub-Saharan Africa and Latin America, experienced increases in income inequality across this period. These data on increasing inequality contrast with a lessening in inequality in the first three decades after the Second World War. These are of course generalizations across multiple countries and certain counter examples are evident. Increases in income inequality in many developing countries and in developed nations like the United States and the United Kingdom, for example, are not matched, according to Cornia, Addison, and Kiisksi (2003, 15), in other places like Germany, Norway, and parts of South-East Asia.

It would be wrong, therefore, to paint optimists and pessimists as two sharply divided camps, since no trend is necessarily universal, a point I shall take up again in Chapter 6 when looking at explanations of global inequality. While more ideologically minded observers have been quick to take up an optimistic or pessimistic story, evidence-based analysis requires more caution. This is especially the case after 2000, when evidence of lessening global inequality has gained greater credibility, but not yet been accepted as a general trend. A notable complication in recent years has been the impact of the global financial crisis beginning around 2007–2008.

Some argue that this crisis was in part a consequence of pre-existing levels of inequality which created a shortfall in demand and increase in household debt (Stockhammer 2012). This position is not very convincing since it places insufficient emphasis on problems in the financial sector to do with the mispricing of risk in the financial derivatives markets. While there are many other structural and institutional causes of the crisis (Holton 2012), it is also important to emphasize its disruptive effects on patterns of economic growth and income. These have still not returned to pre-crisis levels in many countries. Dislocation has also been exacerbated by the combination of crises in global credit mechanisms and sovereign debt crisis. Austerity measures, especially in parts of Europe, have also had a disproportionally high impact on young adults, in terms of unemployment and risk of suicide (Karanikolos et al. 2013). Taken overall then the crisis has deflated income levels from what they otherwise would have been, yet the spatial concentration of the crisis in North America and Europe, rather than Asia and Australia, means that it is unlikely to have increased global inequality.

The work of Milanovic (2007, 2011, 2012) offers the most comprehensive, up-to-date, and methodologically plausible contribution to debates about contemporary trends in global inequality. His work is founded on the methodological proposition that household disposable income is the best unit of analysis to use in studying global inequality. There are several reasons for this. First, census data and national accounts do not give sufficient information on the incomes of individuals, whereas household surveys can and do. Second, disposable income is better than taxable-income as a measure of total income available for consumption. Some income recipients pay no tax, and some receive public income support payments largely separate from the tax system. A third, more sociological point may be added here, namely that most live in multiple-person households, whether as income recipients or income-less dependants such as children or (in many countries) the elderly. Household data gives us a better insight into the life-chances of its members than is given by treating them as individual atoms. Fourth, and last, households rely to varying extents on domestic labour, a major aspect of which is caring for household members. This is mostly done by women. It is also mostly unpaid and hence does not enter into official statistics. Nonetheless, domestic labour is an important contributor to household welfare, alongside the monetized and more obvious contributions organized through markets and public welfare provision (Walby 2009, 287–291).

Good household income survey data has only become available for wealthier industrial countries since 1950 and for the developing world in the last 20–30 years. But it does now cover they key period for which trend in global inequality are in dispute. Based on his analysis of household data, Milanovic (2011, 151ff) has calculated rates of global income inequality between 1988 and 2005 at roughly five-year intervals. His overall conclusion is that the global distribution has 'probably not' become more unequal overall over this period (ibid. 153). This suggests it may have reached a plateau. But does this mean, therefore, that both the optimists and the pessimists are entirely wrong. The answer is that this is not necessarily so, since the overall level of inequality is composed of three elements whose trends point in different directions – some improving, others worsening.

Milanovic distinguishes three analytically distinct components at work within the overall trend in contemporary global income inequality, namely (Table 4.1):

Table 4.1 Three trends in contemporary income inequality

1. Changes in within country inequality.
2. Changing trends in economic growth and income between rich and poor countries.
3. Changing trends in economic growth and income between China and India and rich countries.

Source: Derived from Milanovic, 153–154

The argument here is that the first two of these components have seen overall increases in inequality in recent decades, but that the third component has seen a lessening of inequality. This is because China and India, and certain other parts of East and South-East Asia, are growing faster than the richer countries and this is what has counter-acted deterioration in global inequality elsewhere. When the three components are added together one finds a plateau (2011, 155ff), or possibly declining global inequality (2012, 8). If the pattern detected for the period 1998–2008 is sustained, this would represent 'perhaps for the first time since the Industrial Revolution that there may be a decline in global inequality' (ibid. 7–8).

To be sure, this general trend conceals elements supportive of both the pessimistic and optimistic case. The overall trend is also vulnerable to changes in its components. Thus if the growth performance of China and India were to falter, between-country income inequality would increase. On the other hand as Korzeniewicz and Moran (2009, 106) point out, if the growth rates of China and India continue 'they will eventually change the face of global stratification'. In previous history, individual countries have successfully moved upward in the national stratification hierarchy, such as Sweden in the late 19th century, or Japan after the Second World War. What is different about China and India is their demographic, economic, and geopolitical scale within the global economy.

Several further observations on Milanovic's argument are necessary. The first is that it depends on using a person count rather than a country count to depict an overall rate of global inequality. Since China and India have such large populations, they inevitably skew global data based on a person count. Once you leave them out, the position is far bleaker. Second, China's positive contribution to lessening between-country inequality does not entail any particular view about inequality within China. This is in fact growing considerably in terms of an urban–rural and inter-provincial divide, though the lowest levels of poverty have been overcome (Pogge 2007).

Milanovic's work provides one way of restructuring the complex debate about current trends in global inequality in such a manner as to resolve the wide divergence of opinion in a more integrated fashion. His approach is also more circumspect than many others. There are, in particular, difficulties with jumping too readily to general conclusions about current trends upon which to launch more speculative scenarios about social change. A case in point is Therborn's recent (2012) proposition that patterns of global inequality seem to usher in a 'return of class'.

Therborn takes recent work on global inequality to confirm that 'inter-national' (or between-country) inequality is now decreasing as a result of the rise of China, some other Asian countries, and, in his view, much of Africa and Latin-America. At the same time within-country inequality is increasing, unevenly, but as a general trend. While he acknowledges in other work (Therborn 2006) the multiple dimensions and determinants of inequality, he regards this increase of within-country income inequality as a 'new turn' encapsulated in the idea of 'the return of class'. This rests not merely on changes in income distribution, but, he claims, on the erosion of inequalities of sex and race, a proposition that is not explored in any depth. While globalization brings nations closer together, he argues that increasingly unequal income distributions separate classes from one another. As with all class theory, however, the more difficult question is whether this will re-energize class politics in the form of working-class revolt, create greater demoralization, or increase dreams of middle-class consumerism, fuelled by cheap credit. If class politics is re-energized, this might produce a spatial shift in working-class revolt to places like China. This is an interesting speculation, but very thin conceptually and in terms of evidence.

A more general criticism of the return of class argument is that where you live is more important to your position in the global stratification hierarchy, than your social class. At a general level change of location from a poor to a rich country makes more difference to global inequality patterns, than rising in the social structure in any given country. As far as global stratification is concerned, a good deal depends on how far between-country social mobility is possible, an issue missing from both Milanovic and Therborn. Global migration from poor to rich countries has the potential both to raise living standards for migrants from what they previously were, but also to create an anti-immigrant and strident nationalist politics that undermine class.

A more fundamental difficulty with the work of Milanovic and many others arises over the way distinctions have been made between within-country and between-country inequality. These are not entirely separate processes but interact in highly significant ways. Korzeniewicz and Moran (2009) develop this argument by reaffirming the importance of a global unit of analysis in understanding the dynamics of global inequality. Between-country inequality, in this view, 'is an outcome of the comparative advantages that some nations gain over others in their inter-action' (74). Such advantages depend both on technological innovation and on the absence of rigidities in institutional arrangements. Examples of such rigidities include imperial and colonial controls over populations in colonized areas, or restrictions on immigration into wealthier countries from poorer ones.

Processes such as cross-border migration have implications both for between-country and within-country inequality. Immigration from Europe into the United States in the 19th century tended to create convergence of incomes in the countries involved. However its impact on within-country inequality was mixed. In contexts where labour was in short supply, an influx of migrants reduced inequality. But where large numbers of unskilled migrants entered tighter labour markets, inequalities increased. Restrictions on immigration into wealthier countries like the United States in the 20th century had the effect of reversing the rise of within-country inequality (O'Rourke and Williamson 1999, 138). In the present day restrictions on immigration into wealthier countries from poorer ones have the effect of ruling out one possible mechanism for reducing global inequality between countries. Countries powerful enough to erect barriers against immigration, sacrifice potential reductions in between-country inequality, for their own national interests, one of which is to protect domestic employment and income. And in countries with welfare states, such restrictions also have the effect of protecting domestic redistributive welfare support systems.

Processes of immigration are in a sense the between-country terrain of social mobility, operating in parallel with within-country social mobility which has attracted far more attention from economists and sociologists. Global social stratification requires that both terrains be considered in interaction with each other. Whereas upgrading educational qualifications and skills represents a major route for upward mobility within wealthier nations, immigration can represent the same process on a global level. Even if first generation migrants who lack capital or education are vulnerable to low-paid employment and higher rates of unemployment in the country of settlement, global migration from poorer countries lifts their position within the global income stratification. And this applies both in movement between poorer parts of Africa and Asia to the United States and Western Europe, as well as between very poor and poor nations. In Guatemala, for example, anyone within the poorest 70% of the population would achieve upward mobility if they gained access to most forms of employment in Mexico (Korzeniewicz and Moran 2009, 108).

A very different line of argument takes issue with the 'top-down' approach of official statistics of income typically used by economists to understand types and trends in inequality. What if we were to work from the bottom up, looking at the experience of inequality and poverty. How, for example, do large sections of the world's population live on two US$ per day? This question was tackled in an innovative scholarly study called *Portfolios of the Poor* (Collins, et al. 2009). Based on daily financial diaries kept by several hundred respondents in India, Bangladesh, and South Africa, this study provides somewhat surprising answers to questions of coping with the daily grind.

There are, first of all, three general characteristics affecting the income of those living at this level. First, and quite obviously incomes are low. Second income is episodic because work is uncertain and often seasonal especially in rural areas. Environmental insecurities like floods also play a part in many settings. Income-earning may also be interrupted by religious festivals. Some days no income is earned other days it may be more than US$2. Waged work and self-employment may often be combined. Third, the formal financial instruments accessible to very low income earners through institutions like banks are not helpful to the management of poverty.

How then do people manage? Not, as might be supposed by living hand to mouth, spending sparse amounts of income when it is received? Rather a great deal of attention is given to cash management, saving small sums to pay back debts, to take advantage of opportunities to buy small pieces of land, and to hold against emergencies. Beyond this informal sources of financial support are available whereby neighbouring households or kin borrow or lend small sums to each other. In addition small sums are often held in trust by others as insurance against household members' temptations to relax financial discipline and spend the savings. What surprised the researchers was the extent to which cash flow management was planned by the very poor and how different this picture is to top-down approaches by international agencies like the World Bank who look at annual levels of income and ways of extending formal market-based institutions to assist the poor (ibid. 29).

Informal sources of finance of course have their limits in terms of the scale of available resources and high demands on networks of support. The Grameen Bank in Bangladesh was established precisely to offset these limits by organizing small lines of micro-credit to low-income groups. Initially the focus was on loans rather than savings. And micro-credit was seen very much as a way of supporting micro-enterprises (ibid. 25–26). Collins and his co-authors argue that the financial diaries kept by their respondents indicate a demand for micro-credit for household cash management and to meet adverse contingencies such as medical emergencies and educational costs for children. Formal agencies have been slow to recognize this.

Micro-finance and poverty reduction

While micro-enterprise financing by the Grameen Bank has been criticized for being ineffective in reducing poverty (Khandker 2005), Collins et al. 2009, regard its major contribution as addressing the problem of uncertainty in income flows, a function that formal institutions need to extend further. Quibria (2012) also makes the point that movement out of poverty is a slow uncertain process rather than some instant response to innovations in financial organization or policy. Once again the significance of exploring processes taking place over time is reinforced.

The more general conclusion of *Portfolios of the Poor* is that while not having enough money is bad enough, not being able to manage what little you have is worse. This, it is argues 'is the hidden bind of poverty' (184). It is these two factors which may deprive a child of a place at school or of access to medical help. They also affect whether households can avoid the rapacious clutches of professional moneylenders. The collective self-help of small informal networks of people can help, but does not resolve problems of low and uncertain incomes. Such strategies may also have to face other dimensions of inequality beyond income, such as ethnic discrimination, or lack of systems capable of enforcing legal rights, wider matters which I discuss in subsequent chapters.

A final general methodological issue is the reliability of the procedures and methods typically used in analysing global inequality. I leave aside very technical issues here. The focus is rather on the difficult question of how to compare income across different countries. This is a problem of major significance but has no clear answer. Instead analysts rely on pragmatic as well as technical judgements. Such judgements affect the confidence with which general statements about global income inequality can be made, and therefore the confidence with which particular policies and strategies for reducing global inequality can be formulated. This methodological problem is not banished to an appendix at the end of the book because it is possible that use of different methods affects understandings of levels and trends in global inequality. This is also a practical matter for UN agencies like UNICEF (Ortiz and

Cummins 2011, 11–19), trying to identify and reform gross inequalities affecting the world's children. It is therefore important to follow this issue through.

Comparing income levels between nations requires a common measure that applies in all contexts. This is generally taken to involve the purchasing power that incomes in various countries provide. The difficulty is that the same or similar items have different prices in different countries. Services, for example, are typically much cheaper in developing countries than in wealthier European countries. How, in short, do we compare incomes in euro or pounds sterling with incomes in Chinese yuan or Ukrainian hryvnia, if price levels are not comparable?

There are basically two ways of doing this. The first involves purchasing power parity (PPP) where data on price levels for sets of local goods and services are measured. US prices in dollars for a bundle of goods and services are used as the point of reference, and prices of similar bundles elsewhere expressed as a percentage of the US figure. So if it turns out hypothetically that China's price level is around 42% of the United States, the purchasing power of Chinese income must be multiplied by nearly two and a half times (100/42) to get purchasing power parity (Milanovic 2011, 98–99). Various national income levels across the world are thereby measured in US$PPP. There are however different calculations of PPP levels depending on sources used and estimates made where data is patchy or non-existent.

The majority of economists use this PPP approach. Critics nonetheless argue that PPP figures have high error rates, resulting in constant changes to the ways in which these data are composed. World Bank analysis in 2005, for example, adjusted downward previous estimated income per head in both China and India by more than 30% (Korzeniewicz and Moran 2009, 128). There are also huge gaps, with data appearing only sporadically, every five to ten years, given the extreme difficulty in collecting huge data sets across nearly 200 countries. Retrospective revision makes it hard to use PPP data across time with complete confidence.

The alternative method is to use foreign currency conversion rates (FX) to achieve comparable income levels between countries. This simpler method is generally rejected for two reasons. First, it does not get directly to the purchasing power of populations operating within very different price regimes. Second, the noise of constant volatility in foreign exchange rates creates further difficulties. The second set of problems can be overcome by using average exchange rates over time, but the first objection is more serious.

What then happens if we compare accounts of global income trends using the two different methods? Both show an increase in between-country inequality since the 19th century. The main difference is that the PPP approach produces higher income levels for developing countries in recent years compared with the FX approach (Korzeniewicz and Moran 2009, 63–65, Ortiz and Cummins 2011, 15–16). The PPP data therefore lend themselves more directly to the optimistic argument that global income inequality, taken across all three components has declined in the last two decades. This connection between choice of methods and arguments about trends is not, however, a simple one since proponents of a recent plateau in global inequality, such as Milanovic, also use PPP data. Discussion within UNICEF noted that global inequalities were so high on both measures that no revision of policy perspectives was necessary.

Moving the Analysis of Global Inequality beyond Income Alone

Inequalities of income represent the dominant measure of global inequality among economists and most policy-makers. The broad conclusion among scholars is that global income inequality has increased markedly over the last 200 years. Much recent debate is focussed on the contemporary situation, but neither optimistic nor pessimistic approaches seem to have a general validity. The recent situation is very complex with evidence of improvement in some respects and deterioration in others.

It is important to distinguish between trends in between-country and trends in within-country inequality to be able to make sense of this complexity. These two distinct dimensions to global inequality can and have moved in different directions. For most of the last two centuries between-country inequality has increased, while within-country inequality has generally decreased. This in turn has increased the proportion of global income inequality made up of inequality between nations. Recent trends, however, may have checked the long-run increase in between country inequality, due to the development of populous countries like China and India.

Income is clearly crucial, as is the economic growth and national income profiles of different countries and regions. These indicators are part of a powerful quantifiable approach to the contours of global inequality that cannot and should not be dismissed. And yet they are still very limited in getting at the social experience of inequality. Measurement of income gets only indirectly at questions of the quality of life and what people in various conditions of life typically can and cannot do. This is the basis of the critique of economistic thinking mounted by the 'capabilities' school of social philosophy encountered in previous chapters. In the next chapter the focus of attention is therefore extended beyond discourses focussing primarily on income to examine wider indicators of inequality.

5 Global Social Inequality

Inequality is not simply a matter of differences in income and wealth that trace back to differences in power and the operation of economic and political institutions. It has a far wider scope. One way of grasping far broader senses of inequality is to ask about the positive features of social equality that many see as desirable beyond economic resources. Amartya Sen (1979) famously asked the question 'equality of what?' What forms of equality are most worth having and what obstacles stand in their way? The answers he has given over the last three decades, as foreshadowed in Chapter 1, involve the freedom to fully develop human capacities. Martha Nussbaum (2011, 18) similarly speaks of equality in terms of an enlarged notion of 'what each person is able to do and to be'.

This serves as a starting point for consideration of a wider set of social dimensions of inequality affecting the capacity of people to live a life that they value. Economic thought typically says little about personal values and cultural aspects of life. They are bracketed out of consideration as external (the technical term is exogenous) to the ways in which markets operate and wants are satisfied. Economists avoid the question of where wants come from, believing that expanding economic growth is critical to satisfying most kinds of human needs. The failure of markets to distribute goods in what many regard as a fair or just manner, is of interest, but much of the concern is with trade-offs between efficiency and equity. What is lacking is a broader more sociological account of inequalities arising from limits on human capacities, which market-based economies do not or cannot address.

Where then should a wider approach begin, and what other dimensions of inequality should be included. A highly insightful starting-point is provided by the novel *A Fine Balance,* by the Indian writer Rohinton Mistry (1996). This is set in India in the 1970s and 1980s. It focusses on the complex lives of four characters, whose lives intersect as a result of a dramatic set of contingencies including economic exploitation, inequalities of caste, gender, bereavement, mortality, and physical disablement.

Access to work, housing, and social participation with others in family and community affairs occurs in a setting of destabilizing social change and political turmoil. This includes episodes of forcible sterilization of males, displacement from housing by government slum clearance and redevelopment of poorer housing in favour of up-market accommodation. It also involves disappointment with the fruits of global migration as an alternative to staying in India. The 'fine balance', mentioned in the title, is that between hope and despair.

This balance is constantly shifting in the novel and more broadly we may say in life itself. It is a reminder of the fragility of social existence, but equally of the way that life is of a piece rather than something neatly divided into different economic, political, or cultural spheres. And at the heart of Mistry's work is a narrative account of individual lives, a focus that Nussbaum sees as essential to the broad 'capabilities' approach to human welfare and inequality.

For economists, this novel might be interpreted as the growing-pains of transition to a modern global economy, which, with sustained economic growth should over time lift living standards and improve welfare. Yet a fine analytical balance is also required between evidence supporting an optimistic case, such as poverty reduction or literacy improvement, on the one hand, and contrasting evidence that supports a pessimistic interpretation. This includes continuing problems of gender, racial and culturally based social exclusion, together with continuing political sources of inequality, and failures in policies and programmes.

One very insightful way of categorizing different aspects of inequality is provided by Therborn (2006, Chapter 1). He distinguishes (Table 5.1) between *resource* inequalities, *vital* inequalities, and *existential* inequalities.

The discussion of income inequality in the previous chapter dealt with resource inequalities, especially those to do with material resources. This by no means exhausts the span of resource inequalities. Education, for example, can be thought of as a resource of a broadly social kind. It is not simply about the acquisition of employment or human capital

Table 5.1 Three types of inequality

1. Resources	Income, assets, skills
2. Vital	Bodily health, senses of well-being
3. Existential	Freedom, respect, rights to social and political participation

Source: Derived from Therborn (2006)

skills, but also highly relevant for social and political participation, for health and well-being, and as an aspect of human freedom and dignity.

Vital inequalities deal with human bodies and their well-being, embracing issues of mortality, disability, and the burden of disease. It is important here to emphasize that such vital inequalities apply not simply to humans as biological organisms, but also to the ways in which social beings understand, give meaning to, and value their well-being and health.

The third type of inequality of equal moment to the other two is existential inequality. This concerns personal freedom and social respect and includes issues to do with caste or racial exclusion, patriarchy in gender relations, and interpersonal stigmatization.

Human Development and Global Inequalities

The broader approach to global inequality found in Therborn builds both on earlier social philosophical work on human capacities by Sen and Nussbaum – already mentioned – and more policy-oriented work within the United Nations and other global bodies around the idea of human development as distinct from economic growth. The UNDP, as indicated earlier, has developed Human Development Indicators (HDI's), to extend understandings of inequality beyond income alone, and to determine how far progress has been made towards an enlarged vision of human well-being. The HDI comprises three dimensions, health, living standards, and education. Data on these three are collected using a number of indicators like life expectancy for health, mean years of schooling for education, and gross national income for living standards. These are organized primarily for countries and the index is therefore designed primarily to look at social inequality between-countries.

It appears fairly simple on the surface to show what difference this broader approach makes to understandings of inequality that are not restricted to income alone. Thus nations may have similar profiles of national income per head – New Zealand and the Bahamas are similar in this respect – yet their life expectancy and educational records differ markedly. Income by itself can be misleading as a guide to broader issues of inequality (UNDP 2012a). There remains, nonetheless, a wide-ranging debate on just how far income inequalities are the most critical factor in low life expectancy and educational disadvantage, and how far other contributory factors need to be taken into account. (See also below pp. 99–118.)

Discourses about human development and the enhancement of capabilities, build on earlier discourses of human rights, the most prominent of which is the 1948 UN Universal Declaration of Human Rights. This spoke of rights to dignity, life, liberty, and security of the person, which are at the heart of the idea of overcoming existential inequalities. The declaration spelt out a range of political, economic, and cultural rights, which have been extended further since 1948, to include abolition of the death penalty and the idea that violence against women is a violation of women's human rights (Walby, 345). The more recent human development approach takes a more explicit interest in economic issues and has encouraged more concrete strategies for achieving a reduction in the most glaring social inequalities.

This wider human development approach informs the Millennium Development Goals. These goals, developed from 1990 onwards by the UNDP on behalf of the UN, include specific targets of improvements in human well-being, within which reductions in various dimensions of inequality are crucial elements. There are eight areas around which these goals are set. These are the ending of poverty and hunger, universal education, reduction of gender inequality, better child health, improvements to maternal health, the combating of HIV/AIDS, environmental sustainability, and an improved global countries between the rest of the world and developing countries in issues like governance. It has been said that poverty is a more important target of the Millennium Development Goals than inequality itself. However some goals such as those to with gender and health are measured, in part at least through indicators of inequality. The Millennium Development Goals also place greater weight than the HDI on issues of environmental sustainability.

Looking for the moment at the Human Development Indicators, this three-dimensional evidence base includes both trend figures for the different measures used and an aggregate index which pulls together the different indicators. This is available for individual nations. Over time additional supplementary information is contained in a Composite Poverty Index and a Gender Inequality Index. The UNDP Human Development Reports review these data, indicating changes in the ranking of nations, as well as producing broader surveys of wider themes not necessarily covered in the indicators. In the 2011 report, for example, the chosen theme was 'sustainability and equity', in 2013 it was 'the rise of the south: human progress in a diverse world'.

In the 2011 Report, the leading countries on the HDI were Norway, Australia, and the Netherlands, while the sub-Saharan countries of Democratic Republic of the Congo, Niger, and Burundi stood at the foot of the index (UNDP 2012b). In fact the 10 countries at the bottom of the index were all in sub-Saharan Africa. Interesting some wealthier countries positions in the index were adversely affected by increasing internal inequality. This was true, for example, of the United States.

The broad trend findings in recent reports suggest that improvements in life expectancy and education and not necessarily matched by income trends (UNDP 2012c). Even though gaps between richer and many poorer nations have narrowed somewhat in aspects of education and health, income gaps for many poorer nations have not. This is consistent with a good deal of the analysis of income inequality discussed in the previous chapter, where the positive 'China and India' effect reduces between-country inequality for large numbers of people, while the income inequality gap for much smaller countries in much of sub-Saharan Africa and parts of Asia, is growing. On a broader level, progress in education, health, and (for some countries) income has to be set against worsening of some environmental indicators. These include soil and water quality, extent of forest cover, and scale and rates of carbon dioxide emissions (UNDP 2012c).

Elements of improvement and optimism here dissolve somewhat when gender inequality is taken into account. In the Gender Inequality Index, Scandinavian and other Western European nations come at the top on measures of reproductive health, years of schooling, and parliamentary representation, while countries in the Middle/West Asia such as the Yemen and Afghanistan, and in Africa, such as Chad, Niger, and Mali, come lowest. In the Yemen only 7% of women have a secondary education compared with 24% of men. Meanwhile in much of south Asia, the gender gap in education and labour force participation remains very wide (UNDP 2012b).

I shall return to the wider set of social indicators of inequality such as health, gender, and social participation, later in this chapter. For the moment some general evaluative comments on the HDI index and associated measure of inequality are necessary.

The HDI index, while welcomed as a broader measure of human development (and by extension inequality) than income alone, has been criticized for a range of reasons (see the review by HDR statistician Kovacevic 2011). Some deal with the fit between the chosen indicators and the broad concept of human development. One problem is that the index mixes input measures (like school enrolment) and output measures (like literacy). The criticism here is that output measures are better indicators of development because they refer to performance rather than preconditions for human development. The index is therefore weak in assessing the efficiency with which inputs are turned into outputs (Ryten 2000), or put in more human terms, how far initial enrolees stay in the education system and achieve educational goals. Others criticize the index for underplaying qualitative aspects of development. This applies to issues like literacy, which can involve a wide range of cognitive accomplishments, including numeracy skills or information literacy. Similar qualitative issues apply to assessments of health, including the extent to which capacities can be exercised. I return to this issue below.

Another problem with the index is that it has often ignored within-country inequalities. This neglect has recently been addressed by including information of income inequality within countries based on 20% bands of the population (e.g., top 20%, bottom 20%). These additional data allow comparisons between the various income bands and HDI levels within different countries. Thus in countries ranked as middle income in national terms, for example, the top 20% of income earners, when their life expectancy and educational participation is taken into account, rank at the higher end of the HDI levels achieved by the wealthiest countries. This is once again consistent with inequalities in life expectancy and educational participation being less than inequalities of income. Grimm et al. (2009), supplement this enhanced HDI information, with their own data calculating HDI levels for income bands within a wider range of nations, generating an 'inequality-adjusted HDI' (more accurately a within-country inequality-adjusted HDI). This again finds that in most developing countries outside the HIV-AIDS zone, inequality of life expectancy is lower than other forms of inequality (ibid. 14).

There are however further technical problems with the index. One is the high degree of correlation between the three different dimensions of development. When the components of an index have very high correlations between components, it is unclear what the index adds to our understanding. In such circumstances, one core indicator would serve as a proxy for the others. Some critics, for example, claim that life expectancy alone gives outcomes very similar to the full index (Ivanova, Arcelus, and Srinivasan 1999). Kovacevic, by contrast argues that the high degree of correlation between the different measures is not true of all levels of the hierarchical ranking of countries, weakening at the lower to middle levels.

Walby (2009, 354–355) notes the widening of focus between the HDI and the Millennium Development Goals. However she argues that there is little in the index on human rights, including sexual and reproductive rights. There is also nothing at all on violence, which she regards as one of four dimensions of power and inequality. This reflects the limited extent to which social measures of gender inequality have been developed, but it also has wider significance in social theory and social policy-making. Here violence, while relevant to visions of social progress and greater equality is downplayed and neglected. In human rights thinking, for example, it is only excessive violence by states against individuals and populations that is widely recognized. Violence against women has also received increasing attention, but little thought has been given as to how violence in general might be included in indicators of inequality and human development. Walby suggests that relevant data might include homicide rates, levels of imprisonment within a population, and the timing of legal regulation of violence against women in measures such as laws against rape in marriage.

These problems with the wider measurement of human development are very relevant to understandings of the wide range of issues that affect social inequality. They point both to ways of improving measurement as well as to limits in the capacity of current indices to cover the experience of severe multiple inequalities, like those explored in *A Fine Balance*. I now turn to look in more depth at further statistical data on a number of dimensions of social inequality, including life expectancy and health, gender, and race. An underlying analytical question here, raised earlier in the book, is how far inequality in these wider spheres, is primarily a consequence of income, and how far other causes are at work.

Life expectancy and health

Life expectancy is included in the HDI as a major indicator of social inequality. Being able to lead a full life includes the idea of a long life. And global life expectancy at birth, according to UN statistics, has increased in aggregate from around 53 years in 1960 to around 70 years in 2010. Yet there remain huge (Table 5.2) differences between countries, with the wealthiest countries of Western Europe and North America achieving an expectancy at birth of around 80 years in 2010, while much of sub-Saharan Africa, and countries like Afghanistan languish at a figure of around 48–49 years. There is a significant amount of complexity

Table 5.2 Life expectancy at birth: 2010: Selected examples

World as a whole	70
Sub-Saharan Africa	48–49
India	65
China	73
Western Europe/North America	80

Source: World Bank (2013a)

here, though, since the more economically dynamic developing countries like China, India, Russia, and Brazil have life expectancies of 73, 65, 69, and 73 respectively, which lie between the extremes (World Bank 2013). These improvements have occurred even in countries with large amounts of internal income inequality. There has therefore been more convergence between countries in life expectancy than in income. Nonetheless poverty and low incomes remain major contributors to mortality, and higher incomes are not by themselves any protection against health risk and early death.

It should also be emphasized that there are different age-related patterns at work in life expectancy improvement between richer and poorer countries. Continuing recent improvement in the richer countries is based very much in improvements for the over-50s, whereas in the poorer countries the improvement is far more for the young. General convergence rates do not get at these age-specific trends, and may therefore give a false picture of a narrowing gap between rich and poor for all segments of the population (Deaton 2006, 12).

Life expectancy is however only one of a number of important measures pertaining to health and well-being. Mortality statistics should be combined with morbidity or disability levels to determine how far people suffer from debilitating physical and mental health conditions over significant periods of their lives. This may involve both premature death, but also impairment of human capacity to engage in valued activity. Disability is thus a crucial element in inequality.

Disability-affected life years (DALYs)

One way of measuring this kind of impairment calculates disability-affected life years or DALYs, a measure originally developed for the World Bank around 1990. This concept brings together years lost through premature death with years of healthy life lost to disease and disablement (World Health Organization 2009, v). Calculation of DALYs also takes into account the severity of disease. The underlying significance if this approach is that it improves measures of the global burden of disease.

The 2009 report of the World Health Organization (WHO) on Global Health Risks, underlined continuing health inequalities, as well as the complex and multiple sources of risk (2009). In terms of mortality the six leading risk factors were high blood pressure, tobacco use, high blood glucose, physical inactivity, and overweight and obesity. These increased risks of heart disease, diabetes, and cancers, apply across all income groups. In terms of the burden of disease, the four leading risks (measured in DALYs) were underweight, unsafe sex, alcohol use, and unsafe water, sanitation and hygiene. Underweight, unsafe sex and unsafe water, sanitation, and hygiene are disproportionately concentrated in south-east Asia and sub-Saharan Africa. The profile of alcohol use as a health risk is more complex, being highest for men in Africa, middle-income groups in the Americas, and some high-income countries.

Specific health risks can be separated for analytical purposes but obviously interact and combine in complex ways to affect inequality. This can be demonstrated with environmental risk especially through the effects of climate change. These include extreme events such as droughts and floods, changing patterns of infectious disease, effects on food yields and freshwater supplies, displacement of vulnerable populations (e.g., from low-lying land), and loss of livelihood (McMichael et al. 2008, 192). Such effects are felt unequally across countries and regions. In sub-Saharan Africa, for example, 110 million people are estimated to live in malaria-prone regions, and this number could increase with effects of climate change on microbial patterns and on food supply, worsening poverty. Such predictions may or may not prove accurate, the main point here being that patterns of health are part of a dynamic but crisis-prone set of social and natural processes.

Personal testimony of a Bangla deshi rickshaw driver

A personal narrative of the interaction of risk and crisis is the example of a Bangladeshi rickshaw driver, investigated in Portfolios of the Poor. This story shows how easily health problems quickly become financial problems. A rickshaw driver who had three rickshaws sought medical assistance for throat pain, and sold the rickshaws one by one in search of a cure. Additional debt was then taken on to meet continuing costs. On his death from throat cancer, the family was left with no income, no reserves of saleable assets, and considerable debt. For the poor health risk and financial risks interact in sometimes devastating ways (Collins et al. 2009, 86–87).

The incidence of preventable death among children is also a leading indicator of health inequality. In 2004, WHO estimated that over ten million children died worldwide. Around 80% of these were located in sub-Saharan Africa and South-east Asia. Africa accounts for nine out of every ten worldwide child deaths due to malaria, and nine out of every ten child deaths due to HIV/Aids. Together with around half deaths due to diarrhoea-related disease and pneumonia (ibid. 8). Around 40% of all these child deaths were reported to be from preventable causes such as nutritional deficiencies, underweight, suboptimal breast feeding, and preventable environmental risks. And behind this list of proximate causes of death lie further influences such as lack of access to adequate public health resources, food insecurity, poverty, and political neglect.

There has nonetheless been some improvement in combating deaths of under fives, which fell from 16.6 million in 1970, to 12 million in 1990, and 7.6 million in 2010 (UNICEF 2012, 83), during a period when the world's population has been growing rapidly. Yet there remain gross inequalities in the incidence of under fives mortality, since the number of deaths in sub-Saharan Africa remains high while sharp falls are evident elsewhere, notably in Asia and Latin America. The contrast between rich and poor, captured in ratios of mortality, is especially telling. In 2010 mortality of under fives stood at a figure in excess of 120 per 1,000 live births for most of sub-Saharan Africa, Haiti, and Afghanistan, to around 3–5 per 1,000 for Europe, North America, and Japan (ibid. 87). However if we look at absolute numbers of lives saved, far more of these are in sub-Saharan Africa than Europe, simply because the scale of health challenges is so much greater in the former.

Maternal mortality rates show a similar profile. Thus there is an worldwide decline of 47% in maternal deaths between 1990 and 2010 from 400 to 210 per 100,000 live births. High levels of maternal mortality have nonetheless been concentrated in poorer countries which still average of 240 per 100,000 live births, or 15 times higher than in developed countries (WHO 2012, 2). Pregnancy-related complications claim the lives of over half a million women annually, 99% of which take place in developing societies (Levine and the What Works Working Group 2007, 41). There are however exceptions, such as Sri Lanka, where over four decades up to 2,000 maternal mortality has been reduced from around over 500 per 100,000 live births to around 60 (ibid. 41). Taken overall poorer women across the world continue to have much higher fertility levels than women with higher incomes, and this also increases health risks for women (Ortiz and Cummins 2011, 22).

Looking generally across issues of global health inequality, debates continue as to how far health inequalities are due to income inequalities and how far due to other influences.

Preston (1975), in a much quoted analysis, argued that a significant amount of ill health could be explained by low income. This argument was meant to challenge those at the time who thought that income levels had made little or no contribution to improvements in life expectancy in poor countries, by contrast with public health measures. Preston nonetheless found a strong correlation between income and various levels of health, and later analyses have reinforced and extended this position. The idea that 'Wealthier is healthier' (Pritchett and Summers 1986), sums up much of this work. In both popular and professional discourse it is clear that global health problems are widely believed to be problems of poverty.

The World Health Organization in the late 1990's calculated that less than half the global health improvements between 1952 and 1992 could be explained through income growth. Deaton (2006) while noting that the correlation between low income and health problems has persisted, also sees a need to recognize greater complexity in the determination of health outcomes. For one thing there are countries or regions with low incomes but better health outcomes than is typical for poorer countries. He cites Cuba, Sri Lanka, Costa Rica, and Kerala. Marmot (2005) adds China to this list. These examples suggest that wider social determinant of health, together with policy and professional interventions matter too.

Beyond this, sociologists have added a further political dimension to health determinants in poorer countries, namely state capacity, whether measured in terms of fiscal capability or rule of law mechanisms. Dawson (2010), for example, argues that where states are weak and unable to protect markets and civil society, there are strong impediments to effective public health programmes. This argument is sustained quantitatively through correlations between higher levels of corruption and weakness of financial institutions, on the one hand, and worse child mortality rates for the under fives.

In spite of this wider focus in public health and some sociological literature, the emphasis on income and poverty remains predominant among economists, warranting further consideration. As we saw in Chapter 2, liberal economists assume that economic growth will raise incomes and reduce inequality, leading to convergence between initially poorer and richer countries. Deaton, by contrast, maintains that this linkage between economic growth and health improvement is not automatic. The connections are complex rather than strongly correlated. There are several aspects to this. First, some countries have improved their life expectancy while experiencing little or no growth, such as sub-Saharan Africa from the 1950's to 1990. This he puts down to processes such as greater levels of immunization and cleaner water. Second richer countries have recently continued to improve their health, but their growth rates have declined in recent decades.

Third, there is the argument put by the World Health Organization that countries are poor because they are sick and this impedes growth. This position sounds plausible at first sight, but relies on dubious assumptions that sickness impedes growth for which there is little evidence. Unless it could be shown that sickness systematically reduces the supply of labour or inhibits the impact of educational reform and skill acquisition, this linkage seems doubtful. The recent economic growth in countries in India, in spite of significant sickness levels, supports this argument, even in the midst of the personal tragedies that ill health creates. For both India and China, Drèze and Sen (2002) found that rates of growth and the reduction of child mortality were negatively related. From this evidence there is no reason to suppose that lessening sickness rates in poorer countries contributes to growth.

Marmot (2005) also cautions against over-simplistic accounts of the relationship between poverty and health inequality. Thus 'the form that poverty takes and its health consequences are quite different when considering chronic disease and violent deaths in adults, compared to deaths from infectious disease in children' (1101–1102). The contrast here is between health inequalities due to non-communicable disease and interpersonal violence compared with inequalities due to communicable disease. Such complexities require a much richer account of the social and political determinants of health than is provided by any single general cause. This applies whether the general approach focusses on income and poverty or from too narrow a concern with wider social determinants.

A challenging example of divergent patterns of poverty and inequality, is, in his view the health profile of Aboriginal and Torres Straits Islanders. Unlike the African pattern of poor health due to communicable disease, the prevailing patterns is one of low-levels of infant mortality but high levels of adult mortality from heart disease, cancers, endocrine, nutritional and metabolic diseases including diabetes as well as significant levels of interpersonal violence. Speculating that it would scarcely help to enter such communities and claim that their smoking, obesity, and excessive drinking were killing them, Marmot sees a more helpful line of argument in the search for causes that lie behind harmful behaviour, a search that requires a more complex account of social and cultural as much as economic processes.

Improved conceptualization of social health determinants, and deeper analysis of specific health inequalities are ongoing processes. What is clear is that vital inequality is a significant part of global inequality, and that there is a complex balance to be struck between processes of improvement and outstanding obstacles to improved health status. It is also clear that income inequalities alone are unable to account for health inequalities. Market-based growth-focussed solutions are not sufficient and may be irrelevant. Public health programmes matter, and these depend on underlying state capacities as much as specific policies, points to be explored further in subsequent chapters. Political economy and sociology both contribute to an appreciation of the wider social determinants of health, and their interaction with income patterns.

Attention now turns to existential inequalities, around the theme of freedom and respect.

Existential inequalities: Gender, race, and ethnicity

Human well-being is not restricted to the purchasing power of incomes available to individuals, households, and states, measurable in economic statistics. Bodily health matters a great deal, but this is itself not separable from broader issues to do with the ways that human beings are valued, positively or negatively, and how such valuations are built into access to resources and opportunities for people to live the lives they choose or prefer. Constraints of many different kinds structure life-experience and life-chances, but so do conditions of freedom and respect that are built into social relationships and institutions. This way of understanding broader aspects of social inequality has been highlighted in the late 20th century by writers like Taylor, Habermas, Sen, and Nussbaum. But it also emerges, as have all ideas about freedom and well-being, from social experience, conflict, and movements for social change and reconstruction.

One of the most significant dimensions of existential inequality is that of gender, referring to relations between women and men, where men (or women) enjoy a disproportionate share of some valued resource, aspect of well-being, or valued social role. The gender dimension of global inequality is clear across income, wealth, health, and literacy, as well as economic and social participation, institutions of power and regimes of violence. Collectively this set of inequalities is often described as the global gender gap. In most of these domains it is men who are in better position and women who experience inequality. However in a few domains, such as life expectancy and some aspects of educational attainment it is women who have the advantage, and thus greater gender equality means men narrowing the gap on women.

Gender inequality is not then uniform across all these domains, even in the majority of areas where men are in an advantageous position. Nor is gender inequality static, but has changed over time in quite significant ways. Women are certainly not to be regarded simply as victims of a monolithic set of unequal social arrangements, since there are elements of improvement in their current situation, which women themselves have done much to bring about as active agents of change.

The kinds of indicators that are used in accounts of women's inequality are listed itemized in Table 5.3:

Table 5.3 Possible indicators of gender inequality affecting women

- a gap between male and female wages for comparable work
- a gap between participation rates for men and women in paid employment
- a glass ceiling limiting womens' access to the highest paid and most powerful jobs
- a gap between male and female access to the most productive land
- a gap between male and female participation in political institutions
- a gap between men and women in literacy rates
- a gap between men and women in school enrolments
- non-recognition of womens rights to control fertility and obtain divorce
- greater vulnerability of women to interpersonal violence, both as adults and children
- lack of a gender focus in public policy

The are also two areas where indicators suggest women's advantage over men. These are in life expectancy and educational attainment at secondary and tertiary levels.

Most, but not all of these indicators can be quantified. Measurement of vulnerability to violence and domestic subordination is extremely difficult even where public legislation exists banning certain violent practices, such as trafficking of women, or abortion of female foetuses. Indirect measures may nonetheless be instructive, whether legislation exists or not, as in the skewed distribution of male and female infants in countries where female foetuses are aborted (Guilmoto 2012). This practice – known as gendercide – is evident not merely in India and China, but also according to the UN Population Fund (ibid. 20), in the Balkans. Within these limits I now look at individual items in these lists, and possible interconnections between them.

Beginning with economic inequality, there are a number of salient features of gender inequality. The first is income inequality for economically active women. This is reflected in a gap in income levels between men and women in general, and also when differing acquired skills are taken into account. We do not have systematic data on male and female 'income' for the world as a whole, and analysis therefore rests on countries for which evidence is available, most of which are developed. For the EU and the United States in 2006, this gap ranged from 7–22%, lowest in Denmark and Finland and highest in Ireland and the United States (European Commission 2008). The World Bank also produces data on the gender gap in manufacturing across the world. In 2009 this stood at 23%, varying regionally between 9% in East Asia and the Pacific, to 47% in the Middle East and North Africa (World Bank 2011b). The most recent data from the International Labour Organization (ILO 2013) compare the gender pay gap between 1999–2007 and 2008–2011 to include the effect of the Global Financial Crisis. These data indicate a continued lessening of the pay gap even through the GFC.

The global pay gap figures also have a further technical problem built into them, which may mislead observers into under-estimating inequality. The difficulty is that smaller pay gaps do not necessarily mean women's absolute position has improved. There are at least two cases where this would apply. The first is where smaller pay gaps arise from a decline in male wages where women's wages stay the same. The ILO data shows this happened during the GFC which hit male employment harder in countries like Estonia (ibid. 4–5). Since the gender pay gap is very low for part-time work any worsening of men's conditions of employment is likely to narrow the gap with women, without making women better off. The second, discussed by Walby (2009) is where smaller pay gaps arise in countries with low historic female participation in paid employment, for example, in certain southern European countries. Here, women are not found in some sectors of lower paid work and hence it is only somewhat higher paid women whose incomes are being compared with men. This in turn may give a false impression of lower gender inequality in income than is justified.

Walby (2009, 333–334) maintains that face value gender gaps based purely on incomes do not control sufficiently for variations in female economic participation and should be supplemented with other measures to create a more robust indicator. Looking first at female economic participation rates for 2009, the gap is 26 percentage points for the world as a whole, with regional variations from 49 points in the Middle East and North Africa and 47 points in South Asia to 16 points in Europe

(World Bank 2011b). Once again all these measures have improved over the last 20 years. Dorius and Firebaugh (2010, 1952) have calculated the Gini coefficient for gender income inequality in labour force participation, seeing a decline from 27% in 1960 to 18% around 2000. These inequality levels indicate far more improvement than for global inequality as a whole, yet they only deal with the measurable, and do not, for example, get at issues like poorer working conditions or fewer opportunities for promotion for women compared with men.

Walby, following the UNDP Human Development Index, also uses the female share of earned income as a measure that combines wage levels with female economic participation rates (see also Esping-Andersen 2007, 224). For the OECD countries, regarded as 'highly' or 'medium developed', this increased from 47% to 59% as a whole over the 20 years from 1995 to 2005. An increase is evident everywhere except Eastern Europe (ibid. 335). There remains nonetheless a significant difference in this ratio between more highly developed countries in Scandinavia, the United Kingdom and Australia, with a score of 65–72%, compared to Mexico and Turkey at 35–39%.

Another dimension of gender inequality is that of occupational segregation by gender. One way of examining this is in terms of the proportion of women in top jobs as senior managers and public officials. Here the ratio of female to male incomes was lower, typically in the range 30–42% for countries like the United States (42%) and France (37%), but far lower in Turkey (7%), Korea (8%), and Japan (10%) (ibid. 335). Further analysis using European data up to 2001 and controlling for differences in experience and skill confirms the existence of a glass ceiling for women, though this varies by country and economic sector, being less evident in Scandinavia and in the public sector. This suggests that gender-specific policies in areas like discrimination and in child care affect the picture (Arulamparam, Booth, and Bryan 2006). However it is not universally agreed either that the glass ceiling is strongest at the higher level of hierarchies or that public employment is necessarily more egalitarian than private (see, for example, Bihagen and Ohls 2006 on Sweden). Women's desires for flexibility in entrepreneurial activities may also contribute significantly to erosion of some aspects of the glass ceiling (see, for example, Madichie 2009 on Nigeria).

Women worldwide play a significant role in agriculture, whether paid or part of domestic arrangements. In this sector the 2012 World Development Report of the World Bank, finds that women, particularly those in Africa, operate smaller plots of land, farm less profitable crops, and have greater difficulty in accessing credit than men (World Bank 2012).

This partly reflects womens greater role in producing crops for local consumption, including home gardens rather than world markets. But it is also connected with cultural or legislative restrictions on owning land, which in turn adversely effects the chances of getting credit from financial institutions who demand collateral (FAO 2011).

Attention now shifts to gender inequalities in political representation and participation in government. Here there are extremely high levels of inequality in women's participation in national legislatures, which exceed other forms of gender inequality. Dorius and Firebaugh (2010, 1952) calculate the Gini coefficient for political representation of this kind at 80 in 1980 and 69 in 2005. These levels are higher than the Gini coefficients for global income inequality across the same time frame. The Inter-parliamentary Union (2013) has surveyed women's membership of the lower or single house of national parliaments across the world in February 2013. Only in Rwanda and Andorra are women in a majority. Otherwise there are 30 countries in the world where women represent less than 10% of parliamentarians, and 75 countries where female representation is less than 20%. The latter group includes economically developed countries like United States, Ireland, and Japan, but is mainly composed of less developed countries in the eastern Europe, the Middle East, central, southern and south east Asia, and central America. Gender inequality in this domain is declining but is still more extreme than on the other quantifiable measures surveyed here.

Next, I look at gender inequalities in literacy rates and school enrolments. These are major components in the Human Development Index, and have received considerable scholarly and political attention. According to UNESCO statistics (2010), outlined in Table 5.4 nearly 800 million people reported themselves illiterate in 2008, of whom two-thirds were women. For the world as a whole 83% of adults were classified as literate, comprising 88% for men and 79% of women. Inequalities in literacy were concentrated in a small number of regions, notably South Asia, where adult literacy was 62% and sub-Saharan Africa where it was 63%.

Table 5.4 Adult literacy rates: 2008

World as a Whole	83%
Men	88%
Women	79%
South Asia	62% (men 73% – women 51%)
Sub-Saharan Africa	63%

Source: UNESCO (2010)

In ten sub-Saharan countries, adult literacy was less than 50%. Gender inequality was highest in South Asia, where 73% of men but only 51% of women were literate, and the position was nearly as unequal in sub-Saharan Africa. The trend, as with other indicators reviewed here, was for gender inequality in literacy to lessen over the last two decades. UNESCO calculates that overall literacy rates improved by 8% in the 20 years to 2008, while female literacy improved by 10%, though starting from a lower base. All these data apply to adults. Child literacy discussions are usually subsumed under educational provision.

Literacy, judged from the viewpoint of Therborn's analysis of multiple inequalities, is both an asset or resource available to enhance human well-being while also offering ways of transforming existential inequalities. This is not to underestimate its destabilizing effects on cultures centred on oral transmission. Nor is it to underplay the ways in which literacy is connected with the rationalization of knowledge acquisition and transmission through the printed word and electronic media. Nonetheless its existential impact is a considerable one wherever women have previously been marginalized in patriarchal cultures of gender domination.

These general comments also apply to processes of educational participation. Here there is a similar gender gap between primary education completion rates across the globe and in particular regions. Globally in 2009, 88% of children completed primary education worldwide, but in sub-Saharan Africa, the figure was only 67%. And of these girls were particularly disadvantaged. For every 100 boys completing primary, less than 70 girls completed in countries like Central African Republic, Chad, and Democratic Republic of the Congo. Further gender disadvantage is evident worldwide in secondary education completion rates. Interestingly the gender gap for post-secondary enrolment had been eliminated by 2000, indicating that the gap has closed faster at this higher level than primary and secondary (Dorius and Firebaugh 2010, 1952). This unevenness is however best explained by the greater concentration of post-secondary educational institutions in wealthier more developed countries, to which an increasing number of educated young people from the rest of the world now enrol.

Reduction of gender inequality in school enrolment has generally been faster than reductions in the other indicators discussed here. Dorius and Firebaugh argue that in the last two decades of the 20th century gender inequality in average years of completed schooling narrowed by around 30%. They also find, perhaps surprisingly, that obstacles to change do not seem to map neatly onto cultural or religious affiliations.

Thus advances in both adult literacy for women and school enrolment for girls are not significantly less for Hindu or Muslim countries, notwithstanding prominent counter examples like Afghanistan under the Taliban (ibid. 1955).

I move on now to look at two issues. One is women's rights as they affect control over sexuality and reproduction, the other is violence against women. Such questions involve public health as well as human rights. They concern questions like rights to access safe abortion in cases of unwanted pregnancy or rape, and also issues like access to divorce to achieve separation from abusive partners. Finally there are further issues here to do with the rule of law and personal security and freedom from public sources of violence. Inequalities on these dimensions of human well-being, many of which adversely affect women are, however, far harder to measure than indicators such as income, life expectancy and literature. Neither the Human Development Index nor the Millennium Development Goals have much to say on these questions. The existential impact of such inequalities are very real nonetheless, affecting victims and their families over their life-times, involving traumatization and stigmatization as well as depression and disruption to employment (Walby and Allen 2004).

The traumatic impact of rape

'Its been very difficult for me to get over the rape', a young woman from Guatemala explained to Médecins Sans Frontières health workers. 'I got pregnant so young and had to leave my studies and many other things behind.

Each psychotherapy session helps me find relief and consolation... People don't see or understand the magnitude of sexual violence in Guatemala, and when they do see it, they judge us the victims'.

Source: Médecins Sans Frontières (2013, 13).

Most rape, possibly 90%, affects women, but levels of rape are very hard to determine, as is well-known, due to under-reporting. The UN Office on Drugs and Crime has collated a range of sexual violence (including child abuse) and rape statistics from a number of countries. Reported annual rates of sexual violence, expressed per 100,000 of population, range from 183 in Sweden and around 140 in several Caribbean nations, to around 2000–3000 in countries like Albania and Ukraine (UNODC 2011). These comparisons may however tell us more about levels of efficiency in pursuing reporting, or cultural neglect of rape as a serious human rights violation than real levels of sexual violence. An alternative way of presenting the data is to look at the lifetime incidence of gender-related violence for women, estimated at between 25 and 50% in a report prepared for the World Health Organization (Krug et al. 2002). Ultimately, therefore, there remains a sense that published data represent only the 'tip of the iceberg', and that far better empirical material is needed to grasp the immensity of the problem.

A final aspect of gender inequality that is relevant to all the dimensions previously surveyed involves the extent to which public policy recognizes and addresses issues of gender inequality. Salient policy areas include equal opportunity legislation in labour markets, and access to health and education. They also involve intimate aspects of existential well-being including legal bans on rape in marriage and access to abortion and divorce. There has been a wider extension of access to divorce over the last 30 years, but more variation exists in access to safe abortion. It is estimated that only 40% of the world's women have access to induced abortion within certain gestational limits with no restriction on reason, while at the other end of the spectrum 25% either have no access or only where a woman's death is indicated (Centre for Reproductive Rights 2009). Public policy decisions here have major implications for maternal mortality and morbidity arising from unsafe abortions.

What then is the general trend across these various dimensions of gender inequality? Dorius and Firebaugh (2010, 1951–1952) find that between 1960 and 2005, global gender inequality, has declined across nine welfare criteria that can be measured with reasonable accuracy. Yet levels of inequality vary markedly across different domains. Women actually have a slight advantage with respect to longevity, but are at an extreme disadvantage in political representation. Global gender inequality in labour market and educational participation, and in wage rates, has narrowed significantly though by no means everywhere. The same narrowing has also occurred in relation to gender inequality in literacy.

General convergence between men and women has thus occurred at rather different rates, as has convergence within particular countries. Meanwhile, gender disadvantage remains significant in areas like violence against women, where statistics are unlikely to yield a precise sense of levels of violence or get at the qualitative experience of sustained abuse and the undermining of self-worth. These complexities make it unlikely that one single grand theory of gender inequality applies, and that a more fine-grained approach is necessary. Issues of cause and effect will be pursued in the following chapter.

In addition to gender, race, and ethnicity have been widely seen as further, often interrelated, dimensions of global social inequality. This has been discussed in Chapter 3, where the historical sociology of global inequality identified long-run processes that have influenced patterns of inequality over time. Empire, colonization, and slavery have been linked with very significant racial and ethnic inequalities. These have affected all three categories of vital, resource, and existential inequality – though the existential impact on freedom and respect is perhaps most salient to understandings of the way inequality can undermine self-respect and the capacity to live a full and productive life.

Some initial comments on the ideas of race and ethnicity are necessary at this point, to clarify which kinds of social processes are involved. Race, in particular, is a problematic category, insofar as it draws on 19th century pseudo-scientific notions of human groups distinct in their biology, physical characteristics, and capacities. Racism was built into discourses of this kind, because it was presumed that racial characteristics involved a hierarchy of capacity, intelligence, and social worth. 'Higher' races were thereby believed to have the right to dominate 'lower' races, while racial mixing would lead only to biological weakness and enfeeblement. The intellectual weaknesses of this approach is that there are no strict and invariant biological correlates of supposed races. At best there are only varying probabilities that such correlates apply, at worst the connections are arbitrary. Biological race as a plausible feature of social science and social analysis is thus a fiction. Socially constructed race is not (see also Winant 2004, 39–41).

While the pseudo-science of race is far less prevalent today, racism remains a major issue in global inequality. Racism may be defined as beliefs and actions which privilege members of some social groups and dis-privilege others, according to perceived characteristics of such groups. What matters is not some dubious assumptions about innate racial biology, but the connotations associated with different skin colour and the perceived cultural characteristics associated with it. The salience of race to global inequality is where such connotations are used in a prejudicial way to privilege some 'races' over 'others', whether in access to resources or in worthiness of respect and equal treatment to others. This in turn generates social conflicts to do both with material resources and the cultural meaning and value of social difference.

Meanwhile, the concept of ethnicity dispenses with biology and focuses on perceived cultural characteristics between social groups.

These may be the source of cultural identity and pride, but may equally be used in a prejudicial way leading to unequal access and opportunity. One way of proceeding, then, would be to treat race and ethnicity separately as separate processes in generating social inequality within and across borders. This however runs the risk of objectifying individual races as social realities. The alternative approach is to combine racial and ethnic dimensions to global inequality. This combines recognition of different ways of constructing social inequality, while also accepting shared features of socio-cultural domination.

Among the leading indicators of racial and ethnic inequality are items listed in Table 5.5.

The discussion which follows selects some of the more salient features of this list for further attention, rather than attempting a comprehensive elaboration of every single aspect.

Most studies of racial and ethnic inequality in incomes are based on individual nations, notably the United States. Some comparative national statistics are however available, which allows the possibility of gauging how far such forms of inequality are constant across nations and regions. Darity and Nembhard (2000), in a review of literature, found consistent labour market discrimination across 12 countries in the last three decades of the 20th century for men of colour. This applied both to richer (e.g., Australia, United States) and poorer (e.g., India, South Africa) countries, and to countries with higher (e.g., Brazil, South Africa) and lower (e.g., Canada, Israel) general patterns of inequality. There was also some evidence in the lessening of such inequality over time. Attewell, Kasinitz and Dunn (2010), in their comparison of white/black incomes across the United States and Canada, found that controlling for education, the income-gap in the two cases were roughly similar at around 17%, even though the two countries have somewhat different political and cultural characteristics.

Table 5.5 Possible indicators of racial and ethnic inequality

- inequalities in income and wealth between cultural groups
- higher levels of unemployment by race and ethnicity
- discrimination in access to employment, education, and housing
- social segregation in residential location and public space
- inequalities in health outcomes
- subjection to violence and interpersonal hostility
- racialized constructions of crime leading to higher levels of criminal conviction and incarceration
- intersection of racial, ethnic, and gender disadvantage

Much analysis has gone into analysing the racial wage gap in the United States. Some have charted phases of narrowing in this gap over the past 50 years (see, for example, Smith and Welch (1989), Couch and Daly (2002)). It is widely held that racial inequality is declining in significance, with the earnings gap declining by around 30% in the latter part of the 20th century. This optimistic interpretation is disputed by a number of writers. Western and Pettit (2005) suggest that it is misleading to see narrowing of the racial wage gap as an indicator of general decline in racial inequality. This is largely because wage differences do not measure relative differences in unemployment. Taking unemployment into account the improvement in the racial wage gap declines from 30% to around 10% (ibid. 573).

Understanding joblessness and African-American men

Among young African-American males, rates of joblessness are high. This has been explained partly because of low skill and partly discrimination. In addition, Western and Pettit (2005) emphasize the significance of incarceration for joblessness. In 1999 among black men aged 22–30, more than 30% of joblessness is made up by those incarcerated. The implication is that the racial wage gap by itself gives a false impression of decline in racial inequality.

Economic inequality between ethnic groups is also a feature of global inequality, connected primarily with global migration and settlement over the last two centuries. This issue is however complex since migrant ethnicity may be associated with either disadvantage (ethnic penalty) or advantage (ethnic premium) compared with native populations. In first generations disadvantage may be reflected in higher levels of unemployment and lack of access to better more skilled jobs for most groups. However those with capital, entrepreneurial skill and educational qualifications may do better. Such positive developments may be further consolidated in second and subsequent generations with the further educational up-skilling of migrant children. On the other hand second-generation disadvantage may persist especially in large cities, as indicated in work on ethnic minorities in the United States (Portes and Rumbaut 2001) and on Europe (Heath and Cheung 2007).

The issue of labour market discrimination by race and ethnicity also remains a significant issue. Recent work by Pager, Western, and

Bonikowski (2009) on low-wage labour markets in New York City finds subtle evidence of discrimination. White, Black, and Latinos matched for experience and skill were tracked in job applications across time. The research showed that Black applicants were half as likely as whites to get call backs and job offers. Discrimination along cultural lines may nonetheless differ between economic sectors and forms of employment with differing demand for labour. In an Indian study based on Delhi, Banerjee et al. (2009) found no discrimination in call-back rates between applicants from different castes in the expanding software sector, but rather more discrimination against lower-caste applicants in less buoyant call-centre jobs. Certainly much research on Indian labour markets finds continuing caste and religious discrimination but often of a kind that is subtle, covert and difficult to prove, characterized by Das (2013) through the idea of 'glass walls'.

Educational opportunity is an issue that is central to questions of racial and ethnic disadvantage and to attempts to overcome it. Much of the perceived reduction in the racial wage gap in the United States in the late 20th century was put down to greater educational opportunity as a result of public policy initiatives. Nonetheless, as I have argued earlier, the extent of this narrowing gap has been exaggerated and racial discrimination persists. Mere educational access by itself may not be adequate to address disadvantage if there is differential treatment of racial or case groups within the school system leading to low participation. Artis, Doobay, and Lyons (2003) show this remains a very real problem for low caste children in India. Mistry's novel *A Fine Balance* also includes a literary account of these forms of exclusion.

In the case of ethnicity and education, there is considerable evidence for inequalities in educational attainment among immigrants from ethnic minorities, most clearly in the first generation (Schnepf 2007, Chiswick and DebBurman 2004). The picture for the second generation is more complex with evidence both of educational success, and also continuing disadvantage. Heath and Brinbaum (2007) note that second generation migrants of Turkish, Moroccan, and North African ancestry, or Mexican ancestry in the United States tend to do worse than the general population, while those of Indian ancestry in the United Kingdom, or Greek ancestry in Germany match the population as a whole.

A good deal of this picture is explained by parental economic and educational status, but not all (Schnepf 2007). For groups like those with Turkish or Caribbean ancestry in Europe or Mexican ancestry in the United States, other explanations of disadvantage must be taken into account. These include what Heath and Brinbaum call 'cultural dissonance' (Heath and Brinbaum, 297) where parents may lack cultural capital and language fluency suited to the new context. Conversely for ethnic groups that do as well or better than the general population, characteristics of the migrant group, including economic and cultural values and expectations may help to explain cultural advantage.

The theme of subjection to violence and hostility, whether overt or covert, haunts racial and ethnic inequality. At its most extreme, racial and ethnic genocide, evident most recently in the Balkans and central Africa, testifies to the continuing salience of this kind of gross inequality involving the slaughter of populations and the mass rape of women and children. Racial, ethnic, and gender inequalities in such cases clearly intersect. Regimes of violence, as Walby (2009, 193) argues, may be deployed by social groups or individuals, but also by states. In modern democratic nations, some of the group violence involved in practices like genocide, lynching or ethnic cleansing may have declined, but states may still deploy violence or the threat of it, internally as much as externally in dealing with real or perceived threats to security. Meanwhile ethnic violence and genocide are not absent from the contemporary world and may re-erupt wherever social problems are focussed on the ascribed cultural characteristics of social groups.

Evidently ethnic and racial divisions are not a thing of the past, and have not been undermined by the forces of modernization, secularization, and cosmopolitanism.

Goldberg (2002) has developed an influential theory of the racial state, seeing it as central rather than peripheral to modern states. The argument is that race is a discourse whereby states discuss the meaning of their political constitution and community. Writers like Ronit Lentin (2006) have applied this notion to immigration policies of modern European states like Ireland, interpreting selective rules of exclusion of migrants, harsh detention centres and discourses about illegal immigrants as racist in character.

Contemporary public policies, as already noted with respect to gender inequality, take different standpoints towards racial and ethnic inequality and what to do about it. They may apply both to ethnic or racial groups with a long historical presence within a given territory or to contemporary processes of migration and settlement. Public policies within democratic countries range from assimilation to a dominant culture, through social integration around ideals of social citizenship, to multicultural policies of varying kinds. The latter two options are more explicitly directed at issues of inequality. Relevant policies may subsume racial and ethnic inequalities within more general equal opportunity policies in areas such as access to schooling, as in the United States. Or they may take the form of anti-racist policies directed at areas such as employment, health, and community relations. The EU, for example, is expressly committed to combating racism in law and policy (Bell 2009). Walby (ibid. 286) maintains that social-democratic polities make a bigger impact on ethnic inequalities than countries inclined to neo-liberal policies. This is because social-democracy is more attuned to those issues of social inclusion that are not spontaneously addressed simply by labour market inclusion and economic growth. It is nonetheless clear that social divisions and inequalities based on race and ethnicity still persist even in social-democratic settings (Kraal, Roosblad, and Wrench 2009). One reason for limited policy success may be that EU policy has not fully responded to the intersection of racial and ethnic inequalities, with gender inequality (Lombardo and Verloo 2009).

Conclusions

This long chapter on social inequality covers a huge set of issues across the fields of human development. The multiple dimensions of inequality discussed here demonstrate very clearly how far global inequalities extend beyond income alone. Much of the discussion here has been empirical and descriptive, with the aim of assembling a richer body of up-to-date evidence than is typically available in literature dealing with particular dimensions of inequality. The multidimensional breadth of this endeavour also reflects a more sociological attention to issues wider than public economic activity alone.

Attention to empirical complexity across this chapter on social inequality and the previous chapter on inequalities of income helps to reshape the way explanation of global inequalities should be undertaken. Perhaps the most important task in this reshaping is the challenge empirical complexity poses to explanations which focus on one single overriding prime mover responsible for the overarching patterns of global inequality. Foremost among such prime movers is the argument that globalization or global capitalism is itself the paramount cause of global inequality. Following from this is the belief that opposition to globalization or global capitalism is the key to overcoming global inequality.

There are two interconnected arguments against this proposition. The first, theoretical challenge, is to the proposition that there is only one source of power, inequality and human suffering in the world. The alternative view is that there are multiple sources of power, inequality, identity, and suffering. The second, empirical challenge, is that the diverse and complex patterns of inequality observed historically and in the contemporary world make any notion of a single prime mover implausible and untenable.

In the next chapter, attention returns to explanations of inequality following through on these conflicting interpretations, to produce a broader sense of the range of causal processes that are most salient to explanation of global inequality.

6 Does Globalization Cause Global Inequality?

It is widely held that globalization is responsible for global inequality. But how far is this really the case? Many other causes of inequality have also been identified, such that globalization appears as one cause among many. There is also good reason to believe that globalization reduces inequality in some circumstances. All of this throws doubt on the idea that there is one overarching cause of global inequality, which if addressed in public policy and social action, would allow a simple solution to the multiple inequalities discussed in previous chapters.

In this situation it is important to clarify what it is about globalization that may cause inequality, as well as the processes whereby globalization may diminish certain kinds of inequality. Once again the issues here turn out to be complex. The attribution of causation is never straightforward, and causes do not operate separately in isolation from each other. It is necessary therefore to consider how different kinds of processes interact, rather than operating with a shopping-list of supposedly different and distinct causal factors.

In the first part of the chapter, consideration is given to various mechanisms whereby economic globalization influences global inequality. In the second part attention turns to a broader consideration of demographic, environmental, cultural, and political dimensions of global inequality.

Economic Globalization and Inequality

The relationship between globalization and inequality is far from settled. The most immediate issue here is what is meant by globalization, a process that has many definitions (Holton 2005, 2011). Most focus on cross-border connections and interdependencies across the globe, and much public debate around globalization narrows this focus to economic processes. These include flows of capital, commodities, labour, and technology across borders, associated with free trade and economic deregulation. So globalization, in these accounts, boils down to economic globalization. Yet there are many other political and cultural processes that cross boundaries including forms of governance, science and education, social and political movements, social media, and doctrines of human rights, together with religious and cultural practices. Robertson (1992) sees the globalization of consciousness as a key characteristic of globalization alongside connectivity. So it is not just the economy that is globalized.

When it is said that globalization causes global inequality most observers are thinking of economic globalization. Inequalities arising from economic processes, so it is believed, also structure other inequalities in areas such as health (Navarro 2007, Labonté and Schrecker 2007a, 2007b) or gender (Mills 2003). In this argument economic globalization is bound up with global concentrations of power linked with deregulated markets, multinational corporations and institutions of global governance like the World Bank and International Monetary Fund. These bodies develop and implement policies supportive of free trade, cross-border investment and privatization of state assets. In this way, economic globalization is not simply the spontaneous outcome of markets. For this reason economic globalization is better conceived in terms of the political economy of globalization.

The full consequences of the political economy of globalization, according to its critics, are that it magnifies the inequality generated within global markets by constraining national sovereignty and democracy (Wallerstein 1979, 1991, Sassen 1996, 1998a). Corporate evasion or avoidance of taxation also undercuts measures of social protection and income income support (Palan, Murphy, and Chavagneux 2010). Meanwhile economic globalization shifts cultural practices in the direction of privatized consumerism and social conservatism (Ritzer 2004). This is, of course, a very broad-brush account, from which those sympathetic to the general argument may differ in particular elements. For example, many critics of economic globalization dispute whether it has systematically undermined welfare states (Navarro, Schmitt, and Astudillo 2004), as previously assumed.

Much of this argument is directed towards the contemporary situation. There is however another way of thinking about the connections between globalization and inequality. This looks at globalization across history. We have already surveyed world system theory, perhaps the leading example of historical approaches to global inequality in earlier chapters. Another way of establishing the historical connection between economic globalization and inequality is through an economic history of long-run trends. Thus, as Sutcliffe (2004, 34) points out, many analysts see patterns of long-waves towards and away from globalization over the last 200 years. The 19th century expansion of the global economy up to 1914, is seen to be followed between 1914 and 1950, by a period of economic nationalism involving trade protection and a decline in global flows of capital and labour. Since 1950, a new wave of economic globalization has very much reversed the previous trends. From a historical perspective then it may be that reversals to economic globalization will occur again in the future.

Looked at in this historical manner, does the evidence support a connection between the two waves of economic globalization and growing inequality, or a connection between the retreat from globalization and lesser levels of inequality? The answer is almost certainly no, if we focus on global income inequality which continued to grow throughout the whole period, including periods of de-globalization. In addition, the more recent epoch of intensified economic globalization between 1980 and the advent of the global financial crisis in 2008, sees trends in income inequality pointing in opposite directions (see Chapter 3). Sutcliffe rightly concludes that if the explanatory strategy is based on the search for correlation between a single variable that stands for globalization and another variable that stands for inequality, then the question is unanswerable (ibid.).

There may then be no single general theory capable of accounting for the relationships between economic globalization and inequality. This is why I reject the presumption that global inequality can be explained simply in terms of global capitalism or the capitalist world-system. Such explanations are over-generalized. Globalization should not be thought of as 'a blanket force impacting all nations in a similar manner' (Mills 2009, 6). A more fine-grained approach is required that translates these general blanket forces into more specific and precisely defined processes. As we will see in the discussion below this includes the possibility that the political economy of globalization can in some circumstances undermine forms of inequality, rather than creating or reproducing inequalities. And beyond that some sense of the limits of globalization as an explanatory force are required, which requires some sense of additional or alternative explanations of inequality.

This lack of a plausible general theory connecting globalization and inequality is magnified when we adopt a wider definition of globalization and wider social dimensions of inequality. Most analysts have therefore adopted a different strategy less concerned with overarching general trends across historical epochs, and more concerned with the relationships between different elements of globalization, such as free trade or foreign direct investment, and a range of indicators of inequality. These are not simply to do with wages, but also levels of unemployment, economic volatility, health, and quality of life.

The particular aspects of the political economy of globalization singled out for their effects on inequality may be conceptualized in different ways. Melinda Mills (2009), as indicated in Table 6.1 singles out four particular elements, as follows:

Table 6.1 Checklist of connections between globalization and inequality

- the internationalization of markets and declining significance of borders for economic transactions
- tougher tax competition between countries
- increasing interconnectedness through information and communication technology
- the growing volatility of markets

Source: Derived from discussion in Mills (2009)

In rather broader terms, Labonté and Schrecker (2007b, 2–11), as indicated in Table 6.2, identify seven 'clusters' characterizing globalization:

Table 6.2 Extended checklist of connections between globalization and inequality

- trade liberalization, growth, and poverty
- labour markets and global reorganization for production
- debt crises and marketization under pressure
- financial liberalization and financial crises
- cities restructured by the global marketplace
- globalization, natural resources and environmental exposures
- marketization of health systems

Source: Derived from Labonté and Schrecker (2007b, 2–11)

These checklists offer ways of breaking down excessively generalized approaches to the relationship between globalization and inequality, to achieve a more precise understanding of what aspects of globalization contribute to greater inequality or equality. While it may be possible to reconstruct a more convincing general theory out of such elements, it is far more likely that the causal mechanisms involved are far too complex to account for the multiple forms and trajectories of inequalities discussed in the last two chapters.

I now look at some of the more important lines of analysis designed to explain the relationship between economic globalization and inequality. This draws selectively from the checklists drawn up by Mills, Labonté, and Schrecker.

Economic openness and inequality

Primary attention among economists has been given to the relationship between openness to global economic processes, achieved through free trade and deregulation of markets, on the one hand, and inequality, on the other. Do free trade and foreign direct investment tend to put downward pressure on wages, and encourage governments in the poorest countries to liberalize at the expense of social welfare? In Chapter 2, concerned with general theories, I have emphasized the problem that markets do not necessarily distribute incomes and welfare in an egalitarian manner.

What then does more detailed research say about the impact of trade within globalized markets on patterns of inequality? The answer is that there is no consensus on the existence of a general relationship between openness to trade and global inequality. While ideologues of the free market presume the connection must generally be positive, and critics see the connection as invariably negative, a more judicious conclusion would be that sometimes the connection is positive, sometimes negative, and sometimes neutral. How can this very complex answer be so?

The case for a positive connection between openness to trade and declining inequality has been made in both general and country specific terms. Chakrabarti (2000) using cross-sectional data from 1985 for 173 countries found a negative relationship between trade globalization and income inequality. Meyer (2003) meanwhile found that trade globalization reduces income inequality because it reduces sex segregation of occupations and gender inequality, a key aspect of global inequality. Anderson (2005, 1051) in an extensive review of the literature finds 'almost no support' for the argument that trade openness generally increases inequality. The OECD in a more recent report also find no general evidence that trade openness increases inequality in OECD countries (2011).

Babones and Vonada (2009), in a study covering the period from 1975–1995, find no general connection between trade globalization and inequality across panels of countries analysed cross-sectionally and longitudinally. Yet they also note that some research finds different associations between trade globalization and inequality across different decades, which they find troublesome because it suggests no strong causal connection consistently at work. And for individual countries, the evidence is more mixed. The proportion of foreign trade to GDP in France and Germany, Mexico has increased markedly since 1970 and levels of inequality have remained either constant or declined. In Brazil, China and the post-Soviet states, where the significance of increased trade has also been marked, inequality, by contrast, has increased. Such arguments rest of course on measures of within-country inequality, which is only a limited proportion of total global inequality (see Chapter 4).

Ravallion (2001) had earlier argued that that the lack of a general connection between trade openness and income levels may conceal variations between higher and lower-income countries. Poorer countries may then experience an increase in income inequality associated with openness to trade arising from tariff cuts on imports, and resulting dislocation to local producers. Labonté and Schrecker (2007b, passim) assemble a range of evidence which identifies losers from trade liberalization, more particularly from low-cost imports. These include Zambian manufacturing, Ghanaian poultry production, and Mexican corn-farmers.

Yet this effect is not standard across all case-studies of developing countries. Certainly in Latin America, increased trade openness was associated in the 1980's and 1990's with increased income inequality, but as Szekely and Sámono (2012) and Cornia (2014) suggest this trend has been reversed in the first decade of the 21st century. Similarly in India, increased openness in the 1990's was accompanied first by a rise in income inequality between 1994 and 2000, but this was falling again by 2005 (Krishna and Sethupathy 2011). Some analysts argue that the short to medium term effects of global openness may increase inequality, but that this recedes after economic adjustments are made and domestic policy initiatives like improved education take effect. Szekely and Sámono (2012) make this argument for Latin America, suggesting that trade liberalization is not a medium to long-term obstacle to greater income equality.

Kaplinsky (2005) by contrast finds that certain structural features of an open global economy disadvantage the growth prospects of many lower income countries. This is because global competition in many product markets seeks out low-cost producers pushing down prices for manufactured goods and producer incomes. While China has done well in global markets, emulating the previous generation of East Asian Tigers, this has been achieved through a combination of low labour costs and good product quality. China's massive export boom is thus associated with downward price pressure on goods produced in less efficient locations. To survive in this competitive environment many other lower income countries cannot rely on spontaneous market forces, but require pools of funds to support infrastructural development and training. Yet development aid funds are declining and often short term (see Chapter 7). Meanwhile, a further structural feature of the open global economy that bodes ill for global welfare and inequality reduction is what Kaplinsky sees as a growing excess of productive capacity over employment opportunity.

If Kaplinsky's argument is correct then there are both optimistic and pessimistic implications. The optimistic one is that some developing countries, like China can succeed in finding successful niches within an open global economy. This has not lessened within-country inequality in China, but it has lowered between-country inequality by virtue of China's huge population size. The pessimistic implication is that many cannot and do not find such niches, leaving an uneven picture of successful and inhibited development. So, while economic globalization in the form of free trade and deregulation can help reduce inequality, it can also do nothing much by itself to lessen it. This conclusion is not a comfortable one either for ideological supporters of laissez-faire or for their ideological opponents.

Kaplinsky (48) also usefully distinguishes between *relational* and *residual* aspects of the connection between poverty, low incomes, and globalization. His arguments about economic openness and downward price pressures on producers in poor countries assert relational connections, such that the reproduction of poverty and inequality is intrinsic to some mechanisms of globalization. The residual argument is that poverty and low incomes arise because certain countries have not entered the global economy and gained advantages from it.

It is of course feasible to argue that both kind of effects are at work. This can be illustrated if we look at the spatial scope of trade openness as a potential contributor to greater or lesser levels of inequality. As Thompson (2007, 185) points out the degree of global economic integration involving developing countries is very uneven. It is generally only 25 or so developing countries (including some of the biggest like China and India) that have become more integrated through trade globalization and capital export. Many others, including much of sub-Saharan Africa are only weakly integrated. This means that trade liberalization is likely to be less of an explanation of existing inequality in such settings, and that other causal mechanisms are also at work, both global and local in character. These may include poorly conceived and executed aid programmes, or internal failures in government.

In the light of these considerations, my argument is not of course that trade globalization never increases income inequality. Nor does it mean that other aspects of economic globalization like foreign direct investment or financial liberalization do not increase inequality. What it does mean is that there is no general causal connection between free trade and global inequality, and, that free trade in many circumstances increases wage levels. In such positive circumstances, there is nonetheless evidence that wealthier or more skilled groups in developing countries do better than the unskilled (Beyer, Rojas, and Vergara 1999, Harrison 2007). This, however, depends very much on local political processes including the scope of democratic processes, rather than global market penetration alone.

If periods of intensified trade globalization are accompanied by such diverse trends over time and space, there is clearly a need to take account of other possible causal influences. Some further dimensions of economic globalization that have come in for attention are listed in Table 6.3.

These should not be regarded as entirely separate causal influences since they interact with each other.

Foreign direct investment

Foreign direct investment is a major element in economic globalization, growing faster than world trade. Much of the analytical emphasis has been on capital mobility out of relatively high-cost manufacturing in developed countries into lower-cost developing nations. This shift has been associated with a de-industrialization of developed nations (Gereffi 2009) and a greater emphasis on lower-wage service employment, processes that increasing inequality in such countries (Mills 2009). The connections between economic globalization and de-industrialization are however controversial. Rowthorn and Ramaswamy (1998) argue

Table 6.3 Further relevant features of economic globalization

- foreign direct investment
- inter-sectoral changes in economic structure (e.g., de-industrialization)
- general policies of deregulation
- financial globalization
- labour migration

that economic development and rising productivity are more important explanations of de-industrialization than globalization. Brady and Denniston (2006) are more cautious and take a more historical view. Globalization increased manufacturing in developed countries up to around 1975, with de-industrialization only occurring subsequently. This emerged not as a necessary outcome of outward movements of capital, but rather as global competition increased and lower-cost production elsewhere gained a competitive advantage. It should also be remembered that much global production occurs within corporations, such that higher level functions (such as research, design, and complex assembly) often remain in developed countries while component manufacture may be relocated elsewhere.

The implications for developed countries may indeed be increased unemployment arising from a decline in low-skilled manufacturing work, though an expansion of service work has taken up much of the slack. Increased inequality arises here insofar as service work is poorly paid (Alderson and Nielsen 2002), and also from the greater vulnerability of low-skilled workers to economic restructuring. The work by Buchholz et al. (2009) on globalization and the life-course finds that more highly skilled middle-aged males are most protected from structural change, while younger workers are most exposed. De-industrialization may then have a differential impact across generations and across the life-course, rather than applying uniformly across the working population.

Meanwhile the growth of industrialization in developing nations tends to increase the wages of low-skilled labour (Moran 2003, Thompson 2007, 189). It also offers more opportunities for paid work for women including expanding export-oriented sectors in countries like China, India, and South Africa (Razavi, Pearson, and Danloy 2004). Set against this are often deteriorating elements in work conditions. Examples include the maquiladora manufacturing sectors of countries like Mexico (Labonté and Schrecker 2007b), and insecure sub-contracted cheap labour factories of south-east Asia highlighted in the campaign against Nike's athletic shoe production (Sage 1999, Global Exchange nd).

Taken overall, foreign direct investment is not a major cause of global income inequality because its effects are often positive rather than being consistently negative. It is nonetheless a mechanism by which employment opportunities expand and contract in complex ways across time and space. It does contribute to greater inequality in some contexts, but there is no general evidence of a 'race to the bottom' in wages and labour standards associated with FDI.

Inter-sectoral changes

The issue of inter-sectoral changes in the economy and levels of inequality, takes us back to Kuznets' inverted U-shape curve where inequality starts at a low rate in agrarian societies, increases in the first phases of industrialization and decreases thereafter (see Chapter 2). This approach was developed in an epoch focussed on national economic development and has not fared well in the post-1950 epoch of intensified globalization, where between-country and some within-country inequality has increased. The Kuznets model might well apply to contemporary China where rapid industrialization has created increased within-country inequality. But the model is not very helpful in exploring the broader dynamic effects of globalization and inequality.

Galbraith (2011) recasts Kuznets' emphasis on inter-sectoral change for the contemporary epoch, by emphasizing the significance of global inter-sectoral terms of trade as one among several influences on global inequality. It is important, in other words, to include changes in the relative prices for commodities in sectors such as agriculture, energy, manufacturing, and services including finance in the analysis of inequality. Key prices include the prices of food, energy such as oil, and the price of credit expressed in interest rates. Inequality is especially sensitive to shocks and crises that rapidly raise or lower inter-sectoral prices. Rapid food price rises relative to incomes have been occurring since 2005, and these are particularly damaging to the global poor (Ivanic and Martin 2008). Lack of food security, together with poverty and inequality associated with the rise of agro-fuel production, is a major disturbing development in inter-sectoral changes affecting agriculture (see the critique in Bello 2009). They are negative aspects of structural change in the global economy from the viewpoint of global inequality.

General policies of deregulation

Structural changes in the global economy associated with movements in wages and prices are organized through globalized markets operating through global rules of the game. In the last few decades these rules have included deregulation of markets for commodities and credit, and abandonment of capital controls. Such rules are not simply spontaneous effects of competitive market processes, but linked very much to the interests and policies of the powerful, including global corporations, global regulatory bodies like the IMF, and larger nations. Such processes of deregulation and liberalization – known collectively as the Washington consensus – are clearly aspects of policy-based globalization. Yet it is equally important to recognize that globalization does not mean an end to nation states or their role in constructing global institutions and market rules (Braithwaite and Drahos 2000, Holton 2011). But whatever the precise balance of global and national elements in the world economic order, the system-wide processes that create and reinforce rules of the game, are clearly of great significance for patterns of inequality.

General policies designed to create market deregulation in developing countries may be more significant than the actual operation of deregulated trade, for patterns of global inequality. This occurs when the policies designed to achieve deregulation and economic growth actually strangle economic activity in a counter-productive way. Much of the earlier critique of deregulatory policy concerns the way that global bodies such as the IMF and World Bank have operated stabilization, structural adjustment and market-centred development projects in the world's poorest countries (Stiglitz 2002, chapters 2 and 3).

This line of criticism is nonetheless vulnerable to the charge of caricaturing the work of such bodies in a way that ignores how they have evolved in the last 20 years. A key set of changes here has been a greater focus on good governance, sound political and legal institutions, and improved education and training as critically important features of development processes (Woods 2006, 3). For the World Bank, in particular environmental sustainability (Goldman 2005) and social inequality are now seen as major issues to be addressed in achieving more effective improvements in human welfare.

As I argued in Chapter 2, the problem here is not that markets cannot in principle stimulate growth and the reduction of poverty and inequality. The difficulty is that they are insufficient by themselves in successfully achieving this and that poorly executed top-down global policies, which fail to realize the importance of wider political and cultural dimensions of economic life will often fail. The Fund and the Bank have both learned from problematic aspects of deregulatory policies (Table 6.4).

The assumption that such policy changes would help shift resources into more efficient, market-based growth which would then create greater equality is especially problematic. This is largely because of intervening political, legal, and cultural processes, as listed in Table 6.5.

Babb (2005) in a thoughtful review of the literature notes positive as well as negative features of policies of structural adjustment aimed at market deregulation and liberalization. Positives may include greater government fiscal responsibility and improved systems of taxation,

Table 6.4 Criticisms of the effects of deregulatory policies

- very rapid tariff reductions in poor countries have proceeded without adequate attention to severe consequences for employment and incomes; privatization of state industries has often created collusive monopolies of big business and government rather than efficient markets
- rapid abandonment of basic subsidies of food and fuel have proceeded without alternative provision for low-income earners
- Reduced public social expenditure on health, education, water supply, and sanitation have worsened inequality summarizes a number of the more widespread criticisms.

Table 6.5 Political legal and cultural issues in development

- whether an effective and stable set of legal and political institutions exists
- whether sufficient levels of physical infrastructure and human capital are present
- prevailing cultural attitudes and preferences towards work, credit, and physical mobility
- concerns over the impact of structural change on the integrity of community and on food security

together with stronger property rights for business, though none of these by itself necessary undermines inequality. Negatives, on the other hand, include mismatches between new and old institutions. Examples include Mexican implementation of privatization and financial liberalization without adequate bankruptcy legislation in place (Babb, ibid. 204). Stein (2011) provides many examples of mismatch in sub-Saharan Africa in areas such as credit and finance and market liberalization without adequate transport infrastructure.

Babb (2005) also identifies further negatives including excessive debt burdens on developing countries which undercut social policy and social citizenship, and corruption within elites, which undermines social cohesion and senses of social justice among populations. Further social implications of structural adjustment include adverse health consequences (Breman and Shelton 2001). Such policies also rely on unpaid female labour acting as domestic nurturers and organizers who effectively subsidize market development by dealing with the human costs of adjustment and dislocation (Mills 2003).

A further very telling point on the policy side, emphasized throughout this book, is that the most successful developing countries in terms of breaking out of poverty and economic dependency have not in general followed the nostrums of the Washington consensus. China and India, for example, may be seen as relaxing public controls over economic life as a precondition for their spectacular growth over the last two decades. This in turn has helped to reduce between-country inequalities in the global arena. Yet their advance is scarcely one of free unregulated markets and privatization on the model of the Washington consensus. In China it looks rather more like a state-led capitalism (Wade 2007, 114), based on 'partial liberalization, two-track pricing, limited deregulation, financial restraint, an unorthodox legal regime, and the absence of clear private property rights' (Mukand and Rodrik 2002, 2). India's position is less distinctive but clearly involved only partial and cautious deregulation. These two cases contrast markedly with Latin-America where the Washington consensus was far more influential yet regional growth rates have been very patchy. And in the case of Brazil, one of the expanding BRIC group of nations, capital controls and active social policies again flew in the face of Washington consensus nostrums (Pradilla 2009).

Lastly, the power dimension of global policies of deregulation should be emphasized. Thus it is powerful corporate interests and the wealthier nation states who tend to determine what is regulated, how it is done, and what is not deregulated (Braithwaite and Drahos 2000). The idea that global capitalism is thoroughly committed to deregulation in every respect is an ideological mystification.

Financial globalization

Critics of globalization often point to the destabilizing effect of financial globalization, especially for developing countries, and consequent negative effects on inequality (Labonté and Schrecker 2007b). This is said to follow from the greater integration of such countries into global capital markets. These markets are characterized by huge volumes of short-run capital flows as well as the longer-term flows associated with foreign direct investment, discussed earlier. Financial liberalization exposes developing countries to the volatile patterns of short-term capital flows, based on perceptions as to the relative degree of risk in different countries and sectors. Resulting problems have been manifest in capital flight associated with currency crises involving devaluation and a decline in purchasing power in poorer countries, such as Mexico in 1994–1995, South-east Asia in 1997–1998, and Argentina in 2001–2002.

Prasad et al. (2003), in a paper for the IMF, argue that financial liberalization shows no clear empirical relationship with economic growth. Instead of reducing volatility, financial integration may increase it. Financial globalization certainly increases risks of destabilization. They therefore recommend that it should be approached very cautiously as a policy tool, since it may only work in countries with more effective financial institutions, or after a transition period of adjustment. Meanwhile the Global Financial Crisis of 2008–2013 suggests that there are systematic rather than simply localized sources of volatility and threats to income and economic security within global capital markets (Holton 2012). These effects are magnified where regulation is weakest as in the operation of tax havens where it is estimated that around US$12 trillion of the world's personal wealth was registered in 2007 (Palan, Murphy, and Chavagneux 2010).

A further key issue in financial globalization is that of the debts incurred by poorer countries, and especially their governments, sourced both from global agencies and commercial sources. By the mid 1990's the burdens of these debts had become unsustainable in the sense that the poorest (mostly African) countries lacked the resources to pay them off. Development aid had not generated a dynamic upswing in economic growth, to enable the payment of interest, let alone repayment of the debts themselves. It also inhibited such countries' capacities to utilize such resources for programmes that might offset inequality in areas like education and health.

The World Bank started programmes to relieve debt around 1996. The process gained greater momentum through the Jubilee 2000 movement. This influenced wealthier countries to cancel or reduce some of the sovereign debts of the poorest countries. Through initiatives like the Heavily Indebted Poor Countries (HIPC) programme, it is calculated that nearly US$100 billion of debt has been cancelled (World Bank 2013b). In this way a contributory linkage between financial globalization and global inequality has been partly addressed. World Bank assessments note that reduction in debt payments have increased funds spent in other social development areas. Yet these have achieved only uneven success, with many countries seriously off-target in improvements in literacy or public sanitation. This once again speaks to the complexities arising from the ways that flows of finance influence inequality on the ground – a matter pursued right through this chapter.

Migration

Globalization involves flows of people as well as flows of capital. Since the greater part of global inequality involves inequalities between countries, the direction and impact of global migration flows is of considerable significance for patterns of inequality. This applies both to countries of origin and destination countries as well as to migrants themselves as a particular group. While global migration has not been designed to reduce inequality (Castles 2007), it is unclear how far it may improve or worsen the situation.

While much attention in wealthier countries is given to adverse effects of immigration on the existing native-born population (Borjas 2003), a good deal of research indicates that increased immigration does not adversely affect the overall position of the native-born to any significant extent (see the literature review in Dustmann, Frattini and Glitz 2007). There are a range of reasons why this may be so. First, immigrants generally bear the costs of finding work in a new situation in terms of higher unemployment rates than the general population. Second the native-born may move out of sectors where they compete with immigrants to other jobs. It is also because migrants spend and thus increase aggregate demand, and this is linked with the positive effect of immigration in increasing per capita incomes within recipient countries (Sanderson 2013). What is less clear are the effects on between-country and within-country inequalities.

Migration from a poor country to a wealthier one clearly has implications for between-inequality inasmuch as those working in the new setting will generally be better off. What is less clear is the effect on the poorer developing countries from which they come. It is important that global migrants are not stereotyped as poor and unskilled. Generally it is not the poorest of the poor who migrate (Bastia 2013, 8) but rather people with some resources and networks. While many migrants have low levels of skill, migrant cohorts also comprise a significant amount of educated and skilled labour alongside the unskilled. There is a significant personal benefit to be gained by migration for the educated and more highly skilled in terms of access to higher incomes, but the effect on the country of origin may be less positive. One negative effect is a 'brain drain' where the poorer country loses some of its educated and skilled labour to a wealthier country. Set against this are the remittances that are sent back from the destination country to the home country. If the negative effects are greater than the positive ones, then between-country inequality and within-country inequality in the poorer country would worsen.

There is considerable debate about the socio-economic consequences of remittances. Their scale is not in dispute. The World Bank indicate that remittances to developing countries had grown to US$372 billion by 2011, of which the major recipients were India, China, and Mexico (Ratha and Siwal 2012). The significance of remittances in some smaller countries, like Tajikistan, Nepal, and Lebanon, is considerable where they represent 20% or more of GDP. Overall the value of remittances each year far exceeds overseas development aid and represents around 60–65% of FDI. There remains considerable debate, nonetheless, about what these flows signify. Where, for example, do remittances end up? If they are spent on consumption rather than used to finance business, as is often the case, they may not be directly significant for development and the reduction of inequality. On the other hand, if they are used to support social expenditure in health and education, they may well reduce health inequalities and contribute to human capital formation and a more educated workforce. There is inadequate research at present to determine quite where the balance should be struck in terms of effects on inequality, but remittances certainly make an impact in reducing the otherwise negative effects of brain drain from outgoing skilled migrants.

The overall effects of global migration on inequality are very mixed, rather than supporting very optimistic or very pessimistic interpretations. Nonetheless given the centrality of between-country inequality for global inequality, it remains the case that more rapid immigration from poor to rich countries – currently prevented by restrictions – would make significant inroads into global inequality.

Beyond the Political Economy of Globalization: Towards a Broader Examination of the Causes of Inequality

There is wide recognition among many analysts that global inequalities have multiple intersecting causes rather than being reducible to a single over-arching explanation rooted in the political economy of global capitalism (Suter 2009, Walby 2009, Dorius and Firebaugh 2010). The analytical challenge therefore is to identify further levels of explanation without losing sight of the importance of political-economic processes. So, if economic globalization is not wholly responsible for global inequality what else is?

One simple starting-point in this endeavour is to identify possible causal influences that have been brought forward as significant elements in explaining global inequalities. A provisional listing of these is provided in Table 6.6.

Under each of these headings, a complex mix of spatial scales is involved, ranging from the global and regional to the national and local. Put another way the causes of global inequality are not necessarily global in origins.

Table 6.6 Checklist of broader influences on inequality

- environmental factors including resource endowment, climate change, and environmental policy interventions
- demographic developments and pressures
- cultural relationships and policies associated with racism, patriarchy, and ethnicity
- political institutions and public policy, including issues of corruption, capability, and democratic accountability

Environmental issues are intrinsically global in scope, though the incidence of demographic crises like famine is generally more specific to particular regions. Cultural practices and the politics of culture also operate on a range of scales from global cultural conflicts (Barber 1995) or civilizational wars (Huntington 1996) to national and localized cultural practices which operate to increase or diminish inequality. Meanwhile political institutions and public policy also operate in this way and cut right across the analytical themes identified here from the environment and demography to racism and patriarchy, human rights and equal opportunity, as well as issues of fiscal integrity and corruption. The agenda of issues here is so large that it will not be possible to dig too deeply into any single theme.

Environmental influences on global inequality

There is a wide body of scholarship focussed on the globalization of environmental risk, inequality, and injustice (Beck 2007, 2010, Carmin and Agyeman 2011, Holifield, Porter and Walker 2011). In this work global capitalism and global political economy are pitted against critical social movements and local communities dealing with adverse consequences of the movement of environmental risk across borders.

Globalization and environmental risk

Agyeman and Carmin (2011, 2–3) recount the case of the disposal of European computer waste in Ghana. On arrival waste is dismantled, generally using the manual labour of young workers, including teenagers. Health and safety protection is generally non-existent, so there is no protective clothing. The toxic aspects of the materials involved are generally processed by hand or with rudimentary tools. This exposes workers and surrounding communities to health risks, as well as problems of toxicity entering the soil and groundwater.

The most direct and obvious impact of environmental conditions on inequality is observable in the field of health. In Chapter 5, I argued that many health inequalities between rich and poor countries have narrowed over the last 60 years. Nonetheless the impact of climate change, the globalization of waste, and population pressure on resources such as water, represent major enduring challenges to any attempt to alleviate the inequality of poorer countries.

McMichael et al. (2008) emphasize an important shift in global thinking about environmental health over the last ten years. In the recent past, attention focussed on localized physical, chemical, and microbial hazards, most of which are remediable. They cite World Health Organization estimates that a quarter of the global burden of disease is due to modifiable factors in air, water, soil, and food (Prüss-Üstün and Corvalan 2006). Meanwhile the environmental burden falls disproportionately on low-income countries where risks of heavy metal and chemical residues contamination of foods, and of water-born enteric pathogens are greater than more affluent countries. The disease-burden is especially high in tropical regions, with malaria a large killer, especially of children. Climatic and biological factors here make malaria far harder to eradicate than elsewhere (Sachs et al. 2004) even though greater investment in public health would make a considerable difference.

These local and regional issues remain extremely important, but environmental health thinking has increasingly shifted to larger scale global issues associated with climate change, water shortage, and loss of biodiversity that may be far harder to combat. For Beck (2010), these trends among to the arrival of a world risk society, where the poorest are socially vulnerable to potentially catastrophic environmental trends. However he also warns against a tendency to regard the causes of environmental crisis as simply natural in origin. Discourses of this kind obscure socially generated risks separating the producers of risk from their consequences. Underlying this position is the assumption that seemingly environmental causes of global inequality should rather be attributable to other social causes including global corporate capitalism and the national self-interest of wealthier countries. These are telling points, but they do not entirely dispose of natural environmental causes of climate change.

The overwhelming majority of climate scientists continue to confront climate change deniers over the reality of the issue. But there is a danger that this heated debate receives greater analytical attention than the mechanisms by which adverse effects of climate change affect health and global inequality. Such effects include extreme weather events (including floods, storms, and fires as well as heat waves), changing patterns of infection, and malnutrition arising from adverse effects of warming on food yields. These all have a disproportionate effect on the poorest populations. It is also the poorest groups living on low-lying land, who are most likely to be displaced by floods and rising sea levels. Such effects also have adverse consequences for economic development and livelihoods and thus for inequalities of income as much as health.

However the balance is struck between anthropogenic and natural causes of climate changes, the question remains as to which anthropogenic causes are most salient. Economic globalization may be seen as a major contributor. Mechanisms here include the global corporate power of fossil-fuel businesses over national energy policies, lack of regulation of potentially toxic or polluting activities in poorer nations, and through the impact of free trade on deforestation and reduction of biodiversity. Yet it is by no means clear that these are necessarily connected with global capitalism. Socialist countries have been committed to fossil fuel production on a massive scale, while both the neo-liberal and social-democratic varieties of modernity evident in the Western world remain committed to the exploitation of nature as a social asset. It may then be industrialization or modernity rather than globalization as such that is the major underlying cause of anthropogenic climate change.

There are also paradoxical issues here too. On the one hand increased economic growth including fossil-fuel exploitation may increase the growth rates and aggregate incomes of populations in India and China. This, other things being equal will reduce global inequality – especially that part linked to between-country inequality. On the other hand, the continuing impact of fossil-fuel exploitation on climate change may increase global inequality because of negative environmental effects on the poorest populations adversely effected by increased health risks discussed earlier.

Taken overall then there are both natural and anthropogenic causes of environmental processes that contribute to increased inequality.

Demographic aspects of inequality

Demographic processes connect with inequality in many different ways. Economists see population growth under certain conditions as a spur to economic growth, which then has the potential to narrow income inequalities. Provided population growth does not outstrip food supply (the Malthusian problem), demography expands aggregate demand, though this by itself is unlikely to be the sole or most important contributory factor. Increased productivity linked to technological and organizational innovation is also critical, as is a stable and predictable set of political and legal institutions. Even then the net effect of all this on within-country inequality depends on how far rising per capita incomes are distributed across the population, which itself depends on levels of democratic participation, union density, and other aspects of the distribution of power and influence.

In some contexts, like much of tropical Africa, population growth in rural areas massively outstrips food supply, with the average size of household farms declining, unaccompanied by agricultural intensification (Sachs et al. 2004, 139). This leads both to environmental degradation with the depletion of soil nutrients and the perpetuation of subsistence agriculture. This also helps to perpetuate inequality, though it is not by itself a complete explanation of inequality in sub-Saharan Africa (for further discussion of this issue see chapters 2 and 4).

Looking at the relationship between between-country inequality and population, a good deal depends on the relative per capital income growth achieved in different countries, and whether growth in the poorest countries exceeds growth in the wealthier ones. In general across the period from 1820 to 2000, per capita income growth was far greater in the wealthier countries and regions, than the poorer ones in Africa and Asia, and thus global income inequality on this measure increased. This poorer performance has attracted a range of explanations, which may broadly be divided, as we have seen earlier, into external and internal causes. Population growth and mobility within poorer countries has not had a decisive effect on economic development. This applies whether development problems are explained in terms of the power of external interests over economic resources, failures in deregulatory policies imposed from outside, or internal factors such as lack of stable institutions and thus greater political risk.

There are, however, ways in which population growth in poorer countries can worsen social inequality. Dorius and Firebaugh (2010), in their research into gender inequality, note that recent trends towards greater equality are unevenly spread across different locations. For the period 1970–2000 they find that population growth is significantly higher in countries where gender inequality is higher. While some explain this in terms of the advantages of children to those in poverty, they also consider the relationship between gender inequality and fertility. Where women have less input in family size decisions, fertility tends to be higher, and this seems to be independent of income. If population grows more in such settings than in richer countries, then gender inequality grows as an element of global inequality unless it is offset by other trends towards greater inequality (ibid. 1949).

Finally there is the question of global population mobility already discussed earlier. Here restrictions on immigration from poorer to richer countries, limit global migration as a personal and household vehicle for inequality reduction. In this case it is not economic globalization that restricts population movement, but the interests of populations in wealthier countries anxious to protect their own livelihoods. While capital and commodities flow very freely across borders, labour does not. Immigration restriction is then a form of de-globalization of labour markets that contributes to between-country inequality.

The cultural politics of racism and patriarchy

Cultural relationships have sometimes been seen as a significant source of inequality. Tilly (2001, 360), for example, noted that many anthropologists maintain that 'widely held beliefs, values and practices' that 'promote the differential distribution of advantages', among social groups constitute one major explanation' of racial, patriarchal, and caste-based inequality. While political economic explanations tend to reduce such cultural explanations to the power of dominant economic interests, this forecloses on the possibility that inequalities of race, gender, and ethnicity have autonomous cultural sources. This possibility has already been canvassed in the wider historical sociology of inequality proposed in Chapter 3. The impact of race, ethnicity, and gender on income inequality has also been explored empirically in Chapter 5. I now investigate the coherence of cultural explanations in greater detail, linking them back to global as well as national processes and institutions.

Culture is a notoriously slippery term, stretching from values and attitudes to structures and institutions, sometimes treated almost as politics-free, while at others times, centred on power and inequality. Racism, ethno-centrism, and patriarchy responsible for generating inequality may then be expressed in personal attitudes and interpersonal relationships, but may equally be embedded in structures and institutions. The terrain of culture is however inherently political, forming key elements in structures of power, forms of identity, and processes of social conflict over social inequalities. Racism and patriarchy may be explicit, intentional and deliberate in how they function, but may equally be covert and latent in the way they operate.

One pathway beyond explanations of global inequality that focus on political economy alone is to consider wider debates on modernity and processes of modernization. Modernity has many definitions, and a recent trend has been to think of multiple modernities (Eisenstadt 2000) rather than one single modern pattern. Most approaches to modernity include cultural, political, and legal institutions and practices alongside economic institutions, but the precise form these take varies across different modern nation states.

In classic post-war modernization theory (Parsons 1971) it was a combination of processes like democracy, the rule of law, scientific rationalism, and a culture of individual achievement and acquisitive individualism that were associated with the dynamic evolution of modern society over previous traditional forms of social life. In the process it was thought that poverty, inequality, ignorance, and authoritarianism would be overcome, and with them, the ascriptive cultural prejudices and institutions that fostered the unequal treatment of cultural groups. Yet rather than withering away in the face of modern secular reason, market economies, liberal democracy, and cultures of individual achievement and self-realization, it is clear that race, ethnicity, and patriarchy remain largely intact and in a range of settings across both rich and poorer countries. The much-vaunted cosmopolitanism typically associated with globalization is one significant contemporary trend (Holton 2009). But it is not sweeping all before it. Racist politics of social exclusion is very far from dead while ethno-nationalism has revived across Europe, and ethno-centric tribal conflicts are endemic in central Africa.

One explanation of all of this is that modernity's best efforts to abolish slavery, institute civil and citizenship rights, and implement equal opportunity for all, are still incomplete. Older institutions of white supremacy, privilege and forms of prejudice against others, including Jews and Blacks live on, and require fresh initiatives to combat them. An alternative, more radical line of argument has explained the persistence of racial, ethnic, and gender inequality, as a product of modernity, or at least certain key features of it. Thus a range of social theorists associated with post-structuralism, feminism, and post-colonial thought have challenged the foundations of modernization theory over the last 40 years (Foucault 1973, Said 1978, Pateman 1988, Goldberg 2002, Winant 2001, 2004). These currents of thought are diverse rather than unified. But in one way or another they identify weaknesses in key elements of modernity. These include coercive features of rationalization designed to discipline subordinate social groups as well as both colour- and gender-blindness in supposedly universalistic liberal democratic institutions in dealing with racism and patriarchy.

What then does all of this add to explanations of global inequality?

First, this current of thought offers ways of thinking about global inequality that take the historical legacy of empire, slavery patriarchy, and race seriously without reducing these influences to the simple logic of capital accumulation and capitalism. Explanation of global inequality is, as we have seen, inconceivable without taking seriously negative consequences of market-based economic processes and structures of power. What radical critics of modernity have done is expand the repertoire of explanatory options beyond recourse to reductionist logic of capitalism arguments.

Discussions of race and inequality provide important examples of how this operates. One of the major general features of the work of Foucault and Said is to show how binary cultural divides act as forms of discursive power embodied both in ideas and in forms of discipline, surveillance, and cultural domination. This is sometimes summed up in the term 'othering'. Race and racism represent one important instance of othering, as do religious distinctions between Christians and Muslims, or cultural distinctions between the civilized and backward or barbaric social groups. Racial, religious, and civilizational distinctions of this kind are widespread in the history of European colonization of Latin America, Africa, and Asia. They function to create and reproduce white European supremacy and may therefore be regarded as cultural forms of globalization that are intrinsically connected with global inequality.

Winant (2001) argues that global racial inequality is not explained by the general nature of the capitalist world-system. He speaks rather of a 'world racial system' (ibid. xiv), or 'racial longue durée'(21) consolidated in the 18th and 19th centuries that had autonomous effects of its own on in creating patterns of global inequality between and within countries. This system is closely connected with changing global relations between capital and labour, but it is far more than that. It is also a key element in the formation of empires and the constitution of a hierarchy of nation states. Beyond this it creates new cultural identities that also intensify racial hierarchies. Winant's argument invites the further comment that racial dominance is not explained primarily by supposed needs of capitalism. Put another way, capitalism has no necessary linkage with particular forms of unfree or free labour, particular authoritarian or democratic polities or particular racist or cosmopolitan cultural formations. It can operate in any of these contexts.

In this analysis Winant globalizes the idea of racial inequality, speaking of 'the world as a ghetto'. This represents a move beyond nationally-focussed accounts of racial inequality that tend to dominate the field, towards global–national interactions. For the racial system is dynamic and subject to resistance and change rather than a static all-embracing explanation of global inequality. A watershed in the racial longue durée is located around the time of the Second World War. Henceforth the combined effects of movements for colonial independence, the rise of movements for civil rights and democracy began to make serious inroads into global racial hierarchies which had hitherto contributed much to the rise of between-country inequality. A classic case of global-national interactions in this context is the demise of apartheid in South Africa from a combination and external pressure and internal resistance.

While global racial hierarchy has been eroded by colonial revolution, independence and democracy, the legacy of white racial supremacy has endured, not least in the United States. This has been explored in sociological research on racial discrimination and inequality (see Chapter 5). Racial inequality has also been analysed in new schools of scholarship such as Critical Race Theory (CRT).

Developed among some legal scholars in the United States from the 1970's onwards (Delgado and Stefancic 2001), CRT is one of a number of parallel intellectual currents of research on race and inequality (Pitcher 2011). They focus on the intersection of race, class, gender, and sexual orientation rather than political economy alone, and on the deeply embedded nature of racial thinking and racial exclusion within modern society. Among the rather eclectic mix of themes addressed by CRT, are inequalities in the legal system around the question of whether African-Americans can get justice from white juries, the racial implications of legal narratives, and the naming of the realities faced by those subject to racist behaviour including insults, epithets, and name-calling. This helps to get at qualitative aspects of existential inequality that are hard to measure, but very real nonetheless.

One theme in CRT and other critical currents in scholarship around race is the colour-blindness of many institutions and discourses. Colour-blindness to race is reflected both in liberal-democratic United States and republican France (Salmi 2011). Here issues of whiteness and white supremacy do not surface, either because they would strike at forms of privilege incompatible with the American dream, or because they would undermine proud French ideals of republican virtue. In both cases, racial supremacy is made invisible by national myths, yet its reality is evident in evidence of labour market disadvantage and exclusion (for the United States see Chapter 5, for France, see Silberman, Alba and Fournier 2007).

Massey (2009) provides a powerful way of understanding connections between global inequality and race. His focus is on what is called American exceptionalism. While globalization is seen as creating pressures towards greater inequality around the world, how nation states respond to these pressures matters a great deal to the scale and types of inequality that ensue. The United States is marked out as exceptional because global pressures towards greater inequality have been expressed far more intensely here than elsewhere. This is partly because the tax system favours the wealthy by sharply limiting the scale of income redistribution to the less well-off. Looking at inequality before and after tax, Smeeding (2005) found that US inequality pre-tax was only slightly above countries in Western Europe, whereas after tax inequality came out as far higher in the United States. Republic administrations also adopted policies to weaken unions and reduce the minimum wage. In other words it was national policy rather than globalization that was important in explaining the differential.

Racial inequality enters the picture not simply because of Republican cuts to welfare in the 1990's, but more specifically as a result of racial stigmatization of African-American women as 'welfare queens' maximizing numbers of children to maximize welfare payments. While the Democratic Party committed to civil rights had previously dismantled racial elements in welfare, these have now become re-racialized in Republican discourses about welfare. In Massey's view, the legacy of race, so significant in recent US history, helps to explain the extent of US inequality because it allows a populist politics of racial division to inhibit social protection against the economic pressures associated with globalization.

This argument is of substantive interest as an analysis of globalization and inequality in the United States. Yet it is equally of interest in broader methodological terms, because it integrates together global and national explanations of inequality within a historical framework. Although Massey sees himself as providing a new political economy of poverty in an epoch of globalization, this analysis has wider sociological implications for debates about multiple modernities. This is because it shows two types of modernity at work, one based on economic liberalism and the cultural politics of class and race, the other centred on civil rights, democracy and social protection.

The cultural politics of patriarchy and gender has an analytically similar status to that of race, in the sense that gender divisions are not reducible to the global capitalist economy. This applies even though economic processes have a great influence on income inequalities faced by women. In parallel with a racial longue durée, we may also speak of a patriarchal longue durée. This creates long-run structures of gender-based inequality in income and access to positions of power. But it has also come under challenge, with the rise of feminism. The underlying theoretical point here is that patriarchy, while contingently connected with capitalism, is not simply explained by any intrinsic need of capital for low-female labour, or unpaid domestic labour serving the work-force and socializing children. Capitalism can operate with or without patriarchy. And patriarchy can operate as a powerful cultural force for exclusion of women in any context, including politics and civil society and community life, whether or not pressures of market-based capitalist power operate.

Political institutions, public policy, and inequality

A major analytical theme in much of the literature on global inequality is the extent to which inadequacies in political institutions adversely affect social inequality (see the review in Dawson 2010). This occurs when states fall apart as in contemporary Somalia and the recent history of central Africa. It also happens when states lack the capacity and/or resources to secure social and political order, stabilize property rights, and provide a low-risk social environment suited to economic and social development. Such problems have been evident not merely in parts of Africa, but also in parts of Asia.

Much research on sub-Saharan Africa includes problematic political institutions as an element in explanations of this region's low incomes and poor health compared with the rest of the world. Problems here range from lack of capacity to protect property rights in most countries, endemic corruption, and authoritarian control over populations which inhibits democratic routes towards the alleviation of poverty and reduction of inequality. What is less certain is how exactly such institutional problems have arisen, and how problems with political institutions interact with other explanations of Sub-Saharan inequality arising from globalization, from high disease burdens, and high transportation costs (Sachs et al. 2004, 131–132, van de Walle 2009). Before exploring these, it should also be emphasized that sub-Saharan Africa is not a uniform region, largely because of the historic and continuing impact of white settlement in the South, linked both with mineral and agrarian resource endowment, and state commitment to economic development. While South Africa has higher levels of within-country inequality than most of sub-Saharan Africa, its per capita income growth has reduced some of the between-country gap with wealthier countries.

What then are the adverse connections between problematic political institutions and inequality? Cross-national studies of developing countries generally find positive connections between states able to achieve social order, protect private property and market transactions, and raise taxes, on the one hand, and increase levels of income, economic development (Leblang 1995, Evans and Rauch 1999), and, to a lesser extent, improved child mortality (Lazarova 2006, Holmberg, Rothstein and Nasirtoussi 2009). On the other hand, states who fail these tests, preside over economic stagnation and more persistent inequality. But what exactly are the mechanisms involved? Is state capacity or incapacity more a function of levels of available resources based on tax revenue, reflecting what might be called the fiscal mechanism? Or is it more to do with the capacity of states to wield effective and legitimate authority over a territory such that administration if efficient rather than corrupt and property rights are protected rather than subject to arbitrary interventions by powerful elites (Holmberg et al. 2009)? The latter mechanism comes close to ideas of the rule of law, but Dawson (2010) warns against equating this with strong rule of law institutions that include legal constraints on political power associated with democracy. He prefers the thinner notion of rule by law, as evident in successful states like China, and the United Arab Emirates, where legitimate authority is exercised without democratic processes that limited the exercise of power.

How then do fiscal and rule by/of law institutions influence patterns of inequality? Fiscal mechanisms influence inequality where they connect with public policies in areas like income redistribution or public health and educational provision, whereas rule by law mechanisms tend to operate through impacts on markets and civil society. More efficient markets are capable of increasing incomes though not necessarily distributing it so as to minimize inequality, while support for civil society allows trust, reciprocity, and networks of social capital to emerge. Developing countries with stronger rule of law systems see greater use of social co-operation in civil society to support and enhance livelihoods and self-respect (Esman and Uphoff 1984, Rothstein and Stolle 2008, Collins et al. 2009). This evidence suggests that inequality does not necessarily impede the development of social networks and the operation of social capital.

Dawson (2010) argues that rule of law may have beneficial effects in reducing inequality independent of the scale of resources available to states. In this research the rule of law was measured in terms of an index composed of data on popular observance of the law, the impartiality of legal institutions, and the scale of trust in financial institutions. The positive effects of rule of law institutions, defined in this way, emerge from a cross-national study of child mortality – a key element in global inequality – between 1990 and 2005. Reduction of child mortality was linked both with the rule of law and trade openness but not with direct foreign investment, indicating once again the complexities involved in explaining global inequality. The more general conclusion here is that state capacity as measured by resources at the disposal of the state may not be the best indicator of institutions capable of reducing inequality. This is true if potential revenue is not actually collected or if it is used in ways that do not address inequality whether through corruption or the siphoning off of income for political elite consumption.

A wider historical sociological approach to institutional influences on inequality in developing countries is provided by van de Walle (2009). He addresses the high levels of inequality in contemporary Africa. These cannot be adequately explained in his view by negative impacts from contemporary globalization, since Africa has largely been neglected by foreign investment. His explanation is rather directed at the historical experience of colonization and the negative legacies it has left for post-colonial political institutions. Drawing on work by Engerman and Sokoloff (2000) and others this line of argument begins with the poor or uncertain natural resource endowment of much of Africa (especially the tropics), labour scarcity, and a huge disease burden. Colonization came late to most of this region compared to Latin America where the colonial era lasted over 300 years, compared to less than 100 years in sub-Saharan Africa. White settlement was far less in Africa than Latin America, and colonial political institutions far more limited and alien in Africa which failed in the main to develop domestic institutional and state traditions (except in the southernmost regions) found in the Americas. Exclusion of mass populations from political participation continued into the 20th century. Consequently the colonial state achieved comparatively little in terms of economic and social development, the primary purpose being law and order.

It was this legacy that post-colonial African political institutions took over. Inheriting a state that was 'neither responsive nor developmental' (ibid. 319), new elites were faced with little trained manpower and governing classes tended to come from ethnic groups which the colonial states had had most dealings with. Political power, as pointed out by Diamond (1987), became recognized as the quickest way to become wealthy, and political clientelism and corruption became part of the mechanisms of advancement. Under the rhetoric of socialism, many foreign assets were transferred immediately after independence to the political class. Even land redistribution to Africans often involved the best land going to the wealthiest political families. Van der Walle (2009) is generally scathing about subsequent policy achievements, noting low levels of social spending, and the anti-rural bias in tax policy. This line of argument gives some longer-term perspective to historical legacies of inequality set in train well before the Washington consensus and the epoch of structural adjustment that receives disproportionate attention.

Conclusion

This chapter has covered a wide range of explanations of global inequality. In spite of the huge complexity of this terrain, it is possible to summarize and restate the broad argument made in this chapter in the following six propositions.

First, globalization is not the over-riding general cause of global inequality. This flies in the face of much commentary on the state of the world, but the analyses developed here indicate a much more complex picture.

Second, there is no single over-riding general cause of global inequality, and hence no single and unambiguous political strategy to reduce inequality. Opposition to globalization would not reduce global inequality and would probably increase inequality between nations.

Third, there are connections between aspects of globalization and patterns of inequality, but it is necessary to dis-aggregate specific elements often bundled together under the broad heading of globalization to understand more precisely the effect of various cross-border processes on inequality. The evidence suggests that trade openness and foreign direct investment are mixed in their effects, sometimes negative, sometimes positive. Economic globalization also influences patterns of inequality through policies of deregulation, structural adjustment, and privatization. These may have long-term positive effects, but the shorter to medium-term effects are often negative, especially where interventions are badly conceived and misread the need for social and political preconditions to be met before market-supporting reforms can operate successfully. This is why organizations like the World Bank have over time shifted their focus from much-criticized and narrow forms of structural adjustment to a more explicit concern with social development and inequality.

Fourth, the connections between global capitalism and inequalities of power are very real. A political economic approach to the global organization of production and exchange to the global distribution of power and global inequalities of access to policy-making matters a great deal. Poorer countries and their citizens get a raw deal from richer-nations who restrict immigration in their own self-interest. However political economy is weak in explaining the cultural politics of inequality with particular reference to race and gender. It is also inadequate in exploring the dynamics of civil society as it affects ways of living with and overcoming inequality.

Fifth, explanations of global inequality should include demographic and environmental influences in their own right. Environmental risk falls disproportionately on the poor, while inroads into inequality are hard to make without social policy interventions that engage with demographic challenges of an expanding global population.

Sixth, rather than continuing the search for a grand theoretical synthesis of all the various explanations of global inequality, it is more plausible to leave aside this holy grail, in favour of an open-ended multicausal approach organized around middle-range theory. This in turn suggests the need for a more subtle approach to policy recommendations capable of reducing inequality. It is to this latter question that I turn in the final chapter.

7 What Is to Be Done? Policy Responses to Global Inequality

What can be done about global inequality? This key question immediately raises many others. The agenda of questions, challenges, and answers is vast.

How far can global inequality be reduced? And what changes are required in the way markets function, and in the public policies adopted by global organizations and nation states? Can development aid play a positive role in this process? And what underlying political processes are relevant to understanding whether policies and aid programmes succeed or fail? Who are the major players in social action to do with global inequality? And why is it that so much emphasis has been given to top-down initiatives and rather little to bottom-up processes of political mobilization among those whose lives are dominated by the human costs of inequality? And how does all this translate into policies? Which policies and strategies for implementation, if any, are working, and what changes and shifts in policy responses are likely to speed up the reduction of the various dimensions of inequality discussed in this book?

The Uncertain Place of Egalitarianism in the Modern Global Order

That we ask these questions at all reflects characteristic features of modernity. Firstly, equality and human rights have emerged as core political and social values, intrinsic to full democratic citizenship and social participation, and therefore something that political institutions and public policy should foster. Secondly egalitarianism transforms inequality from something regarded as natural and immutable to a social problem amenable to amelioration through social intervention. Yet ideals of a more egalitarian world have yet to be matched by institutional arrangements or policies that make an unequivocal difference to the profound global inequalities that exist today.

This is partly because arguments in favour of egalitarian obligations towards the world's poorest populations are not shared by all social groups and interests. Reduction of absolute levels of poverty seems to be quite widely shared, but the reduction of inequality within and between countries is nowhere near as prominent in debates and conflicts the current state of the globe. Nor is resistance to greater egalitarianism simply to do with powerful and wealthy interests and groups across the modernizing world, for it extends to less well-off residents of wealthier countries who resist increased immigration of the World's poor in defence of their own income and wealth. Resistance to increased taxation for any purpose by rich and poor is also widespread. This reflects broader features of global modernity in which self-interest and possessive individualism are major economic and cultural values. This undercuts much of the political thrust of egalitarianism.

Unlike the earlier modernization theorists of the 1950s and 1960s, more recent theorists (Eisenstadt 1999, 2000, Walby 2009, 26–27) argue that modernity does not come in a singular form. Different modern societies do not converge on an identical bundle of market-based, democratic, and individualist institutions and cultural practices under the security of the rule of law. Rather modernity comes in different versions. These reflect contrasting regional and national histories and path-dependencies, and contrasting ways of connecting and balancing market freedom, democratic rights, individualism, and community obligation. Such variations mean, not simply that patterns of inequality will vary across modern nation states, but that there will be different approaches to the obligations of individual nations and their citizens to address global inequality between nations. Policy conflicts between neo-liberal and social-democratic approaches reflect these underlying contrasts and variations both in national settings and in the international arena.

Analysing what to do about global inequality, however, also requires an approach that stretches beyond national boundaries and varieties of capitalism and modernity at a national level. Conflicts of values apply trans-nationally as well as domestically. Economic globalization in terms of economic self-interest embodied in free trade and capital mobility, has clearly meant intensified cross-border transactions, but cosmopolitan concerns for forms of human welfare and dignity that operate across borders have proven far harder to implement and secure (Nussbaum 2011).

This is not because cosmopolitanism is too abstract and remote from everyday life concerns about global inequality, nor is it because cosmopolitanism as a way life might seem to fit better with wealthier social classes who can afford to be more generous than poorer classes on the margins of survival. Newer less philosophical and more sociological accounts of cosmopolitanism show how it can emerge in micro-level contexts at all points in the social structure, able to foster co-operation across boundaries, and blend local or national affiliations with obligations to a wider world (Holton 2009). Such connections may be less blatant or egregious than the clamour of nationalist assertion, but they do capture the world view of many, both within international organizations, and within social movements aiming at human rights, reduction of poverty and cultural oppression, and improved global health and welfare. The clash between neo-liberal and cosmopolitan values at a global level clearly underlies much of the policy debates over the Washington consensus and controversies over development aid.

Why Single Focus Approaches to Global Inequality Reduction Don't Work

In the previous chapter a number of causes of persistent global inequality were identified. These help explain why global inequality has increased over the last 150–200 years. The complex multi-causal nature of the determinants of inequality also means that no single policy nostrum is adequate to a fundamental reduction of global inequality. This applies to all the favourite single-shot policy recommendations in play, whether they focus on free markets and deregulation, rejection of globalization, or the replacement of capitalism by socialism.

Openness to global markets through international trade and capital mobility has sometimes been a positive force for long-term economic development and thus the opportunity to reduce inequality, but only up to a point. This is partly because economic globalization by itself contains no automatic or explicit mechanisms for redistributing the fruits of economic growth so as to reduce global inequality. It is also because the enforcement of market solutions on poor developing countries lacking supportive social and political institutions generally fails to secure self-sustaining economic growth let alone redistribution of resources to the most needy. Social and political regulation of some kind is required in all contexts, whether to cope with the destabilizing effects of markets on financial security and social cohesion, or to democratize political processes that otherwise tend towards authoritarianism and corruption. Most of the successful developing economies in recent years, such as China and India have emerged through a policy mix of market-based and state-sponsored initiatives, though even here political and social reform still holds back internal reductions in inequality.

For some, the concentrations of corporate power and elite-based policy-making associated with economic globalization, lead to policy options in which globalization itself is rejected in favour of national democratic autonomy from global economic penetration. The well-known demonstrations in Seattle at the 1999 meeting of the World Trade Organization generally favoured economic protection of home industries and jobs, over free trade. Economic nationalism may seem like an understandable policy response in a context of social crisis. Protectionist strategies, however, are most unlikely to stimulate economic productivity, a major source of income growth and potential inequality reduction within home countries. They also invite global economic warfare and the collapse in export markets as seen in the world depression of the 1930s. This in turn makes no inroads into between-country inequality.

Since globalization in some blanket sense is not the primary cause of global inequality, general opposition to globalization is not a coherent policy response. Rather the focus of attention should be on a wide set of possible policy responses, sensitive to those aspects of globalization that have failed and those that have not. In all of this the major obstacle to the creation of a 'sane globalization' (Rodrik 2011, 253) is the current failure to make economic globalization consistent with the social goals of human development.

A final policy approach involves not the rejection of globalization, but the rejection of capitalism and capitalist globalization, precisely because of the current failure to make globalization consistent with human development. This position is reflected in social movements sometimes referred to in terms of alter-globalization and represented in the World Social Forum, set up in opposition to the elite-based World Economic Forum (Smith 2004). Much of the impetus here comes from a sense of the positive dynamic of civil society in encouraging the transformation of global inequalities of power and human welfare from below. Examples of largely successful campaigns associated with this approach include the Jubilee 2000 movement against global debt burdens suffered by poor countries, and campaigns against the involvement of global corporations in sweatshop employment in the world's poorest countries.

This third strategy has indeed helped influence debates, policies, and practices on the ground on many aspects of global inequality, promoting a widening agenda of human development issues largely ignored by corporations and the elite-politics of global organizations. It therefore seems more plausible than the other two options of neo-liberalism and anti-globalization. The idea of a more socially responsible globalization is nonetheless ambivalent in its relationship with capitalism and markets, with some currents seeking to replace capitalism and others to reform it. This parallels the ambivalence of the labour movements of industrial capitalism in the 19th and 20th centuries around issues of revolution or reform.

The existence of multiple causes of global inequality, political and cultural as much as economic, suggests that anti-capitalism by itself is inadequate as a policy response. This is recognized among many critics and global civil society movements. Specific campaigns target political authoritarianism and corruption, as well as racism and patriarchy, none of which would be resolved simply by abolishing capitalism. Many also recognize that environmental protection and sustainability are key aspects of struggles against global inequality. This is because it is often the poorest populations that experience the negative impacts of climate change, pollution, and toxic waste (Urry 2011).

However, there remains the thorny problem of how to make global capitalism more compatible with human development. At the centre of this problem is the conundrum of how best to harness the economic dynamism and rising productivity that properly regulated markets are capable of generating with enhancements to democracy and human rights.

Development Aid and Policy Responses to Global Inequality

Development aid is a major global strategy aimed at social as well as economic objectives, some of which, directly or indirectly, influence patterns of global inequality. Unlike the three single focus strategies discussed in the previous section, development aid, at least in theory, is capable of targeting multiple inequalities. Development aid is nonetheless a term that stretches across a wide range of political, military, and technical projects as well as areas to do with poverty, and inequalities of income, health, education, and social inclusion. This multidimensionality complicates the evaluation of its impact on global inequality. However the key question here is whether development aid actually works?

Aid of this kind involves flows of resources from national governments, international bodies like the World Bank, and private bodies, including charities and other NGOs to governments and non-official bodies in poorer countries. Table 7.1 indicates that official flows vastly exceed private aid donations by a ratio of over 4 to 1.

Table 7.1 Sources of foreign aid, 2012 (US$)

Official flows from governments and agencies	135 billion
Private flows from non-government sources	32 billion
Private funds offered through markets	307 billion
TOTAL	474 billion

Source: Author's own table derived from OECD 2013

The leading official donor countries are the European Union and the United States, while the largest agency involved is the World Bank. The largest single destination for official aid is Africa at around 38%, and Asia at around 25%. Total development aid reached a peak in 2010 and has declined by around 5% in current prices since then.

The table also includes the scale of private funds offered to recipient countries and interests within them, much of it in the form of foreign investment or commercial loans to governments. This exceeds the scale of development aid by nearly 2 to 1. The predominance of market-based inflows of funds over development aid, means that any analysis of policy responses to global inequality needs to take account both of capital markets, how they function and whether they are properly regulated, as well as the role and effectiveness of development aid.

There is a vast debate on whether development aid works (Bauer 1972, Cassen 1994, World Bank 1998, Tarp 2000, Riddell 2007, 2009, Wilkinson and Hulme 2012). Much of this is characterized by highly ideological and political discourses, which are prejudicial and highly selective in terms of perceptions of success or failure. The rational kernel of arguments can be summarized as follows in Table 7.2:

Table 7.2 Arguments around development aid

Positive

1. Most aid does succeed in meeting its objectives especially in the short-term (Cassen 1994), even if some is wasted through poor organization or syphoned off by corrupt practices. Development aid does not necessarily or inevitably fail.
2. Aid does contribute positively to economic growth (Clemens et al. 2004, Minoui and Reddy 2010). But this relationship depends on supportive political institutions in recipient countries (Burnside and Dollar 2004).
3. Aid has been successful in addressing inequality in areas like public health and education (see Chapter 5).
4. Even if some aid doesn't work, this is an argument for doing it better rather than not doing it at all (Riddell 2009).

Table 7.2 (Continued)

Negative
1. Much aid doesn't get to the poorest where it is most needed. It benefits elites more.
2. Too much aid is syphoned off through corruption and local political involvement (Bauer 1972).
3. Aid programmes are not typically accountable to their intended recipients and wider audiences. Donors interests come first.
4. The positive contribution of aid to economic growth is dubious (Easterly 2006).

How then to strike a balance between the positives and negatives? The stark choice between abandon aid altogether and continue with it on more or less the existing basis is not one that most observers and activists subscribe to. The issue is rather one of how best to reform aid and make it more effective. There is a great deal that scholarly analysis can do to facilitate this process.

One important example is clarification of the relationship between development aid and economic growth. This is especially important because growth is a vital precondition for the reduction of both poverty and material or resource inequality. Growth raises aggregate incomes and positively influences flows of tax revenue available for redistribution. Whether redistribution happens though, is another matter depending in large measure on political and institutional arrangements. Farmers' incomes may not benefit if the terms of trade for their produce worsens. Corruption and institutional weaknesses are also crucial variables here. If there is no effective tax system then it is hard to use fiscal revenue created by growth that has been stimulated by aid for any tangible purpose.

The reasons why scholars disagree about whether development aid stimulates economic growth are partly methodological. Should calculations assume that the effects of aid are contemporaneous, and that all types of aid should be bundled into an aggregate measure? Much of the pessimistic case about aid and growth rests on these assumptions. Minoui and Reddy (2010) by contrast allow for longer-term impacts and differentiate between different types of aid. They find a long-term positive relationship between aid and growth. Others such as Burnside and Dollar (2004) argue that the positive potential of aid will tend to be realized where political arrangements are stable and conducive to growth, but that this can be undercut by corruption and incompetence.

One simple way of reconciling much of the disagreements in the very wide-ranging debates that are only touched on here is to argue that there is neither a generally valid positive or negative relationship between development aid and economic growth. Rather development aid can boost growth in certain circumstances and therefore aid for growth should not be abandoned as a strategy.

Yet even where development aid contributes to economic growth, this only represents a necessary not a sufficient condition for inequality reduction. Growth can and does often leave inequalities untouched or even worsened. Bangura (2012, 203) also argues that the most highly unequal societies need very high growth rates to overcome poverty and make inroads into inequality.

Moving beyond growth, debates on development aid also include a complex set of discussions about both the aims and content of development aid programmes and the political processes whereby goals are set and programmes implemented. Much of this centres on critical evaluation of the Millennium Development Goals, discussed in Chapter 5. Wilkinson and Hulme (2012), in an edited collection entitled *The Millennium Goals and Beyond*, summarize an agenda of issues that should be prioritized in the evaluation process. I have selected from their listing the following key points expressed in my own terminology in Table 7.3:

Table 7.3 Reforming the millennium development process

1. Ensure equitable economic growth
2. Reduce inequalities between individuals and groups within and between countries
3. Promote national ownership of development aid through socially inclusive mechanisms that take national priorities seriously
4. Include climate change and the mitigation of its effects
5. Ensure rights of women to freedom from violence
6. Adopt more rigorous processes of reporting, monitoring, and accountability in assessing the effects of development aid

Source: A selective summary of Wilkinson and Hulme 2012, 229–230

Beyond this, it is important to set issues of global development aid within broader considerations that apply to two key dimensions of global action on inequality. The first is the framework of global governance as it affects global inequality. The second is the policy framework that translates global development goals into concrete policies and which sets the rules of the game for global transactions between corporations, governments, and the world's poor as these affect global inequality.

Multi-Level Governance as It Effects Within-Country and Between-Country Inequality

A necessary starting point here in looking at policy-making and the rules of global transactions is the distinction between within-country and between-country inequality. As we have seen the lion's share of global inequality is made up of between-country inequality. This trend has been a historical feature of the epoch of market-centred economic globalization. The ideological supposition that free markets organized within the liberalizing agenda of the Washington consensus will eventually and necessarily make inroads into global inequality is therefore spurious and untenable. Alternative policy interventions within the global arena have therefore attracted increasing attention within a range of settings. These include international organizations like the United Nations, World Bank, and World Health Organization, within the policies supported by nation states within the global arena, as well as a host of non-government organizations like Oxfam and Greenpeace. The deliberations and policies that emerge in this complex set of interconnected settings are influenced not simply by national self-interest and corporate lobbying, but also by changing norms by movements for political and social reform and academic analysis and commentary.

It may seem paradoxical therefore to find that much applied research and public comment on inequality and its reduction, still concentrates on within-country inequality (Beck 2007). Individual nation states in other words remain a central point of reference in analysing inequality and in pursuing questions about which policies create and which policies reduce patterns of inequality. While many acknowledge global as well as national sources of inequality, much of the policy focus is on the competing approaches of neo-liberalism and social democracy and their respective consequences for social inequality within wealthier nations.

There are certainly good reasons why nation states remain central reference points for policy initiatives affecting between-country as well as within-country inequality. Firstly nation states have been challenged but not undermined by economic globalization (Holton 2011). While varying considerably in wealth, power, and influence, the larger or wealthier nation states remain key actors in international organizations, including the G8, G20, World Bank, and World Trade Organization. Such bodies influence the rules of the game within the global economy and strategies for poverty reduction and social reform. Alongside multilateral activities of this kind, national political autonomy remains a reality both for wealthier countries and the more successful developing nations, like

China, India, and Brazil. Nation states are therefore a major presence in decisions which affect global inequality, even though the global polity is also influenced by decisions taken by corporations, and campaigns organized by non-government organizations.

Secondly nation states are regarded by many citizens as the foundation of democracy. When this assumption is combined with national identity as the strongest form of political affiliation, it is no surprise to find that it is national inequalities that most exercise citizens within individual nations. National identity has not been undermined by economic globalization, and may even have strengthened in part as a response to perceived threats to national sovereignty in policy-making. For many, national interests come first, although this may not in any way preclude a concern for others across the world. National affiliation and global concern are not mutually exclusive.

A third element in this nation-centred focus is the absence of a world state with effective power and democratic legitimacy (Nussbaum 2011). This is further associated with a growing scepticism about the capacity of global and regional forms of governance – whether the World Bank or the European Union – to resolve problems of inequality, injustice, and environmental crisis. Many citizens have turned their attention inwards and hardened their stance towards perceived threats from outside – such as global immigration from poor to richer countries, or the global politics of corporate elites.

In this situation, it might seem that restructuring of global governance to make inroads into social inequality is politically hopeless, and that the most that can be expected is action at a national level. There are nonetheless two general observations which can be made about this kind of scenario.

The first highlights the shortcomings of individual country responses alone. Even if internal levels of inequality were radically reduced in individual countries acting independently, this would still leave the world a highly unequal place. This is because of the huge income and wealth gaps between developed and developing countries, which mean that the poorest groups in richer countries are better off than all but a small segment of the population of poorer countries (Rodrik 2011, 135). This is why discussions of global inequality that focus primarily on within-country inequality reduction in Western nations like the United States or the United Kingdom, or regions like the EU, miss much of the point.

A second observation is that global governance, while much criticized, does exist. Actually existing global governance falls short of a world state, but represents something more than an arena dominated by the national pursuit of self-interest. Co-operation in multi-level governance occurs in part because some problems, such as warfare, financial stability, environmental sustainability, and global inequality and injustice, are too large for individual nations by themselves to resolve. The global polity that we have therefore reflects a willingness of national governments and corporate interests to co-operate with one another in pursuit of individual and shared aims. It also reflects the influence of social movements and civil society organizations on the agenda of international organizations in areas such as global justice, inequality and human rights, and in the monitoring and combating of practices like sweatshop wage rates in poor countries, sexual violence against women, and racial or ethnic abuse and discrimination. The UN Millennium Development Goals (MDG) represent an aspirational achievement of this global polity of organizations, networks, and activists, as well as a yardstick against which policies may be evaluated and processes of implementation assessed. Yet, the MDGs also have shortcomings, as I argued earlier, one of which is the predominant focus on poverty rather than inequality.

Future strategy is not then a simple matter of replacing the Washington consensus with Millennium Development Goals as they currently stand. Certainly the social focus of the MDG, now incorporated into the work of agencies like the World Bank, is a better general approach than the economism of the Washington consensus. Incomes matter to reducing social inequality, but so do health, education, and a reduction of violence and discrimination, none of which follow necessarily from purely market-centred processes. Rich countries, including their governments, corporations, and citizens, would however need to take far more radical initiatives in terms of their relations with the rest of the world if between-country inequality is to be radically reduced. This is not simply a matter of what policies individual countries take, but also and more importantly how global arrangements and policies are organized.

If the Washington consensus built around economic deregulation and liberalization in pursuit of economic growth is no longer adequate, how should a new order founded on human development best be organized? And how will the architecture of a new order address between-country as well as within-country inequalities? What new forms of global governance are emerging and how best can nation states play a productive role within them? What has been achieved so far and what is lacking? How far can social-democratic perspectives on inequality-reduction be transposed from a national or regional framework to a global one, and what new institutions and policies would be required?

These are very big questions that will be pursued across the remainder of the chapter. Discussion here begins with global governance and then moves on to national and local-level initiatives. This approach combines a sense of macro and micro-level approaches and possible connections between them.

Transforming and Reforming Global Governance

The multiple forms of inequality discussed in this study do not map neatly onto individual nation states, but criss-cross national borders in very complex ways (Walby 2009, 444). The challenges involved here involve policy as well as social theory. This point may be deepened by looking at two dimensions of globalization. The first is the cross-border mobility of capital as it affects taxation and the scope for global redistribution of resources. The second involves income differences between rich and poor countries, pressures towards global migration from poor to rich, and the politics of immigration.

Mobility of capital, taxation, and global resource redistribution

Wealth generation takes place globally, but taxation is organized on a national basis. This contrast in scales is fundamental to global inequality, because the resources necessary to make serious inroads into inequality are currently not available for global redistribution. This is partly because private economic interests seek to minimize the payment of tax through a variety of transfers across borders seeking out low-tax or no-tax regimes in which to hold funds and declare profits from worldwide activities. Tax havens, as analysed by Palan, Murphy, and Chavagneux (2010) are not a marginal feature of the global economy, but integral to the operation of corporations, banks, hedge funds, and capital markets. They calculate that about 50% of international bank lending and 30% of the world' stock of foreign direct investment is registered in jurisdictions like the Cayman Islands, Bermuda, or Jersey (5–6). Tax havens are then intrinsic to global inequality, since they skew the benefits of globalization towards the rich and away from most others.

The limited availability of fiscal resources for redistribution is also partly because states feel themselves to be in a weak bargaining position vis-à-vis corporations who have the choice where to locate investment that creates jobs and taxation revenues for governments. Governments therefore offer tax concessions and tax holidays in order to attract inward investment. These two processes reduce the fiscal buoyancy of nation states and their fiscal capacity to target social inequality. This in turn undermines the viability of what might be called social-democratic forms of global governance.

Flows of global capital and finance to the value of five trillions of US$ circulate around the globe each day, but are not taxed as such. The disjunction between global wealth-generation and national fiscal policy-making also exists because of a failure of neo-liberal global governance both in terms of institutional architecture and policy. The failure, discussed throughout this book, is one of excessive market autonomy from social and political development. This in turn reflects a separation between policy-making designed to support market liberalization and the free movement of capital and trade, and policy-making designed to support human development in its fullest sense, and attuned to democratic aspirations for social change.

The underlying presumption behind neo-liberal strategies is that market liberalization will create the economic expansion and wealth-generation capable of making serious inroads into economic deprivation. Market liberalization could help enable poverty reduction, but it is left to nation states to fix levels of taxation and determine the scope of redistribution of income. What the Washington consensus approach never claimed to be was a framework for the reduction of global inequality per se.

The gradual erosion of confidence in this approach over the last 20 years is manifest in recent shifts within the policy priorities of the World Bank, away from market liberalization as the predominant route to improvements in global welfare. The Bank, financed by loans from the capital market, is now more explicitly focussed on human development goals, issues of educational disadvantage, and gender inequalities, than it was 20 or 30 years ago (Beneria 2012, Mills 2012). It is also more attuned to addressing the democratic deficit identified by many critics as a disabling feature of the earlier epoch of Washington consensus policy-making. This has resulted in far closer relations with non-government organizations and a broader more deliberative style of operation capable of including multiple voices. However the remit of the Bank does not extend to global finance and issues of taxation, which are dealt with by other institutions including central banks organized through the Bank for International Settlements, and the Organization for Economic Co-operation and Development.

New thinking on the need for ways of mobilizing fiscal resources for purposes of global development and inequality reduction have arisen not from the institutions of global governance, which only have a limited potential for self-generated reform. It has emerged rather from wider debates on the idea of a tax on global financial transactions, often referred to as a Tobin Tax after the economist James Tobin. Tobin's original argument had nothing directly to do with global inequality. It was directed rather at limiting speculative cross-border financial movements made possible from the 1970s onwards in the new deregulated system of fluctuating exchange rates. The tax was then designed to help stabilize exchange-rates, but received criticism as being unworkable largely because it required multilateral agreement from all parties to be effective.

An entirely different version of the idea of a tax on global financial transactions emerged in the context of the Asian financial crisis of 1997–1998, and has gathered momentum ever since, fuelled most recently by the global financial crisis of 2008–2012 (Brock 2011). This transformed Tobin's idea from a policy to achieve foreign exchange stability into a policy for global social justice, a way of raising money to finance human development. This thinking emerged not from 'above' via the institutions of global governance, but from 'below' via social movement based critics of globalization. Some kind of transactions tax nonetheless gained support not merely from NGOs like United Kingdom-based Stamp Out Poverty, but also from previous supporters of economic globalization. These included Larry Summers (Summers and Summers 1989) and George Soros (2002), reflecting disillusionment with the failings of the Washington consensus. Some see the tax as best operated by the United Nations as a way of encouraging multilateral participation. In the meantime, 11 countries within the EU are currently considering a financial transactions tax. Most business interests remain hostile, as do key governments such as the United Kingdom.

The example of a global financial transactions tax is instructive for what it reveals about failings in the architecture and policies of neo-liberal global governance in mobilizing resources for global inequality-reduction. It is also instructive in showing how a fertile climate of ideas exists in how to reform the global economy in ways that might assist in the reduction of between-country as well as within-country inequality. Global tax policy to address issues of 'tax escape' (Brock 2011, 6–7) or avoidance and evasion is a key emergent feature of this new climate. There are in other words alternatives to the status quo, able to offer alternatives to single-shot one-dimensional policies of neo-liberalism, anti-globalization, and anti-capitalism. Having said this, it is also clear that a global financial transactions tax, even if it could be implemented, would only provide financial means to address inequality. It would not by itself be sufficient to address inequalities based on gender and race, or deal with multiple political sources of inequality connected with authoritarianism and obstacles to democratic participation.

Global migration and the politics of immigration control

One of the main obstacles in the way to making radical inroads into global inequality is the collective self-interest of wealthier countries. This involves both powerful economic interests and ordinary citizens. While the former oppose taxes on global transactions while often being supportive of more immigration, the latter fear that increased immigration from poor to wealthier countries will drive down wages and increase unemployment in richer countries. The net effect is to sharply limit the political agenda in richer countries to less radical measures directed more at global poverty reduction than redistribution of wealth to lessen global inequality per se.

The political rhetoric of rich-country self-interest involves a range of additional arguments against radical action. One is that poor countries are often highly unequal themselves, which is true, and thus should put their own houses in order first. One way of doing this would be to raise labour standards in poorer countries perhaps linking the WTO trade regime with labour issues. The linking of trade and labour standards may seem a progressive measure to reduce inequality, but has been rejected by leading developing countries like Brazil and India, who fear it would reduce employment and worsen inequality (Anuradha and Dutta, nd). They face the dilemma that increased standards mandated in this way would simply mean a move of work to lower-cost producers, encouraging rather than preventing a 'race-to-the-bottom'.

A second connected argument is that the governments of many poor countries are also corrupt, which is also true, which means that economic transfers without domestic institutional changes towards greater democracy are likely to be wasted rather than reaching their intended target. These arguments help to undercut any rich country momentum towards more radical policy approaches. They also draw a convenient veil over rich-country corruption.

The issue of global migration as a potential means of global inequality reduction will not however go away. Rodrik (2011, 266) argues that 'Even a minor liberalization of the advanced countries' restrictions on the use of foreign workers would produce a large impact on global incomes'. The minor liberalization he has in mind is a revolving temporary work visa scheme that would expand rich country workforces by 3%, without rights to permanent settlement. This would distribute income to some of the poorest members of the global population instantly. The Indian Government, while opposing WTO-mandated labour standards, has called for richer countries to reduce immigration controls and increase the immigrant intake. This issue, like many others is deadlocked within the structures of global governance, arising from perceived conflicts of interest between rich countries and poor ones.

Meanwhile many hundreds of thousands of individuals, families, and groups in poor countries and regions embark on very dangerous and sometimes fatal attempts at illegal immigration. The weight of both legal and illegal immigration pressures has tightened immigration controls in Europe, North America, and Australia, associated with increasingly hostile public opinion towards immigration and immigrants. While opposition to immigration may include racial aspects, much opposition is based on arguments that inflows of migrants depress wages.

Whether and how far this particular effect is really the case is however open to dispute. The World Bank (2006) calculated that rich-country wages would decline by only one half of 1% under a programme of immigrant labour market expansion. Other economists have recently produced similar calculations showing either a small negative or small positive effect of immigration on native-born wages (Ottaviano and Peri 2008, Manacorda, Manning, and Wadsworth 2012). Such calculations may well have a rational basis, but they are unlikely to shift the perceptions of electorates and politicians in richer countries, especially under prevailing conditions of economic insecurity arising from the Global Financial Crisis. Once again a radical policy initiative that might well be effective in reducing economic inequality is politically unacceptable.

If there is to be little if any movement towards the two major policy prescriptions discussed earlier, then the question arises as to whether any major progress in global inequality reduction at the level of global governance, is feasible.

Is Transformation of Global Governance Possible?

Several models of global governance are clearly discredited. These include the idea of a world state able to take global action, transcending national interests in the process. This has never actually been tried because it is seen as thoroughly unrealistic, and looks like it never will be. Two interconnected models that have been tried are the neo-liberal Washington consensus and an elite-based model of top-down political, economic, and legal change, associated with international institutions around the UN dominated by collections of nation states.

The former, as we have seen repeatedly in this book, has failed to secure reductions in between-country inequalities, as well as failing to secure sustainable development of poorer countries. The latter has had some successes in multilateral progress towards improvements in health and education in many poorer nations. It has also helped to institutionalize global norms like human rights and environmental sustainability. Yet it is widely criticized for its lack of democratic accountability and transparency. The European Union, an evolving form of cross-national governance, has had a rather mixed impact on regional inequality (Petrakos 2008), but this is partly an effect of new poorer nations joining since 2004, rather than a policy failure. In any case the EU has been projected as an important step towards cosmopolitan governance and cosmopolitan democracy (Held 1995, Beck and Grande 2007). Yet it has also been criticized for elite-based political deliberation with weak democratic input, while national conflicts over policy-making remain endemic.

Does this mean then that global governance of any kind is impossible, and that attention should revert simply to policy initiatives from nation states, corporations, and civil society organizations? Is global modernity to be restricted to economic and cultural relations, while politics will remain profoundly national in scope?

It might sometimes seem so. However there remains a complex though often disjointed set of institutions and social movements that operate across borders, and which constitute an imperfect, but nonetheless significant arena for global governance. Nothing stands still. It remains possible to learn from previous failures, as the World Bank has done in the emerging post-Washington consensus world. Failed institutions can be redesigned and rebuilt. Nation states, corporations, and social movements all have reasons to co-operate across national boundaries in an epoch when so many problems, from the economic development and financial crisis, to social inequality and environmental crisis are global in scope.

One way of analysing the current dislocations and challenges facing global governance is through Rodrik's conception of a trilemma at the heart of global policy-making (2011, 200–201). We are used to the idea of dilemmas, where two desirable objectives such as efficiency and equality often appear to stand in each other's way. In Rodrik's trilemma, there are three elements involved, namely global markets, nation states, and democracy. His argument is that it is not possible to have all three of these simultaneously.

Global markets can be combined with nation states, as is currently the case, but with a huge democratic deficit. Such arrangements are typically elite-based and top-down in form, with economic globalization able to outflank democratic accountability in a way that is remote from popular concerns and protests.

Alternatively it is possible to roll-back economic globalization, as in the 1930's, combining nation states with a more responsive democratic politics, but at the cost of reduced economic dynamism and pressure on living standards. Of course economic nationalism at that time was equally compatible with fascism and Stalinism, destroying economic institutions. There is therefore no necessary linkage with greater democracy or strategies for inequality reduction.

The option of combining global markets with greater democracy leaving nation states on the margins has not been pursued very far and may not be feasible for two reasons. First nation states and political parties would have to give up the ideal of national sovereignty. Second, markets and democracy run according to different logics. Free markets run on minimal regulation according to very rapid forms of economic adjustment through price mechanisms, whereas democracy works on a far slower deliberative time frame. This mismatch might be resolved if democracy set and monitored the rules of global trade, but the absence of any successful model of global democratic governance makes this option seem difficult.

Cohen and Sabel (2005) offer one way of making progress in this direction through the notion of global accountability. This is directed not at the traditional idea of a nationally bounded citizenry, but at a global public who may have little clear idea of what lies behind global problems and crises. The obligation therefore falls on global regulators to explain what is going one, and to encourage wider global deliberation. It is hard, nonetheless, to see such top-down initiatives operating successfully without input from below. Another option involves forms of corporate social responsibility in which corporations talk with NGOs to try to meet concerns about adverse effects of corporate activity, such as abusive work conditions in poor countries or lack of equal opportunity. The scope of such activities is however limited by profound inequalities of power, and NGO criticisms are likely to be more effective in broader campaigns that seek to mobilize public opinion.

Rodrik's trilemma enhances sociological accounts of variation within modernity, which focus on different ways in which globalization, national political autonomy, and democracy have been balanced. China, as repeatedly noted in this study, combines strong forms of state intervention with global market involvement, but at the cost of internal democratic representation and significant internal inequality. Neo-liberal states like the United States, by contrast, operate with a stronger emphasis on market forces to the detriment both of state regulation and full deliberative democracy. It would be remiss to play down the significance of representative democracy and its impact on greater equal opportunity within the United States. However, its high level of internal inequality suggests that it has only fully managed one of the three policy objectives in Rodrik's trilemma, with both national sovereignty and internal democracy compromised by free market dominance.

This judgement makes a great deal of sense if we consider the domestic impact of the Global Financial Crisis on the United States. Here Wall Street and Big Business were rescued financially by taxpayers and citizens, whose economic fortunes had already been adversely affected by rising unemployment, mortgage repossession, and falling pensions.

Rodrik remains sceptical that the trilemma can be resolved without the involvement of nation states as key players. What is even more important is greater regulation of economic globalization, bringing it into greater harmony with both the nation state and democracy. He is not however convinced that the EU demonstrates a successful balance between the three, largely because of the EU's own democracy deficit and the fragmentation of EU policy-making into different and conflicting national interests during crises.

What he doesn't look further into, at this point, is the contrast between social-democratic and neo-liberal options in resolving the trilemma and thereby tackling global inequality in a rather different manner. Instead he lays down a set of very general propositions that should inform policy-making in a post-trilemma context. These include the following (Rodrik 2011, 237–247):

- markets must be deeply embedded in systems of governance
- there is no one way to prosperity
- countries have the right to protect their own social arrangements, and institutions
- countries do not have the right to impose their institutions on others
- the purpose of international economic arrangements must be to lay down the traffic rules for managing the interface among national institutions

This list deserves further evaluation. First, the Washington consensus governance is clearly dead. Second Rodrik doesn't quite know where to go next, except to reaffirm national sovereignty in the face of global capitalism. It is nation states who have rights in this vision, not citizens. Nor is there any explicit recognition of normative or cultural conflicts and their role in reconstructing globalization. The bland phrase 'traffic rules' remains in their place suggesting a merely technocratic regulation of economic life. Meanwhile countries that practise cultural authoritarianism of a racial or religious kind to the detriment of social inequality would in this scenario be left free of pressure to change. This is the point at which an economistic approach to global reconstruction runs out of steam, and the point where broader and deeper sociological considerations become relevant.

Neo-liberal Versus Social-Democratic Policy and the Reduction of Global Inequality: A Sociological Perspective on Policies to Reduce Global Inequality

Sociologists do not speak with one voice, and have devoted more effort to theorizing globalization and changing social structures than to policy analysis directly relevant to global inequality reduction. The sociological critique of neo-liberalism and political economy outlined in Chapter 2 is crucial to the approach taken in this book. Theory matters a great deal in any attempt to understand social life and to work out how different policy objectives might be realized. It is however comparatively rare to find work that links theory and practice in an explicit manner, able to engage with policy debates, policies, and campaigns.

Beck's prominent work on a cosmopolitan approach to social inequality has been reviewed earlier. It has undoubted merits, not least in demonstrating that cosmopolitan co-operation across boundaries is both an emergent feature of social change and a fruitful utopia capable of inspiring political action. Yet it remains very generalized and aspirational, and is often hard to connect in any direct way with the complex multi-level world of policy-making and political action that we have encountered in this book. A more impressive and wide-ranging contribution is to be found in Walby's major study *Globalization and Inequalities* (2009).

Walby's situates global inequalities within a reworked understanding of the complexities of modernity in an epoch of globalization. Complexity, as we have seen earlier, is concerned with multidimensional aspects of inequality and difference across the whole of life, including gender and ethnicity, as well as class. Violence and the struggle to be free from coercion and insecurities associated with it, is an integral part of the challenges of addressing global inequalities in income, health, and political inclusion (Wilkinson 2004, Yodanis 2004). The effects of violence alongside other inequalities of power play out in relation to struggles over income and labour standards, access to health and education, and freedom from patriarchal, racial, and ethnic inequality.

From this broader sociological perspective, the response to global inequalities involves a far wider canvas than that elaborated by Rodrik. He rightly focusses on reform of global governance, economic policy reconstruction, and stronger norms of political accountability. But sociologists like Walby and Beck also focus on human rights and on a more radical deepening of democracy in ways that are gender-inclusive, which engage with cultural difference, and which also integrate environmental processes into an understanding of global inequalities. In this way, economic, social, and environmental policy issues are linked together. In so doing, a far more prominent place is given to initiatives in civil society for global inequality reduction.

Rather than treating civil society as 'noises off stage', and merely contextual to the grand games of elite-based governance, this current of thought places this sector closer to the heart of reform. Walby's reworked conception of contemporary democracy has multiple institutions and actors within it. These include states, but also 'nations, organised religions, hegemons [by which she means geopolitical entities with disproportionate amounts of power such as the United States], and global institutions' (157). Civil society, meanwhile, serves an additional layer in the global polity, both in the familiar sense of largely localized movements operating from below, and through what are termed 'waves' of action on a regional or global scale (233–249).

Major examples include the Reformation, 19th-century Socialism, Nationalism, and several episodes of Feminism, as well as Environmentalism, and contemporary Fundamentalism. Such waves are associated with tipping-points in social change when developmental pathways may be transformed or shifted into different trajectories. Clearly the examples cited point in many contrasting directions from war and conflict to social cohesion and peace. They also indicate the contested nature of political and cultural debate about the desirability of democracy and various goals of greater equality.

The future, as Walby expressly argues in her conclusion is highly contested, not only because civil society is internally divided, or because nation states have conflicting interests, but also because the United States, the EU, and China aim at differing kinds of hegemonic power (433–435). Instead of the aura of confidence in progress towards greater global equality which surrounds many of the publications of international institutions around the UN, Walby sounds a more muted and cautious tone.

Where then are the shifting developmental pathways beyond the failed neo-liberal Washington consensus. What potential is there for a renewed social democracy in addressing global inequalities? And how far should general theories of the optimal strategies and policies be informed by a pragmatic focus on what works?

The Reworking of Social Democracy and Future Social Change

Conflicts between economic liberalism and socialism or social-democracy have a long history starting in the 19th century, pre-dating contemporary policy conflicts between neo-liberalism and social-democracy. Both sides of this debate have evolved over time, and in this sense represent moving targets. Neither can be dismissed simply by reference to older arguments, both need to be reassessed anew as they evolve (Sandbrook et al. 2007).

Changes in economic liberalism in the last 50 years have brought themes like property rights, risk and uncertainty, and the functioning of institutions closer to the heart of economic theory. Liberal economists are also divided on broad policy strategies, stretching from free marketeers following in the footsteps of Milton Friedman on the one side to radicals like Amartya Sen, on the other. Disagreement and dissent among economists has not however undermined a widely held utopian faith in unregulated markets as the best method of improving human freedom, welfare, and by implication inequality.

Social-democracy in its broadest sense has evolved too, partly by moving the analysis of social inequality beyond class and industrial relations, to wider forms of social inequality, and partly by grappling with problems of cultural difference and what they mean for democracy. It has its own variants of utopianism, notably the belief that a sense of social responsibility embedded in enlightened public policy can triumph over economic self-interest.

The presence of utopian underpinnings in these two conflicting approaches probably explains why both neo-liberalism and social-democracy are so resilient. Egregious market failure during the Global Financial Crisis has not diminished the élan of free marketeers, nor have sovereign debt crises and regulatory failures undermined social-democratic visions of a better world. Walby sees neo-liberalism and social-democracy as two variants of modernity (278ff). While economic globalization is a powerful social force, it has neither destroyed the nation state, nor led to the convergence of national institutions and policies around a common set of economic, political, and cultural arrangements. Emphasizing the importance of historical pathways from past to present, Walby argues that variations between neo-liberal nation states like the United States and social-democratic ones like Sweden and the Nordic countries may be explained in forms of path-dependency that have not been offset by globalization. Such contrasts persist because 'the form and institutions of the state can be deeply sedimented and have effects long after the moment at which the form of institutions was forged' (263).

In common with a wider body of research, Walby maintains that neo-liberal nations have higher levels of within-country inequality than social-democratic ones. They also tend to be more violent (396–408), and this correlates with a shallower penetration of democratic processes across society. Democratic deepening means more than universal suffrage or the abolition of barriers that restrict access to political participation for particular social group, vital though they are. It also involves the application of democratic processes across all institutions, including institutions of welfare as much as political decision-making or industrial relations. The greater its democratic depth, the more likely a country is to institute class and gender based public expenditure. Walby also argues that 'employed women' who have become increasingly unionized represent 'new champions' for social democracy (413–415). They also support a range of public services such as child care. A strong body of evidence suggests employed women are more left-leaning than other women both in Europe and the United States providing electoral support for social-democracy and policies targeting gender inequality.

But where does social-democratic policy-making of a national kind, leave issues of *global* inequality reduction?

In the first place, it is directed more to within-country than between-country inequality. In this sense it contributes to a lessening of global inequality only inasmuch as it reduces inequality within specific countries. Secondly, it has the merit of taking a broader approach to multiple inequalities, that are not addressed directly simply by reference to economic and income inequality. Third it depends rather more on national rather than global initiatives. Global actions enter the picture, at best indirectly, inasmuch as UN bodies monitor levels of inequality and set norms for change such as the Millennium Development Goals. Fourth, social-democracy is not explicitly present at a global level, in spite of the edifice of successive Socialist Internationals, with global aspirations inherited from the 19th century (Colas 1994). The discursive framework that operates across global institutions refers rather to 'Human Development' an ideal that has non-Western as well as Western origins. 'Human Development' is also not 'Social-Democracy' by another name, in that a number of Asian and African nations find Western notions of democracy problematic. How far such reservations will be swept away by new waves of civil society activism across the Middle East and other regions is yet to be determined.

A neglected feature of discussions of social-democracy is the failure to consider initiatives in poorer countries within the global South. This is addressed in the important volume *Social Democracy in the Global Periphery* (Sandbrook et al. 2007). This examines policy initiatives in Costa Rica, Chile, Mauritius, and the Indian state of Kerala since 1990. The argument is that small countries can take significant steps towards greater equality and more successful development. Potential obstacles such as vested economic interests at home, political corruption, and the external pressures of globalization and international bodies like the IMF and World Bank are not insignificant. They can however be partly overcome or at least muted in their influence.

The key institution here is a democratic developmental state, backed by political support from a range of urban and rural groups, and often drawing on historic traditions of social democracy. The main structural precondition here, in their view, has been sufficient prior integration into the global economy to dissolve the semi-feudal dominance of older landed elites, and some degree of effective state organization. The political strategies that have emerged since 1990 aim not at an immediate transition from capitalism to socialism, but a more flexible relationship between global markets and pro-active peripheral state policies committed to democracy and a reduction in social inequality. Such policies include accessible education, health and sanitation, progressive taxation, targeted social programmes, labour-market regulation, and in some cases land reform (25–26, 234). Successes are measurable in terms of improved literacy, lower infant mortality rates, and higher life expectancy, together with enhanced forms of democratic participation (see also Drèze and Sen 2002).

This argument has good empirical support. There are indeed potential social-democratic pathways to global inequality reduction within the global South. This strategy nonetheless requires to be alert to potential problems of internal corruption and external constraints on state fiscal policies arising from global debt markets.

Beyond General Policy Strategies: Pragmatism and Implementation

One of the interesting findings of research into patterns of inequality is that countries at very similar levels of development may exhibit rather different levels of inequality. Why then do some do better than others in relation to reducing inequality? We have seen in chapters 3, 4, and 5 that many of these variations have to do with historical legacies and path dependencies. Yet contemporary processes and policies are clearly also relevant. And beyond policy-making itself, there are many further issues about the implementation of measures that address inequality, whether these originate in public policy initiatives or from other social origins outside government.

From a pragmatic perspective, it is often asked 'What works and what doesn't?' This question arises in part from the observation that progress towards inequality reduction is more successful in some countries, regions, and places than others (see Chapter 5). Why should similar policy initiatives have a variable impact? What factors affect implementation in different context, and what role do civil society initiatives on a cross-border and local level play here?

Much discussion of these questions has been directed at global inequalities in health and how these may be better overcome. A significant example is provided by the What Works Working Group – a network of public health professionals, academics, and administrators associated with the Centre for Global Development think-tank in Washington, DC. This expert group has produced in-depth case-studies of national, regional, and global initiatives that produce measurable improvements to health over a significant period of time (Levine, What Works Working Group, and Kinder 2004, Levine and What Works Working Group 2007). This work is based on World Health Organization's findings that income growth between 1952 and 1992 explains less than half global health improvement in poorer countries (WHO 1999). So what does work and why?

The WHO study focussed on technological innovation and diffusion, including new drug vaccines, and nutritional supplements, as well as the spread of health-related knowledge. Levine and The What Works Working Group, however, argue that technological innovation only works when there is an effective system to deliver new health products at an affordable price (2007, xxix). This in turn depends on mobilizing political leadership in developing countries, good management on the ground, NGO involvement as 'watchdogs and advocates' for improvements in services, and community participation, including village level volunteers to distribute health products and raise public awareness. Through a combination of these elements, success is possible even in the very poorest settings in Africa and Asia.

These arguments are based on clear empirical evidence that often challenges stereotypes about how to lessen global inequality. Governments in poor countries, for example, can and have made a difference, contrary to sweeping diagnoses of inefficiency and corruption. In Sri Lanka, maternal mortality has halved every 12 years since 1935 through services designed and delivered within the health system (41–48). Meanwhile in South America, health ministry co-operation across boundaries helped to diminish the impact of Chagas disease (89–96). The stereotypical assumption that the only successful campaigns have been those that are highly centralized is also misleading. Thus in many cases communities play an active role in programme success. Examples here include local community distribution of ivermectin treatments for river blindness across central and eastern Africa (49–56), or village grandmother distribution of nutrition supplements in Nepal (25–32).

The positive arguments here are not meant to imply that steady progress is being made in reducing all health inequalities. The implication is rather than some health inequalities are being successfully addressed, and most importantly that general macro-level policy prescriptions are not enough. There may indeed be no general policy mix that would work in all contexts. What may be needed instead is a middle-range approach able to recognize that success comes in all shapes, and must be attuned to the specificities of political and cultural context for programme delivery.

This contrasts with the general economic and development policy approaches associated with the Washington consensus. It also contrasts with the idea that development aid on a massive scale will necessarily produce positive results. Funding matters, but what is critical is not so much its scale as its predictability and cost-effectiveness. Finally the middle-range pragmatic approach in areas like health, elaborates the practical merits of a human development perspective on global inequality reduction. This is done by linking broader social and cultural as well as economic conceptions of human welfare with context-specific implementation. Improving public health has the capacity to bring a wide range of benefits including wider social and community participation as well as greater economic potential for those able to leave fuller lives (Drèze and Sen 2002, 39–40).

Yet pragmatism and middle level approaches have their limits. The successful initiatives described in the work of Levine and the What Works Group depend in part on the capacity and willingness of national political institutions to take effective action, backed up by a very mixed coalition of supportive agents of change. Successes in controlling the extremely debilitating river blindness disease (onchocerchiasis) in sub-Saharan Africa, for example, relied on a long-term coalition of 19 African governments, the World Bank, UN Development Programme, and Food and Agriculture Organization, 21 international donors, over 30 NGO's, the Merck pharmaceutical corporation, and, last but not least, the participation of 80,000 rural communities, co-ordinated through the African Programme for Onchocerchiasis Control (Levine and What Works Working Group 2007, xxvii). Coalitions like this, based on political authority, expert knowledge, and human and financial resources, are hard to build and very hard to sustain.

One of the key variables in all of this is political willingness to act, whether in health, education, or in relation to gender and racial inequalities. Nearly 20 years ago, Drèze and Sen (2002) took stock of cross-national variations in economic and human development across the developing world and their implications for inequalities in human freedom. Political willingness to act partly explains why China had done more than India in economic development and literacy improvement, or why different states of India varied in terms of inequality reduction. This does not mean that the drive of political institutions will be sufficient to create successful policies and programmes to reduce inequality. Nonetheless political action, drawing on civil society as well as the state, does seem to represent a necessary feature of inequality reduction processes whether in developing or more developed countries. This judgement is confirmed in work on reducing violence against women, and enhancing greater gender equality (Walby 408).

Drèze and Sen (2002) also emphasize that comparisons across developing countries are crucial in making progress towards enhanced human development goals. This position contrasts with the Western-centred approaches emanating from Europe and North America in which poorer countries are advised they must adopt Western pathways to modernity if they are to prosper and enhance human welfare. For Drèze and Sen there is also much that developing countries can learn from each other. This in turn points to an eastward shift in contemporary patterns of global influence away from an exclusive western focus.

Conclusion

It is hard to summarize a chapter on development aid and policy recommendations without resorting to ideological preferences or truisms. The arena of debate on global inequality reduction is full of conflicts over objectives, policy recommendations, and how best to implement and evaluate change. There remains a highly uncertain and unfinished quality to debates arising from the erosion of the Washington consensus. There are also difficulties in applying social democratic, cosmopolitan or environmental perspectives in a globalizing world, in which nation states representing sectional interests remain key institutions.

Underlying social conflicts over class, gender, race, and ethnicity, continue to matter a great deal to the perpetuation of global inequality, but such conflicts play out in relations between nations as well as within them. There is no escape then from thinking globally about inequality, however much practical action demands effective national and local action. Global governance, however it is organized, will continue to rely on regional and national institutions, and these in turn depend on civil society as much as markets or states, to achieve effective change. There is then an irreducible dialogue between global and local in processes and policies that aim to reduce global inequality, an insight that stems theoretically from work on globalization, developed originally by Roland Robertson (1992) and elaborated further in Holton (2005, 2009).

This book draws on the work of scholars working in economics and history, as well as sociology, and is founded on a strongly interdisciplinary approach to understanding social life. Economists have played a key role in understanding what causes or hinders economic growth and how incomes are distributed through markets regulated through different policy regimes. Nonetheless economic growth is insufficient by itself as a basis for political strategies directed at reduction of inequality, in spite of the relevance of income to so many aspects of social life and human welfare. The alternative conception of human development, developed by a range of social scientists, is a broader and more satisfactory way of thinking about social, political and cultural aspects of inequality and ways of thinking about how inequality might be reduced. This is where sociology plays a more explicit role, both in relation to the familiar issues of class, gender, race, and ethnicity, and in relation to the study of globalization and modernity.

History also matters too, because globalization and global inequality have a long history, and because particular historical legacies contribute to current patterns of inequality. The idea of path-dependency is crucial to any understanding of why social inequality varies between nations. But it is also relevant to policy, in that national and regional histories affect the evolution of policy-making including the issues to which governments give most priority. This applies both to the economic policies that reflect the agrarian, industrial, and service sectors of national economies, and to the influence of religious and secular ideologies as they affect concerns for, individualism and community.

From this rich and complex set of issues it is possible to distil a limited set of general recommendations and observations, similar to that provided by Rodrik. These represent the final concluding thoughts of this study, drawn from the multidisciplinary perspectives developed throughout this book. They may be listed as follows (Table 7.4):

Table 7.4 Recommendations and observations for reducing global inequality

1. Reduction of global inequality requires social, political and cultural change, not simply policies that aim to foster economic growth.
2. Markets need to be intelligently regulated to embody human development objectives without destroying economic innovation.
3. A global financial transactions tax would enable rich country resources to be made available for inequality reduction in poorer countries. Further regulation of tax havens is required to alleviate the fiscal crisis of state finances.
4. Without some reduction in the power and influence of richer countries over processes of immigration, it will be very difficult to make rapid inroads into global inequality. Rich country immigration controls should be relaxed.
5. The widest possible social and political participation in social development is crucial to the legitimacy and effectiveness of inequality reduction, and this inevitably challenges vested interests and cultures of violence.
6. Policy conflicts are inevitable in a modern world in which individualism, egalitarianism, and democracy are simultaneously present. Nonetheless global inequality and environmental sustainability, require political actors to think big and think long term if global inequality is to be reduced in the midst of instabilities and uncertainties associated with climate change.

Bibliography

Agyeman, J. and Carmin, J-A. (2011), 'Introduction: Environmental Injustice Beyond Borders' in Carmin, J-A. and Agyeman, J. (eds.), *Environmental Inequalities Beyond Borders: Local Perspectives on Global Injustices*, Cambridge, MA: MIT Press, 1–15.

Alderson, A. and Nielsen, F. (2002), 'Globalization and the Great U-turn: Income Inequality in 16 OECD Countries', *American Journal of Sociology*, 107, 1244–1299.

Anand, S. and Segal, P. (2008), 'What do we Know about Global Income Inequality', *Journal of Economic Literature*, 46(1), 57–94.

Anderson, E. (2005), 'Openness and Inequality in Developing Countries: A Review of Theory and Recent Evidence', *World Development*, 33(7), 1045–1063.

Anuradha, R. and Dutta, N. (nd), Trade and Labor under the WTO and FTA's, *Centre for WTO Studies*, at www.wtocentre.iift.ac.in/Papers/Trade20%Labor.pdf accessed 24 June 2013.

Appiah, K.A. (2006), *Cosmopolitanism. Ethics in a World of Strangers*, London: Penguin.

Arrighi, G. (1994), *The Long Twentieth Century: Money, Power, and the Origins of Our Times*, London: Verso.

Artis, E., Doobay, C. and Lyons, K. (2003), *Economic, Social and Cultural Rights for Dalits in India: Case Study on Primary Education in Gujarat*, Workshop on Human Rights, Woodrow Wilson Centre, Princeton University, 2003, at www.academia.edu/1914495 accessed 12 April 2013.

Arulamparam, W., Booth, A. and Bryan, M. (2006), 'Is There a Glass Ceiling Over Europe? Exploring the Gender Pay Gap Across the Wage Distribution', *ILR Review*, Cornell University, 60(2), 163–186.

Atkinson, A. (1970), 'On the Measurement of Inequality', *Journal of Economic Theory*, 2, 244–263.

Attewell, P., Kasinitz, P. and Dunn, K. (2010), 'Black Canadians and Black Americans: Racial Income Inequality in Comparative Perspective', *Ethnic and Racial Studies*, 33(3), 473–495.

Babb, S. (2005), 'The Social Consequences of Structural Adjustment: Recent Evidence and Current Debates', *Annual Review of Sociology*, 31, 199–222.

Babones, S. (2008), 'Income Inequality and Population Health: Correlation and Causality', *Social Science and Medicine*, 66, 1614–1626.

Babones, S. and Vonada, D. (2009), 'Trade Globalization and National Income Inequality – are they related?' *Journal of Sociology*, 45(5), 5–30.

Bahun-Radunović, S. and Rajan, V.G.J. (eds.) (2008), *Violence and Gender in the Globalized World*, Aldershot: Ashgate.

Balibar, E. and Wallerstein, I. (1991), *Race, Nation, and Class: Ambiguous Identities*, New York: Verso.

Banerjee, A. Bertrand, M., Datta, S. and Mullainathan, S. (2009), 'Labour Market Discrimination in Delhi: Evidence from a Field Experiment', *Journal of Comparative Economics*, 37(1), 14–27.

Bangura, Y. (2012), 'Combating Poverty in Africa', in Wilkinson, R. and Hulme, D. (eds.), *The Millennium Development Goals and Beyond*, London: Routledge, 192–208.

Baran, P. (1957), *The Political Economy of Growth*, New York: Monthly Review Press.

Barber, B. (1995), *Jihad versus McWorld*, New York: Ballantine.

Bastia, T. (2013), 'Migration and Inequality: An Introduction', in Bastia, T. (ed.), *Migration and Inequality*, Abingdon: Routledge, 3–23.

Bauer, P. (1972), *Dissent on Development*, Cambridge, MA: Harvard University Press.

Beck, U. (2000), *What is Globalization?*, Cambridge: Polity Press.

Beck, U. (2007), 'Beyond Class and Nation: Reframing Social Inequalities in a Globalizing World', *British Journal of Sociology*, 58(4), 679–705.

Beck, U. (2010), 'Re-mapping Social Inequalities in an Age of Climate Change: For a Cosmopolitan Renewal of Sociology', *Global Networks*, 10(2), 165–181.

Beck, U. and Grande, E. (2007), *Cosmopolitan Europe*, Cambridge: Polity Press.

Bell, M. (2009), *Racism and Equality in the European Union*, Oxford: Oxford University Press.

Bello, W. (2009), *The Food Wars*, London: Verso.

Beneria, L. (2012), 'The World Bank and Gender Equality', *Global Social Policy*, 12(2), 175–178.

Bennett, J. (2006), *History Matters: Patriarchy and the Challenge of Feminism*, Manchester: Manchester University Press.

Berman, A. and Shelton, C. (2001), Structural Adjustment and Health: A Literature Review of the Debate, Its Players, and Presented Evidence, Commission on Macroeconomics and Health (CMH), *CMH Working Paper* WG6:6, Geneva: Commission on Macroeconomics and Health.

Bernstein, S. (2011), 'Legitimacy in Inter-Governmental and Non-State Governance', *Review of International Political Economy*, 18(1), 17–51.

Beyer, H., Rojas, P. and Vergara, R. (1999), 'Trade Liberalization and Inequality', *Journal of Development Economics*, 59(1), 103–123.

Bhalla, S. (2002), *Imagine There's No Country: Poverty, Inequality and Growth in an Era of Globalization*, Washington, DC: Institute for International Economics.

Bihagen, E. and Ohls, M. (2006), 'The Glass Ceiling – Where is it? Women's and Men's Career Prospects in the Private vs Public Sector in Sweden, 1979–2000', *Sociological Review*, 54(1), 20–47.

Blau, P. and Duncan, O. (1967), *The American Occupational Structure*, New York: Wiley.

Borjas, G. (2003), 'The Labour Demand Curve is Downward-Sloping: Re-examining the Labour Market Impact of Immigration', *Quarterly Journal of Economics*, 118(4), 1335–1374.

Bourguignon, F. and Morrison, C. (2002), 'Inequality Among World Citizens: 1820–1992', *American Economic Review*, 92(4), 727–744.

Brady, D. and Denniston, R. (2006), 'Economic Globalization, Industrialization and Deindustrialization in Affluent Democracies', *Social Forces*, 85(1), 297–329.

Braithwaite, J. and Drahos, P. (2000), *Global Business Regulation*, Cambridge: Cambridge University Press.

Braudel, F. (1972), 'History and the Social Sciences', in Burke, P. (ed.), *Economy and Society in Early Modern Europe*, New York: Harper, 11–42.

Brock, G. (2011), 'Reforms to Global Taxation and Accounting Arrangements as a Means to Pursuing Social Justice', *Global Social Policy*, 11(1), 7–9.

Buchholz, S., Hofäcker, D., Mills, M., Blossfeld, H.-P., Kurz, K. and Hofmeister, H. (2009), 'Life Courses in the Globalization Process: The Development of Social Inequalities in Modern Societies', *European Sociological Review*, 25(1), 53–71.

Burch, E. and Ellanna, L. (1994), *Issues in Hunter Gatherer Research*, Oxford: Berg.

Burnside, C. and Dollar, D. (2004), 'Aid, Policies, and Growth: Revisiting the Evidence', *World Bank Policy Research Paper* O-2834, March.

Carmin, J-A. and Agyeman, J. (eds.) (2011), *Environmental Inequalities Beyond Borders: Local Perspectives on Global Injustices*, Cambridge, MA: MIT Press.

Cassen, R. (1994), *Does Aid Work?* Oxford: Clarendon Press.

Castells, M. (1996), *Network Society*, Oxford: Blackwell.

Castles, S. (2007), 'Can Migration Be an Instrument for Reducing Inequality?' paper delivered to the Metropolis Conference, Melbourne, October 2007, at www.imi.ox.ac.uk/pdfs/SC%20%plenary1%20Metropolis% accessed 13 April 2013.

Castles, S. and Miller, M. (1993), *The Age of Migration*, Basingstoke: Macmillan.

Center for Reproductive Rights, (2009), *The World's Abortion Laws*, at http://www.reproductiverights.org/sites/crr.civicactions.net/files/documents/pub_fac_abortionlaws2009_WEB.pdf accessed 21 March 2013.

Chakrabarti, A. (2000), 'Does Trade Cause Inequality', *Journal of Economic Development*, 25(2), 1–21.

Chase-Dunn, C. (1998), *Global Formation: Structures of the World Economy*, Lanham, MD: Rowman and Littlefield.

Chase-Dunn, C. and Lawrence, K. (2010), 'Alive and Well: A Response to Sanderson', *International Journal of Comparative Sociology*, 51, 470–480.

Chen, X. (ed.) (2009), *Shanghai Rising: State Power and Local Transformations in a Global Megacity*, Minneapolis: University of Minnesota Press.

Chiswick, B. and DebBurman, N. (2004), 'Educational Attainment: Analysis by Immigrant Generation', *Economics of Education Review*, 23(4), 361–379.

Clemens, M., Radelt, S., Bhavnani, R. and Bazzi, S. (2004 revised 2011), 'Counting Chickens When They Hatch: Timing and the Effects of Aid on Growth', Centre for Global Development, *Working Paper* 44. at http://www.cgdev.org/sites/default/files/2744_file_CountingChickensFINAL3.pdf. accessed 5 May 2014.

Clifford, J. (1992), 'Travelling Cultures', in Grossberg, L., Nelson, C. and Treichler, P. (eds.), *Cultural Studies*, London: Routledge, 96–116.

Cohen, J. and Sabel, C. (2005), 'Global Democracy', *International Law and Politics*, 37, 763–797.

Colas, A. (1994), 'Putting Cosmopolitanism into Practice: The Case of Socialist Internationalism', *Millennium: Journal of International Studies*, 23(3), 513–534.

Collins, D., Morduch, J., Rutherford, S. and Ruthven, O. (2009), *Portfolios of the Poor: How the Worlds Poor Live on $2 a Day*, Princeton: Princeton University Press.

Cooper, F. (2001), 'What is the Concept of Globalization Good For? An African Historians Perspective', *African Affairs*, 110, 189–213.

Cornia, G. (ed.) (2014), *Falling Inequality in Latin America*, Oxford: Oxford University Press.

Cornia, G., Addison,T. and Kiiski, S. (2003), 'Income Distribution Changes and their Impact in the Post World War Two Period', *UNU-Wider Discussion Papers* 2003/28.

Couch, K. and Daly, M. (2002), 'Black-White Wage Inequality in the 1990's: A Decade of Progress', *Economic Inquiry*, 40(1), 31–41.

Credit Suisse, (2012), *Global Wealth Report 2012*, Zurich: Credit Suisse Research Institute.

Darity, W. and Nembhard, J. (2000), 'Racial and Ethnic Inequality: The International Record', *American Economic Review*, 90(2), 308–311.

Das, M. (2013), *Exclusion and Discrimination in the Labour Market*, background paper for the World Development report. New York: World Bank.

Davies, J., Sandstrom, S., Shorrocks, A. and Wolff, E. (2008), *World Distribution of Household Wealth*, Discussion Paper 2008/03, Helsinki: UNU-WIDER.

Davies, J., Sandstrom, S., Shorrocks, A. and Wolff, E. (2011), 'The Level and Distribution of Global Household Wealth', *Economic Journal*, 121, 223–254.

Dawson, A. (2010), 'State Capacity and the Political Economy of Child Mortality in Developing Countries: From Fiscal Sociology Towards the Rule of Law', *International Journal of Comparative Sociology*, 51, 403–422.

Deaton, A. (2006), 'Global Patterns of Income and Health: Facts, Interpretations, Policies', National Bureau of Economic Research, Working Paper, 12735, at http://www.nber.org/papers/w12735HYPERLINK 'http://www.nber.org /papers/w12735" HYPERLINK "http://www.nber.org/papers/w12735' accessed 4 March 2013.

Delgado, R. and Stefancic, J. (2001), *Critical Race Theory: An Introduction*, New York: New York University Press.

Demissie, F. (2007), 'Imperial Legacies and Postcolonial Predicaments: An Introduction', *African Identities*, 5(2), 155–165.

Diamond, L. (1987), 'Issues in the Constitutional Design of the Third Nigerian Republic', *African Affairs*, 86(343), 209–226.

Dollar, D. (2007) 'Globalization, Poverty and Inequality since 1980', in Held, D. and Kaya, A. (eds.), *Global Inequality*, Cambridge: Polity Press, 73–103.

Dorius, S. and Firebaugh, G. (2010), 'Trends in Global Gender Inequality', *Social Forces*, 88(5), 1941–1968.

Drèze, J. and Sen, A. (2002), *India: Development and Participation*, second edition, Oxford: Oxford University Press.

Dubnow, S. (2000), *A History of the Jews in Russia and Poland*, Newhaven CT: Avotaynu.

Duclos, J-Y., Arrar, A. and Giles, J. (2010), 'Chronic and Transient Poverty: Measurement and Estimation, with Evidence from China', *Journal of Development Economics*, 91(2), 266–277.

Dustmann, C., Frattini, T. and Glitz, A. (2007), 'The Impact of Migration: A Review of the Economic Evidence', *Final Report*, Department of Economics, University College, London, at www.ucl.ac.uk/~ucdpb21/reports/WA_Final_Final.pdf accessed 3 April 2013.

Easterly, W. (2006), *The White Man's Burden: Why the West's Efforts to Help the Rest have Done So Much Ill and So Little Good*, New York: Penguin.

Eisenstadt, S. (1999), 'Multiple Modernities in an Age of Globalization', *Canadian Journal of Sociology*, 24(2), 283–295.

Eisenstadt, S. (2000), 'Multiple Modernities', *Daedalus*, 129(1), 1–29.

Elliott, J. (1999), 'Putting Global Cities in their place: urban hierarchy and low-income employment during the post-war era', *Urban Geography*, 20(12), 95–115.

Engerman, S. and Sokoloff, K. (2000), 'History Lessons: Institutions, Factor Endowments, and Paths of Development in the New World', *Journal of Economic Perspectives*, 14(3), 217–232.

Enloe, C. (1989), *Bananas, Beaches, and Bases: Making Feminist Sense of International Politics*, London: Pandora Press.

Epstein, C. (2007), 'Great Divides: The Cultural, Cognitive, and Social Bases of the Global Subordination of Women', *American Sociological Review*, 72(1), 1–22.

Epstein, G. (ed.) (2005), *Financialization and the World Economy*, Cheltenham: Elgar.

Esman, N. and Uphoff, M. (1984), *Local Organizations: Intermediaries in Rural Development*, Ithaca NY: Cornell University Press.

Esping-Andersen, G. (1990), *The Three Worlds of Welfare Capitalism*, Cambridge: Polity Press.

Esping-Andersen, G. (2007), 'More Inequality and Fewer Opportunities? Structural Determinant and Human Agency in the Dynamics of Income Distribution', in Held, D. and Kaya, A. (eds.), *Global Inequality*, Cambridge: Polity Press, 216–251.

European Commission, (2008), *Report on Equality between Women and Men*, at http:ec.europa.eu/employment_social/publications/2008/keaj08001_en.pdf accessed 14 August 2013.

Evans, P. and Rauch, J. (1999), 'Bureaucracy and Growth: A Cross-National Analysis of the Effects of "Weberian" State Structures on Economic Growth', *American Sociological Review*, 64(5), 748–765.

Ferraro, V. (2008), 'Dependency Theory: An Introduction', in Secondi, G. (ed.), *The Development Economics Reader*, London: Routledge, 58–64.

Food and Agriculture Organisation. (2011), *The State of Food and Agriculture 2010–11: Women in Agriculture: Closing the Gender Gap for Development*, Rome: FAO.

Food and Agricultural Organisation. (2013), *Hunger* [statistics from the 2012 Hunger Report] at www.fao.org/hunger/en accessed 13 February 2013.

Foucault, M. (1973), *The Birth of the Clinic*, New York: Pantheon Books.

Frank, A.G. (1971), *Capitalism and Under-Development in Latin America*, Harmondsworth: Penguin.

Frank, A.G. and Gills, B. (1993), *The World System: Five Hundred Years or Five Thousand*, London: Routledge.

Frederickson, G. (1981), *White Supremacy: A Comparative Study in American and South African History*, New York: Oxford University Press.

Frederickson, G. (2001), 'Race and Racism in Historical Perspective: Comparing the United States, South Africa, and Brazil', in Hamilton, C.V. (ed.), *Beyond Racism: Race and Inequality in Brazil, South Africa, and the United States*, London: Lynne Reinner Publishers, 1–27.

Fryer, R. (2010), 'Racial Inequality in the 21st century: The Declining Significance of Discrimination', National Bureau of Economic Research, *Working Papers*: 16256.

Gaiha, R. and Deolaiker, A. (1993), 'Persistent, Expected and Innate Poverty: Estimates for Semi arid Rural South India, *Cambridge Journal of Economics*, 17(4), 409–421.

Galbraith, J.K. (2011), 'Inequality and Economic and Political Change: A Comparative Perspective', *Cambridge Journal of Regions, Economy and Society*, 4, 13–27.

Gereffi, G. (2009), 'Development Models and Industrial Upgrading in China and Mexico', *European Sociological Review*, 25(1), 37–51.

Gilroy, P. (1987), *There Ain't No Black In The Union Jack*, London: Hutchinson.

Global Exchange, (nd), *Nike Campaign*, at http://www.globalexchange.org/fairtrade/sweatfree/nike accessed 4 April 2013.

Goldberg, D. (2002), *The Racial State*, New York: Wiley.

Goldman, M. (2005), *Imperial Nature: The World Bank and Struggles for Social Justice in the Age of Globalization*, New Haven: Yale University Press.

Gottschalk, P. and Smeeding, T. (1997), 'Cross-national Comparisons of Earnings and Income Inequality', *Journal of Economic Literature*, xxxv, 633–687.

Grimm, M., Hartgen, K., Klasen, S., Misselhorn, M., Munzi, T. and Smeeding, T. (2009), 'Inequality in Human Development: An Empirical Assessment of Thirty-Two Countries' Current Research Paper, Georg August Universität Göttingen, *Discussion Papers*, number 6.

Guilmoto, C. (2012), *Sex Imbalances at Birth: Current Trends, Consequences and Policy Implications*, Bangkok: UNFPA.

Hall, P. and Soskice, D. (eds.) (2001), *Varieties of Capitalism: The Institutional Foundations of Comparative Advantage*, Oxford: Oxford University Press.

Halpern, D. (2001), 'Moral Values, Social Trust, and Inequality: Can Values Explain Crime', *British Journal of Criminology*, 41, 236–251.

Hardt, M. and Negri, A. (2000), *Empire*, Cambridge, MA: Harvard University Press.

Harrison, A. (ed.) (2007), *Globalization and Poverty*, Chicago: Chicago University Press.

Heath, A. and Brinbaum, Y. (2007), 'Explaining Ethnic Inequalities in Educational Attainment', *Ethnicities*, 7(3), 291–305.

Heath, A. and Cheung, S. (eds.) (2007), *Unequal Chances: Ethnic Minorities in Western Labour Markets*, Oxford: Oxford University Press.

Held, D. (1995), *Democracy and the Global Order: From the Modern State to Cosmopolitan Governance*, Cambridge: Cambridge University Press.

Held, D. and Kaya, A. (eds.), (2007), *Global Inequality*, Cambridge: Polity Press.

Hoff, K. (2003), 'Paths of Institutional Development: A View from Economic History', *World Bank Research Observations*, 18(2), 205–226.

Holifield, R., Porter, M. and Walker, G. (eds.) (2011), *Spaces of Environmental Justice*, Chichester, Wiley-Blackwell.

Holmberg, S., Rothstein, B. and Nasirtoussi, N. (2009), 'Quality of Government: What You Get', *Annual Review of Political Science*, 12, 135–161.

Holton, R. (1992), *Economy and Society*, London: Routledge.

Holton, R. (2005), *Making Globalization*, Basingstoke: Palgrave Macmillan.

Holton, R. (2008), *Global Networks*, Basingstoke: Palgrave Macmillan.

Holton, R. (2009), *Cosmopolitanisms: New Thinking, New Directions*, Basingstoke: Palgrave Macmillan.

Holton, R. (2011), *Globalization and the Nation-State*, second revised edition, Basingstoke: Palgrave Macmillan.

Holton, R. (2012), *Global Finance*, London: Routledge.

Hopkins, A.G. (ed.), (2002), *Globalization and World History*, London: Pimlico.

Huntington, S. (1996), *The Clash of Civilizations and the Remaking of World Order*, New York: Simon and Schuster.

International Commission on Development Issues, (1980), [Brandt Report], *North-South: A Programme for Survival*, London: Pan.

International Labour Organization. (2013), *Global Wages Report, 2012–3, Wages and Equitable Growth*, Geneva: ILO.

International Trade Union Confederation (ITUC). (2008), *The Global Gender Pay Gap*, Paris: ITUC, available at www.ituc-csi.org/IMG/pdf/gap-1.pdf.

Interparliamentary Union. (2013), 'Women in National Parliaments', at www.ipu .org/wmn-e/classif.htm accessed 13 March 2013.

Ivanic, M. and Martin, W. (2008), 'Implications of Higher Food Prices for Poverty in Low-Income Countries', World Bank Development Research Group, *Working Paper*, 4594, Washington: World Bank.

Ivanova, I., Arcelus, F.J. and Srinivasan, G. (1999), 'An Assessment of the Measurement Properties of the Human Development Index', *Social Indicators Research*, 46, 157–179.

Jackson, G. and Deeg, R. (2008), 'Comparing Capitalisms: Understanding Institutional Diversity and its Implications for International Business', *Journal of International Business Studies*, 39, 540–561.

Jaumotte, F., Lall, S. and Papageorgiu, C. (2008), 'Rising Income Inequality: Technology or Trade and Financial Globalization', *IMF Working Paper* WP/08/185, Washington, DC: IMF.

Jerven, M. (2013), *Poor Numbers: We Are Misled by African Development Statistics and What To Do About It*, Ithaca: Cornell University Press.

Jessop, B. (2010), 'Cultural Political Economy and Critical Policy Studies', *Critical Policy Studies*, 3(3–4), 336–356.

Jessop, B. and Sum, N-L. (2014), *Towards a Cultural Political Economy: Putting Culture in Its Place in Political Economy?*, Cheltenham: Elgar.

Kaplinsky, R. (2005), *Globalization, Poverty, and Inequality*, Cambridge: Polity Press.

Karanikolos, M., Mladovsky, P., Cylus, J., Thomson, S., Basu, S., Stuckler, D., Mackenbach, J. and McKee, M. (2013), 'Financial Crisis, Austerity, and Health in Europe', *Lancet Online*, 27 March, at www.dx.doi/10.1016/S0140=6736(13)6010202-6 accessed 17 April 2014.

Kennedy, S. and Martinuzzi, E. (2014), 'Focus on Low Earners at Davos is Key to Economic Growth', *Independent.ie*, 24 January, at www.independent.ie/business/world/focus-on-low-earners-is-key-to-economic-growth/29945546.html accessed 3 March 2014.

Khandker, S. (2005), 'Microfinance and Poverty: Evidence Using Panel Data from Bangladesh', *World Bank Economic Review*, 19(2), 263–286.

Kilroy, A. (2009), 'Intra-Urban Spatial Inequality: Cities as "Urban Regions"', Washington DC: World Bank, at www.openknowledge/worldbank.org/handle/10986/5991 accessed 29 March 2014.

Korzeniewicz, R. and Moran, T. (2009), *Unveiling Inequality: A World-Historical Perspective*, New York: Russell Sage Foundation.

Kovacevic, M. (2011), *Review of HDI Critiques and Potential Improvements*, Human Development Research Paper 2010/33, New York: UNDP.

Kraal, K. Roosblad, J. and Wrench, J. (2009), *Equal Opportunities and Ethnic Inequality in European Labour Markets*, Amsterdam: Amsterdam University Press.

Krishna, P. and Sethupathy, G. (2011), 'Trade and Inequality in India', *NBER Working Paper Series*, Working Paper 17257, Cambridge MA: NBER, at www.nber.org/papers/w17257 accessed 30 March 2013.

Krug, E., Dahlberg, L., Mercy, J., Zwi, A. and Lozano, R. (eds.) (2002), *World Report on Violence and Health, volume 1*. Washington, DC: World Health Organization.

Krugman, P. and Lawrence, R. (1993), 'Trade, Jobs, and Wages', *NBER Working Paper*, 4478, Washington, DC: NBER.

Kumari, V. (2008), 'Microcredit and Violence: A Snapshot of Kerala, India', in Bahun-Radunović, S. and Rajan, V.G.J. (eds.) (2008), *Violence and Gender in the Globalized World*, Aldershot: Ashgate, 41–55.

Kuznets, S. (1955), 'Economic Growth and Income Inequality', *American Economic Review*, 45(1), 1–28.

Labonté, R. and Schrecker, T. (2007a), 'Globalization and Social Determinants of Health: Introduction and Methodological Background (Part 1 of 3)', *Globalization and Health*, 3(5), 1–10.

Labonté, R. and Schrecker, T. (2007b), 'Globalization and Social Determinants of Health: The Role of the Global Marketplace (Part 2 of 3)', *Globalization and Health*, 3(6), 1–17.

Lazarova, E. (2006), 'Governance in Relation to Infant Mortality Rate: Evidence From Around the World', *Annals of Public and Cooperative Economics*, 77, 385–394.

Leblang, D. (1995), 'Political Capacity and Economic Growth', in Arbetman, M. and Kugler, J. (eds.), *Political Capacity and Economic Behaviour*, Boulder, CO: Westview Press, 109–125.

Lentin, R. (2006), 'From Racial State to Racist State? Racism and Immigration in 21st Century Ireland', in Lentin, A. and Lentin, R. (eds.), *Race and State*, Cambridge: Cambridge Scholars, 187–208.

Levine, R., The What Works Working Group and Kinder, M. (2004), *Millions Saved: Proven Successes in Global Health*, Washington, DC: Centre for Global Development.

Levine, R. and the What Works Working Group, (2007), *Case Studies in Global Health: Millions Saved*, Sudbury, MA: Jones and Bartlett Learning.

Lombardo, E. and Verloo, M. (2009), 'Institutionalizing Intersectionality in the European Union: Policy Developments and Contestations', *International Feminist Journal of Politics*, 11(4), 478–495.

Lopez, J. and Scott, J. (2000), *Social Structure*, Buckingham: Open University.

Mackay, A. and Dawson, L. (2003), 'Assessing the Extent and Nature of Chronic Poverty in Low Income Countries: Issues and Evidence', *World Development*, 31(3), 425–439.

Maddison, A. (2006), *The World Economy: A Millennial Perspective* (vol 1), *Historical Statistics* (vol 2), Paris: OECD.

Maddison, A. (2007), *Contours of the Global Economy, 1-2030AD: Essays in Macroeconomic History*, Oxford: Oxford University Press.

Madichie, N. (2009), 'Breaking the Glass Ceiling in Nigeria: A Review of Womens' Entrepreneurship', *Journal of African Business*, 10(1), 51–66.

Manacorda, M., Manning, A. and Wadsworth, J. (2012), 'The Impact of Immigration on the Structure of Wages: Theory and Evidence from Britain', *Journal of the European Economic Association*, 10(1), 120–151.

Mann, M. (1986), *The Sources of Social Power*, vol 1, Cambridge: Cambridge University Press.

Mann, M. (1987), 'Ruling Class Strategies and Citizenship', *Sociology*, 21(3), 339–354.

Mann, M. (1993), 'Nation-states in Europe and Other Continents: Diversifying, Developing Not Dying', *Daedalus*, Summer, 115–140.

Mann, M. (1997), 'Has Globalization Ended the Rise and Rise of the Nation-State?' *Review of International Political Economy*, 4(3), 472–496.

Mann, M. and Riley, D. (2007), 'Explaining Macro-Regional Trends in Global Income Inequalities, 1950–2000', *Socio-Economic Review*, 5(1), 81–115.

Marmot, M. (2005), 'Social Determinants of Health Inequalities', *Lancet*, 365, 1099–1104.

Martell, L. (2010), *The Sociology of Globalization*, Cambridge: Polity Press.

Massey, D. (2009), 'Globalization and Inequality: Explaining American Exceptionalism', *European Sociological Review*, 25(1), 9–23.

Mavrotas, G. (ed.) (2010), *Foreign Aid for Development: Issues, Challenges and the New Agenda*, Oxford: Oxford University Press.

McCulloch, N. and Baulch, B. (1999), 'Distinguishing the Transitory from the Chronically Poor – Evidence from India', *IDS Discussion Paper* no: 97, Brighton: Institute of Development Studies, University of Sussex.

McKay, A. and Lawson, D. (2003), 'Assessing the Extent and Nature of Chronic Poverty in Low-Income Countries: Income and Evidence', *World Development*, 31(3), 425–439.

McMichael, A., Friel, S., Nyong, A. and Corvalán, C. (2008), 'Global Environmental Change and Health: Impacts, Inequalities, and the Health Sector', *British Medical Journal*, 336(7367), January 26, 191–194.

Médecins Sans Frontières. Australia. (2013), 'Restoring Lives Shattered by Violence', *The Pulse*, February, 12–13.

Menocal, M. (2002), *The Ornament of the World: How Muslims, Jews, and Christians Created a Culture of Tolerance in Medieval Spain*, Boston: Little Brown.

Meyer, L.B. (2003), 'Economic Globalization and Women's Status in the Labor Market: A Cross-National Investigation of Occupational Sex Segregation and Inequality', *Sociological Quarterly* 44, 351–383.

Mignolo, W. (2000), 'The Many Faces of Cosmopolis: Border Thinking and Critical Cosmopolitanism', *Public Culture*, 12(3), 721–748.

Milanovic, B. (2007), *Worlds Apart: Measuring International and Global Inequality*, Princeton: Princeton University Press.

Milanovic, B. (2011), *The Haves and the Have-Nots: A Brief and Idiosyncratic History of Global Inequality*, New York: Basic Books.

Milanovic, B. (2012), 'Global Income Inequality By the Numbers: In History and Now – An Overview', *World Bank Policy Research Paper* no 6259, Washington: World Bank.

Mills, L. (2012), 'Book Review: Kate Bedford, *Developing Partnerships: Gender, Sexuality and the Reformed World Bank*', *Global Social Policy*, 12(1), 86–88.

Mills, M.B. (2003), 'Gender and Inequality in the Global labour Force', *Annual Review of Anthropology*, 32, 41–62.

Mills, M.C. (2009), 'Globalization and Inequality', *European Sociological Review*, 25(1), 1–8.

Minoui, C. and Reddy, S. (2010), 'Development Aid and Economic Growth: A Long-Term Positive Relation', *Quarterly Journal of Economics and Finance*, 50(1), 27–39.

Mistry, R. (1996), *A Fine Balance*, London: Faber and Faber.

Moran, T. (2003), 'Beyond Sweatshops: Foreign Direct Investment and Globalization in Developing Countries', *Cornell University ILR Review*, 56(4) Article 88 at http://digitalcommons.ilr.cornell.edu./ilrreview accessed April 17 2013.

Mukand, S. and Rodrik, D. (2002), *In Search of the Holy Grail: Policy Convergence, Experimentation, and Economic Performance*, NBER Working Paper Series, Working Paper 9134 at www.nber.org/papers/9134 accessed 14 April 2013.

Mycroft, A. (2010), 'The Enduring Legacy of Empire', in Dimova-Cookson, M. and Stirk, P. (eds.), *Multiculturalism and Moral Conflict*, London: Routledge, 170–191.

Navarro, V. (ed.). (2007), *Neoliberalism, Globalization, and Inequalities: Consequences for Health and Quality of Life*, Amityville, NY: Baywood Publishing.

Navarro, V., Schmitt, J. and Astudillo, J. (2004), 'Is Globalisation Undermining the Welfare State', *Cambridge Journal of Economics*, 28(1), 133–152.

North, D. (2005), *Understanding the Process of Economic Change*, Princeton: Princeton University Press.

Nunn, N. (2008), 'The Long-Term Effect of Africa's Slave Trades', *Quarterly Journal of Economics*, 123(1), 136–176.

Nussbaum, M. (2000), *Women and Human Development: The Capabilities Approach*, Cambridge: Cambridge University Press.

Nussbaum, M. (2011), *Creating Capabilities: The Human Development Approach*, Cambridge, MA: Harvard University Press.

O'Connell, H. (2012), 'The Impact of Slavery on Racial Inequality in Poverty in the Contemporary US South', *Social Forces*, 90(3), 713–734.

Offe, C. (1985), *Disorganized Capitalism*, Cambridge: Polity.

Ong, A. (1993), 'The Gender and Labour Politics of Post-Modernity', *Annual Review of Anthropology*, 20, 279–309.

Organization for Economic Co-operation and Development (OECD), (2011), *An Overview of Growing Income Inequalities in OECD Countries*, Paris: OECD, available at http://www.oecd.org/els/social/inequality accessed 29 March 2013.

Organization for Economic Cooperation and Development (OECD). (2012), *Gender Equality: Data*. Tables available at www.oecd.org/gender/data.

Organization for Economic Co-operation and Development (OECD). (2013), Total flows by donor, *StatExtracts* at stats.oecd.org/Index.aspx?datasetcode=TABLE1 accessed 26 February 2014.

O'Rourke, K. and Williamson, J. (1999), *Globalization and History: The Evolution of a Nineteenth Century Atlantic Economy*, Cambridge, MA: MIT Press.

O'Rourke, K. (2002), 'Globalization and Inequality: Historical Trends', *Annual World Bank Conference on Development Economics*, 39–67.

Ortiz, I. and Cummins, M. (2011), *Global Inequality: Between the Bottom Billion – A Rapid Review of Income Distribution in 141 countries*. UNICEF Social and Economic Working Paper, New York: UNICEF.

Ottaviano, G. and Peri, G. (2008), 'Immigration and National Wages: Clarifying the Theory and the Empirics', *Nota de Lavoro/Fondazione Eni Enrico*

Mattei: Global Challenges, 77 at www.econstor.eu/bitstream/101419/53292/1/643931120.pdf accessed 24 June 2013.

Pager, D., Western, B. and Bonakowski, B. (2009), 'Discrimination in a Low-Wage Labor Market: A Field Experiment', *American Sociological Review*, 74(5), 777–799.

Palan, R. Murphy, R. and Chavagneux, C. (2010), *Tax Havens: How Globalization Really Works*. Ithaca: Cornell University Press.

Parsons, T. (1971), *The System of Modern Societies*, New York: Prentice-Hall.

Pateman, C. (1988), *The Sexual Contract*, Cambridge: Polity Press.

Petrakos, G. (2008), 'Regional Inequalities: Reflections on Theory, Evidence, and Policy', *Town Planning Review*, 79(5), vii–xiii.

Pitcher, B. (2011), 'Developing International Race Theory: A Place for CRT?' in Hylton, K., Pilkington, A., Warmington, P. and Housee, S. (eds.), *Atlantic Crossings: International Dialogues on Critical Race Theory*, Birmingham: C-SAP University of Birmingham, 154–175.

Pitcher, B. (2012), 'Race and Capitalism Redux', *Patterns of Prejudice*, 46(1), 1–15.

Pogge, T. (2002), *World Poverty and Human Rights: Cosmopolitan Responsibilities and Reforms*, Cambridge: Polity Press.

Pogge, T. (2007), 'Why Inequality Matters', in Held, D. and Kaya, A. (eds.). *Global Inequality*, Cambridge: Polity Press, 132–147.

Polanyi, K. (1957), *The Great Transformation*, Boston: Beacon Press.

Portes, A. and Rumbaud, R. (2001), *Legacies: The Story of the Immigrant Second Generation*, Berkeley: University of California Press.

Pradilla, A. (2009), 'The Brazilian Consensus' at http://works.bepress.com/andrea_pradilla/3 accessed 26 August 2013.

Prasad, E., Rogoff, K., Wei, S. and Kose, M. (2003), *Effects of Financial Globalization on Developing Countries: Some Empirical Evidence*, IMF Occasional Paper 220, Washington, DC: IMF.

Prebisch, R. (1950), *The Economic Development of Latin America and its Principal Problems*, New York: United Nations.

Preston, S.H. (1975), 'The Changing Relation Between Mortality and Level of Development', *Population Studies*, 29(2), 239–248.

Pritchett, L. and Summers, L. (1986), 'Wealthier is Healthier', *Journal of Human Resources*, 31(4), 841–868.

Prüss-Üstün, A. and Corvalan, C. 2006), *Preventing Disease Through Healthy Environments*, Geneva: World Health Organization.

Quibria, M. (2012), *Microcredit and Poverty Alleviation: Can Microcredit Close the Deal*, United Nations University – World International Development Economics Research (UNU-WIDER), *Working Paper 2012/78*.

Ratha, D. and Siwal, A. (2012), 'Remittance Flows in 2011', *World Bank: Migration and Development Brief*, 18, at http://www.siteresources.worldbank.org/INTPROSPECTS/resource/334934-1110315165/MigrationandDevelopmentBrief18.pdf accessed 3 April 2013.

Ravallion, M. (2001), 'Growth, Inequality, and Poverty: Looking Beyond Averages', *World Development*, 29(11), 1803–1815.

Ravallion, M., Chen, S. and Sangruala, P. (2007), 'New Evidence on the Urbanization of Global Poverty', *Population and Development Review*, 33(4), 667–701.

Razavi, S., Pearson, R. and Danloy, C. (eds.). (2004), *Globalisation, Export-Oriented Employment and Social Policy*, Basingstoke: Palgrave Macmillan.

Reis, E. (2006), 'Inequality in Brazil: Facts and Perceptions', in Therborn, G. (ed.), *Inequalities of the World*, London: Verso, 193–219.

Riddell, R. (2007), *Does Foreign Aid Really Work?* Oxford: Oxford University Press.

Riddell, R. (2009), 'Is Aid Working? Is this the Right Question To Be Asking?' Open Democracy, 20 November, www.open-democracy.net/roger-c-riddell/is-aid-working is-this-right-question-be-asking accessed 28 February 2014.

Ritzer, G. (2004), *The Globalization of Nothing*, Thousand Oaks, CA: Pine Forge Press.

Robertson, R. (1992), *Social Theory and Global Culture*, London: Sage.

Rodrik, D. (2011), *The Globalization Paradox: Why Markets, States, and Democracy and Can't Coexist*, Oxford: Oxford University Press.

Rostow, W. (1960), *The Stages of Economic Growth: A Non-Communist Manifesto*, Cambridge: Cambridge University Press.

Rothstein, B. and Stolle, D. (2008), 'The State and Social Capital: An Institutional Theory of Social Trust', *Comparative Politics*, 40(4), 441–459.

Rowthorn, R. and Ramaswamy, R. (1998), 'Growth, Trade and Deindustrialization', *Working Paper of the International Monetary Fund* 98/60.

Ryten, J. (2000), The Human Development Index and Beyond: Which Are the Prerequisites for a Consistent Design of Development Indicators – Should There Be a Human Development Index? International Association of Official Statistics Conference '*Statistics, Development and Human Rights*' Montreux, 4–8 May 2000.

Sachs, J. and Warner, A. (1997), 'Sources of Slow Growth in African Economies', *Journal of African Economies*, 6(3), 335–376.

Sachs, J., McArthur, J., Schmidt-Traub, G., Kruk, M., Bahadur, C., Faye, M. and McCord, G. (2004), 'Ending Africa's Poverty Trap', *Brookings Papers on Economic Activity*, 1, 117–240.

Sage, G. (1999), 'Justice Do It! The Nike Transnational Advocacy Network: Organisations, Collective Actions, and Outcomes', *Sociology of Sport Journal*, 16(3), 206–235.

Said, E. (1978), *Orientalism*, New York: Penguin.

Sala-i-Martin, X. (2002), 'The Disturbing "Rise" of Global Income Inequality', *Department of Economics Discussion Paper Series*, 0102–44, New York: Columbia University.

Sala-i-Martin, X. (2006), 'The World Distribution of Income: Falling Poverty…and Convergence, Period', *Quarterly Journal of Economics*, 121(2), 351–397.

Salmi, K. (2011), ' "Race Does Not Exist Here". Applying Critical Race Theory to the French Republican Context', in Hylton, K., Pilkington, A., Warmington, P.

and Housee, S. (eds.), *Atlantic Crossings: International Dialogues on Critical Race Theory*, Birmingham: C-SAP University of Birmingham, 176–195.

Sandbrook, R., Edelman, M., Heller, P. and Teichman, J. (2007), *Social Democracy in the Global Periphery: Origins, Challenges, and Prospects*, Cambridge: Cambridge University Press.

Sanderson, S.K. (2005), 'World-system Analysis After Thirty Years: Should It Rest in Peace?', *International Journal of Comparative Sociology*, 46, 179–213.

Sanderson, S.K. (2011), 'Alive and Well Or Just Alive: Rejoinder to Chase-Dunn and Lawrence', *International Journal of Comparative Sociology*, 51, 431–438.

Sanderson, M. (2013), 'Immigration and Global Inequality: A Cross-sectional Analysis', in Bastia, T. (ed.). (2013), *Migration and Inequality*, Abingdon: Routledge, 24–42.

Sassen, S. (1996), *Losing Control? Sovereignty in an Age of Globalization*, New York: Columbia University Press.

Sassen, S. (1998a), *The Mobility of Labour and Capital: A Study of International Investment and Labour Flow*, Cambridge: Cambridge University Press.

Sassen, S. (1998b), *Globalization and its Discontents*, New York: New Press.

Sassen, S. (2001), *The Global City: New York, London, Tokyo*, second edition, Princeton: Princeton University Press.

Sassen, S. (2007), *A Sociology of Globalization*, New York: Norton.

Sassen, S. (2011), *Cities in a World Economy*, fourth edition, Thousand Oaks: Pine Forge Press.

Sayer, A. (2001), 'For A Critical Cultural Political Economy', *Antipode*, 33(4), 637–708.

Schnepf, S. (2007), 'Immigrants Educational Disadvantage: An Examination Across Ten Countries and Three Surveys', *Journal of Population Economics*, 20(3), 527–545.

Sen, A. (1979), 'Equality of What?' The Tanner Lecture on Human Values, at www.uv.es/~mperezs/intpolecon/lecturecomp/Distribucion%20Crecimiento/Sen%20Equaliy%20of20%what.pdf accessed 13 August 2013.

Sen, A. (1985), *Commodities and Capabilities*, Amsterdam: North Holland.

Sen, A. (1996), *Inequality Re-examined*, New York and Cambridge, MA: Russell Sage Foundation and Harvard University Press.

Sen, A. (1999), *Development as Freedom*, New York: Knopf.

Sharman, J. (2011), *Havens in a Storm, the Struggle for Global Tax Regulation*, Ithaca: Cornell University Press.

Silberman, R., Alba, R. and Fournier, I. (2007), 'Segmented Assimilation in France? Discrimination in the Labour Market against the Second Generation', *Ethnic and Racial Studies*, 30(1), 1–27.

Smeeding, T. (2005), 'Public Policy, Economic Inequality and Poverty: The United States in Comparative Perspective', *Social Science Quarterly*, 86(s1), 955–983.

Smith, J. (2004), 'The World Social Forum and the Challenges of Global Democracy', *Social Networks*, 4, 413–421.

Smith, J. and Welch, F. (1989), 'Black Economic Progress After Myrdal', *Journal of Economic Literature*, 27(2), 519–564.

Soros, G. (2002), *Soros on Globalization*, Cambridge, MA: Public Affairs for Perseus Books.

Stein, H. (2011), 'World Bank Agricultural Policies, Poverty, and Income Inequality in Sub-Saharan, Africa', *Cambridge Journal of Regions, Economy and Society*, 4, 79–90.

Stiglitz, J. (2002), *Globalization and its Discontents*, London: Allen Lane.

Stockhammer, E. (2012), 'Rising Inequality as a Root Cause of the Present Crisis', *Political Economy Research Institute, Working Papers series* no. 282, Amherst: University of Massachusetts.

Summers, L. and Summers, V. (1989), 'When Financial Markets Work too Well: A Cautious Case for a Securities Transactions Tax', *Journal of Financial Services Research*, 3(2–3), 261–286.

Sutcliffe, R. (1999), 'The Place of Development in Theories of Imperialism and Globalization', in Munck, R. and O'Hearn, D. (eds.), *Contributions To a New Paradigm: (Re)Thinking Development in the Era of Globalization*, London: Zed Books, 135–154.

Sutcliffe, R. (Bob), (2004), 'World Inequality and Globalization', *Oxford Review of Economic Policy*, 20(1), 15–37.

Sutcliffe, R. (2007), 'The Unequalled and Unequal Twentieth Century', in Held, D. and Kaya, A. (eds.), *Global Inequality*, Cambridge: Polity Press, 50–72.

Suter, C. (2009), 'Searching for the Missing Pieces of the Puzzle: Introduction to Special Issue', *International Journal of Comparative Sociology*, 50(5–6), 419–424.

Szekely, M. and Sámono, C. (2012), *Did Trade Openness Affect Income Distribution in Latin America?* UNU-WIDER Working Paper 2012/03 Helsinki: UNU-WIDER.

Tarp, F. (ed.). (2000), *Foreign Aid and Development: Lessons Learnt and Directions for the Future*, London: Routledge.

Therborn, G. (2006), 'Meaning, Mechanisms, Patterns, and Forces: An Introduction', in Therborn, G. (ed.), *Inequalities of the World*, London: Verso, 1–60.

Thompson, G. (2003), *Between Markets and Hierarchies: The Logic and Limits of Network Forms of Organization*, Oxford: Oxford University Press.

Thompson, G. (2007), 'Global Inequality, the "Great Divergence", and Supranational Regionalization', in Held, D. and Kaya, A. (eds.). (2007), *Global Inequality*, Cambridge: Polity Press, 176–203.

Therborn, G. (2011), 'Global Inequality: The Return of Class', at http://isa-global-dialogue.net/tag/goran-therborn accessed 24 April 2013.

Tilly, C. (2001), 'The Relational Origins of Inequality', *Anthropological Theory*, 1(3), 355–372.

Trivett, V. (2011), '25 US Mega Corporations: Where they Rank if They were Countries', Business Insider, June 27 at www.businessinsider.com/25-corporations-bigger-than-countries-2011-6?Op=1 accessed 18 February 2013.

UNDP. (2012a), 'Human Development Index', *Human Development Report, 2011* at http://www.hdr.undp.org/en/statistics/hdi accessed 24 February 2013.

UNDP. (2012b), '2011 Human Development Index' at http://www.hdr.undp.org/en/media/PR2-HDI-2011HDR-English.pdf

UNDP. (2012c), 'Patterns and Trends, Progress and Prospects', *Human Development Report, 2011* at http://www.udr.undp.org/en/reports/global/hdr2011/summary/trends accessed 24 February 2013.

UNESCO Institute of Statistics. (2010), *Adult and Youth Literacy: Global Trends in Gender Parity*, www.uis.unesco.org/Factsheets/Documents/Fact_Sheet_2010_Lit_EN.pdf accessed 13 March 2013.

UNESCO Institute of Statistics. (2011), *Global Education Digest, 2011: Regional Profile sub-Saharan Africa*, at www.uis.unesco.org/Education?Documents/GED2011_SSA_RP_EN.pdf accessed 13 March 2013.

UNICEF (2012), Statistical Tables, at www.unicef.org/sowc2012/pdfs/All-tables-including-general-notes-on-data.pdf accessed 20 March 2013.

UNODC. (2012), *CTS2011: Sexual Violence*, http://www.unodp.org/documents/data_and_analysis/statistics/crime/CTS12_sexual_violence.xls accessed 14 February 2013.

Urry, J. (2011), *Climate Change and Society*, Cambridge: Polity Press.

van de Walle, N. (2009), 'The Institutional Origins of Inequality in Sub-Saharan Africa', *Annual Review of Political Science*, 12, 307–327.

van Wilsem, J. (2004), 'Criminal Victimisation in Cross-national Perspective', *European Journal of Criminology*, 1(1), 89–109.

Verloo, M. (2006), 'Multiple Inequalities, Intersectionality, and the European Union', *European Journal of Women's Studies*, 13(3), 211–228.

Wade, R. (2003), 'What Strategies are Viable for Developing Countries Today: The World Trade Organization and the Shrinkage of 'Development Space', *Review of International Political Economy*, 10(4), 621–644.

Wade, R. (2007), 'Should We Worry about Income Inequality?' in Held, D. and Kaya, A. (eds.), *Global Inequality*, Cambridge: Polity Press 104–131.

Walby, S. (2009), *Globalization and Inequalities*, London: Sage.

Walby, S. (2011), 'Globalization and Multiple Identities', *Advances in Gender Research*, 15, 17–33.

Walby, S. and Allen, J. (2004), *Domestic Violence, Sexual Assault and Stalking: Findings from the British Crime Survey*, London: Home Office Research Study, 276.

Wallerstein, I. (1974), *The Modern World System: Capitalist Agriculture and the Origins of the European World-Economy in the Sixteenth Century*, New York: Academic Press.

Wallerstein, I. (1979), *The Capitalist World Economy*, Cambridge: Cambridge University Press.

Wallerstein, I. (1991), *Geopolitics and Geoculture*, Cambridge: Cambridge University Press.

Wallerstein, I. (2011), 'Structural Crisis in the World System', *Monthly Review*, 62(10), at http://monthlyreview.org/2011/03/01/structural-crisis-in-the-world-system accessed 10 September 2013.

Walton, P. and Gamble, A. (1972), *From Alienation to Surplus Value*, London: Sheed and Ward.

Western, B. and Pettit, B. (2005), 'Black-White Wage Inequality, Employment Rates, and Incarceration', *American Journal of Sociology*, 111(2), 553–578.

Whelan, C., Layte, R. and Maitre, B. (2004), 'Understanding the Mismatch Between Income Poverty and Deprivation: A Dynamic Comparative Analysis', *European Sociological Review*, 20(4), 275–302.

Wilkinson, R. (2004), 'Why is Violence More Common Where Inequality is Greater?' *Annals of the New York Academy of Sciences*, 1036, 1–12.

Wilkinson, R. and Hulme, D. (eds.). (2012), *The Millennium Development Goals and Beyond*, London: Routledge.

Willson, A., Shuey, K. and Elder, G. (2007), 'Cumulative Advantage Processes as Mechanisms of Inequality in Life Course Health', *American Journal of Sociology*, 112(6), 1886–1924.

Winant, H. (2001), *The World is a Ghetto: Race and Democracy Since World War Two*, New York: Basic Books.

Winant, H. (2004), *The New Politics of Race: Globalism, Difference, Justice*, Minneapolis: University of Minnesota Press.

Winch, D. (1996), *Riches and Poverty: An Intellectual History of Political Economy in Britain 1750–1830*, Cambridge: Cambridge University Press.

Winker, G. and Degele, N. (2011), 'Intersectionality as Multi-level Analysis: Dealing with Social Inequality', *European Journal of Women's Studies*, 18(1), 51–66.

Wolf, M. (2004), *Why Globalization Works*, London: Yale University Press.

Woods, N. (2006), *The Globalizers: The IMF, World Bank, and Their Borrowers*, Ithaca: Cornell University Press.

World Bank, (1998), *Assessing Aid: What Works, What Doesn't and Why?* Washington DC and Oxford: World Bank/Oxford University Press.

World Bank, (2006), *Global Economic Prospects: Economic Implications of Remittances and Immigration*, Washington: World Bank.

World Bank. (2011a), *Migration and Remittances Factbook*, Washington: World Bank.

World Bank. (2011b), *The Little Data Book on Gender*, Washington: World Bank.

World Bank. (2012), *World Bank Development Report 2012: Gender Equality and Development*, Washington: World Bank.

World Bank. (2013a), 'Life expectancy at birth', at http://www.data.worldbank.org/indicator/SP.DYN.LE00.IN accessed 26 feb 2013.

World Bank. (2013b), 'Debt Relief for 39 Countries on Track to Reach $114billion', at www.worldbank.org/en/news/feature/2013/12/16/debt-relief- 39-countries-track-reach-114-billion accessed 21 March 2014.

World Health Organization. (1999), *The World Health Report 1999: Making a Difference*, Geneva: World Health Organization.

World Health Organization. (2009), *Global Health Risks: Mortality and Burden of Risk attributable to selected major risks*, Geneva: World Health Organization.

World Health Organization. (2012), *Trends in Maternal Mortality: 1990 to 2010*, Geneva: World Health Organization.

Yodanis, C. (2004), 'Gender Inequality, Violence Against and Women, and Fear: A Cross-National Test of the Feminist Theory of Violence Against Women', *Journal of Interpersonal Violence*, 19(6), 655–675.

Young, I.M. (1989), 'Polity and Group Difference: A Critique of the Ideal of Universal Citizenship', *Ethics*, 99, 250–274.

Index